Progress to First Certificate

New Edition

Leo Jones

CAMBRIDGE
UNIVERSITY PRESS

Published by the Press Syndicate of the University of Cambridge
The Pitt Building, Trumpington Street, Cambridge CB2 1RP
40 West 20th Street, New York, NY 10011-4211, USA
10 Stamford Road, Oakleigh, Victoria 3166, Australia

© Cambridge University Press 1983, 1990

First published 1983
Tenth printing 1988
Second edition 1990
Fifth printing 1992

Printed in Great Britain
by Scotprint Ltd, Musselburgh, Scotland

ISBN 0 521 37959 8 Student's Book
ISBN 0 521 37958 X Self-study Student's Book
ISBN 0 521 37957 1 Teacher's Book
ISBN 0 521 37096 5 Set of 2 cassettes

CE

Contents

Thanks

No book of this kind can be produced by one person alone and in this case countless people have generously contributed their ideas and advice.

In particular, I'd just like to say how grateful I am to the following friends, colleagues and teachers:

Jeanne McCarten for guiding the New Edition through from start to finish and for her encouragement, perfectionism and good ideas

Jill Mountain and Kit Woods for their detailed comments on the first edition and for subsequently reading, evaluating and suggesting improvements to the first draft of this New Edition

Alison Silver for her editing expertise and sensible suggestions

Peter Taylor and Studio AVP for their professional skills in producing the recorded material

Peter Ducker for his meticulous work on the illustrations and design

Sue Gosling for her help and advice

And thanks to the following teachers whose detailed comments on the first edition and helpful ideas led to many valuable changes in the New Edition:

Susan Barber, Lake School of English in Oxford

John Bradbury, FIAC Escola d'idiomes moderns in Sabadell, Catalonia, Spain

Susan Garvin, British Institute of Florence, Italy

Roger Johnson and Nick Kenny, British Council in Milan, Italy

Fern Judet, Swan School in Oxford

Lynne White, Godmer House School of English in Oxford

And thanks to the following teachers who kindly wrote about their experiences of using the first edition, some of whom gave us their students' feedback:

H. G. Bernhardt, Tony Buckby and colleagues, J. Carvell, Emily Grammenou, Michael Hadgimichalis, Pearl Herrmann, Jill Jeavons, Katherine Karangianni, Marie Anne Küpper-Compes, Bryan Newman, Cathy Parker and colleagues, Véronique Rouanet, Claire Springett, Andrew Tymn, Robin Visel and J. T. Ward

Finally thanks to the numerous other teachers in many different countries (and their students) who have given us useful informal feedback on the first edition.

Thank you, everyone!

From the first edition

I'd like to express my thanks to Sue Gosling and Christine Cairns for all their encouragement and help during the planning, writing and rewriting of this book. Many thanks also to the teachers who used the pilot edition and made so many useful and perceptive comments. Thanks are due in particular to staff at the following schools and institutes: the British Centre in Venice, the British Institute in Paris, the British School in Florence, the Newnham Language Centre in Cambridge, the Studio School of English in Cambridge and the Université II in Lyons.

Acknowledgements

The author and publishers are grateful to the authors, publishers and others who have given permission for the use of copyright material identified in the text. It has not been possible to identify the sources of all the material used and in such cases the publishers would welcome information from copyright owners.

Dover Publications, Inc. for the pictograms throughout the book from *Handbook of Pictorial Symbols; 3,250 Examples from International Sources* by Rudolf Modley; J. Sainsbury for the pictogram on p. 31; Harrods Ltd for the photograph on p. 3; Stambouli frères s.a. for the advertisement on p. 9; Discoveries for the advertisements (top left, centre, bottom) on p. 11; Première (Issue 2) for the advertisement (top right) on p. 11; *Punch* for the cartoons on pp. 16, 23, 30, 35, 44, 50, 58, 67, 79, 81, 84, 90, 93, 110, 121, 131, 146, 150, 159, 166, 168, 171, 199, 205, 208; *The Illustrated London News* Picture Library for the extract on p. 25; Penguin Books Ltd for the extract on p. 32 from the *Penguin Book of the Natural World*, the extract on pp. 118–9 from *Call for the Dead* by John Le Carré © Victor Gollancz 1961, the cover on p. 125 of *Jupiter's Travels* by Ted Simon © Penguin Books 1980, and the cover on p. 126 of *The Human Factor* by Graham Greene © Penguin Books 1978; *The Guardian* and The Meteorological Office for the chart on p. 38 and the weather summary on p. 213 © The Meteorological Office, based on Crown copyright information; Barnaby's Picture Library for the photograph (top left) on p. 43; Oxfam for the photograph (top right) by Jeremy Hartley on p. 43; Camera Press Ltd for the photograph (bottom right) on p. 43; Venice Simplon – Orient-Express for the map on p. 46; British Airways for the advertisement on p. 53 and the photograph (right) on p. 163; British Railways Board for the map on p. 54; Ordnance Survey and W. Heffer & Sons Ltd for the map on p. 56; *The Observer* for the photographs on p. 61 (top), p. 96 (left) and p. 163 (centre); Greek National Tourist Organisation for the photograph on p. 61 (bottom) by Yannis Scouroyannis; *The Guardian* for the article by David Sharrock on p. 64, the article on p. 73 © Associated Press, the article by Jane McLoughlin on p. 158, the article by Derek Brown on p. 165, the article by Michael White and the map on p. 172 © *The Guardian*; BBC Education for the diagram on p. 77; The Consumers' Association for the article on p. 80; The Health Education Council for the extract on p. 87 and the photograph (right) on p. 96; *The Economist* for the chart on p. 88; *Radio Times* for the extract on p. 94; Kuoni Travel Ltd for the extract on p. 102; *The Daily Telegraph* Colour Library for the photograph (top left) on p. 106; Silk Cut Travel Ltd for the photographs (centre left and right) on p. 106; HF Holidays Ltd for the photographs (top right and bottom left) on p. 106; Yugoslav National Tourist Board for the advertisement (top) on p. 107; Wings Ltd for the extract on p. 109; Longman for the extract on p. 118 from *Call for the Dead* by John Le Carré © Longman Group Ltd; Grafton Books for the cover on p. 123 of *To Be the Best* by

Barbara Taylor Bradford; Grafton Books and Warner Bros Inc. for the cover on
p. 125 of *Empire of the Sun* by J. G. Ballard; Michael Joseph Ltd for the cover on
p. 123 of *Zoya* by Danielle Steele; Sidgwick & Jackson for the cover on p. 123 of
Savages by Shirley Conran; Corgi Books for the cover on p. 123 of *Alaska* by
James A. Michener; Collins Publishers for the covers of *Glamorous Powers* by
Susan Howatch on p. 123 and *Send No More Roses* by Eric Ambler on p. 126;
Mills & Boon Ltd and Harlequin Enterprises B.V. for the cover on p. 125 of *Hills
of Kalamata* by Anne Hampson; Reinhardt Books for the extract on pp. 127–8
from *The Captain and the Enemy* by Graham Greene © Graham Greene; Jeremy
Pembrey for the photographs on pp. 144, 163 (left), 176 (left and right), 220 and
225; Midland Bank PLC for the extract on p. 149 from 'Cheque In'; *Cambridge
Evening News* for the photograph (top) on p. 169; *The Guardian* for the
photograph (left) on p. 169; S & G Press Agency Ltd for the photograph (centre
right) on p. 169; Barnaby's Picture Library for the photograph (bottom right) by
Brian L. Arundale on p. 169; Dateline for the extract on pp. 180–2; Curtis
Brown Ltd for the extract on pp. 187–8 from *Mr Norris Changes Trains* © 1935
by Christopher Isherwood; Hutchinson Publishing Group Ltd and Random
House Inc. for the extract on p. 195 from *Hutchinson History of the World* by
J. M. Roberts; Jorvik Viking Centre for the extract on p. 196; Jarrold Colour
Publications for the photograph (right) on p. 203; Department of Tourism, York
for the photograph (left) on p. 203; Leeds Castle Enterprises Ltd for the extract
on p. 207; John Topham Picture Library for the photographs on pp. 213 (centre)
and 215 (centre); Benetton and Brigitte Jacquety Ltd for the photograph (top) on
p. 215; Spillers Foods for the photograph on p. 219 by Arthur Siddy from Spillers
Kattomeat Calendar 1988; Syndication International Ltd for the photograph on
p. 223.

Photographs by the author: pp. 43 (bottom left), 69, 106 (bottom right), 213
(top).
Illustrations by Leslie Marshall on p. 26; Trevor Ridley on pp. 28, 191; Clyde
Pearson on pp. 135, 204, 205; David Mostyn on pp. 214, 216, 224; Chris Pavely
on pp. 218, 220, 225; Thomas Jones on p. 218; Zoë Jones on p. 221.
Artwork by Julie Sailing, Wenham Arts, Joanne Barker, Joanne Currie, Peter
Ducker and Hardlines.
Art direction by Peter Ducker MSTD

Welcome!

This book is designed to prepare you progressively for the Cambridge First
Certificate in English examination (FCE). The exercises and activities will
help you to learn and not just test your knowledge. The nature of the
exercises and activities changes gradually through the book until, by the
time you reach Unit 14, you'll be answering questions which are just the
same as the ones you'll have to answer in the exam itself. Towards the end
of the book, the exercises become more like tests with, for example,
multiple-choice questions to answer.

To help you to prepare for the FCE exam, the sections in each unit
concentrate on different parts of the exam:
▶ Paper 1: Reading Comprehension
    Vocabulary and Reading exercises
▶ Paper 2: Composition
    Composition exercises (towards the end of each unit)
▶ Paper 3: Use of English
    Exercises on Grammar, Word study, Verbs and idioms, Prepositions
    and Problem solving (directed writing)
▶ Paper 4: Listening Comprehension
    Listening activities, based on the cassettes
▶ Paper 5: Interview
    Communication activities, Pronunciation exercises, Picture
    conversations and discussion questions

Each unit is based on a different topic and all the exercises and activities in
the unit are related to the topic. These topics are the ones that are most
likely to come up in the exam – but, perhaps more important, they are
topics which will interest you and give you plenty to talk about.

Activities shown with 🔳 are Communication activities, where you
and your partner are given different information that you must
communicate to each other. These are printed at the end of the book but
they are 'mixed up' so that your partner can't see your information.

📼 indicates that there is recorded material on the cassettes.
A star ★ indicates advice, points to remember or exam tips.

In class, you will be doing many of the activities in pairs or small groups,
so that everyone gets plenty of practice in speaking English. But there will
also be quite a lot of HOMEWORK that you will be expected to do. This will
involve writing compositions, preparing reading passages that you will be
discussing in class and doing exercises that will be checked later in class.
    Don't be surprised if your teacher decides to leave out some sections –
the book is designed to be used selectively in this way.

Good luck during your exam course – enjoy using *Progress to First Certificate*!

1 Shopping

1.1 Shopping habits

Vocabulary

A Work in groups or pairs. Ask your partners these questions:
- What kinds of shops are there near your school or college?
- Which ones have you been in?
- Where are the best shops in this town for food, clothes, books, music or shoes?
- What kind of shops do you never or hardly ever go into? Why?
- What kind of shops do you go into at least once a month? Why?
- Which particular shop do you go to most often?

B Find the missing words to complete each sentence. In some cases there are several possible answers. The first one is done for you as an example:

1 In a shop you can use a credit card or charge card, or you can pay in c.**ash**.
2 If you're paying by cheque, don't forget to put your s................ at the bottom.
3 Someone who owns a small shop and who serves people in it is called a s................
4 Someone who is employed to serve customers in a shop or store is a s........... a...........
5 The salesperson in a shop usually serves the customers from behind a c...........
6 Salesperson: 'Can I h.......... you?' Customer: 'No, it's all right, thanks. I'm just l..........'
7 This real leather handbag was reduced in the summer s................, so I only had to pay £5.95 – it was a real b................!
8 The assistant added up the prices to find the t................ price we had to pay.
9 In case you want to exchange something, remember to keep the r................
10 If the radio goes wrong within twelve months, remember it's still under g................
11 A large store may lose some of its stock as a result of theft or s................
12 If you want something for your headache you can get it at a c................
13 It's unwise to buy new shoes or sandals without first t................ them on.
14 I wanted to buy some walking boots but they hadn't got my s................
15 I've tried on this coat and it doesn't f................ me, it's a bit too ....
16 I'm going to ask if they have any yellow cotton socks in s................
17 Yellow socks won't m................ your sweater and anyway yellow doesn't s................ you.
18 To find out how to wash a garment, look at the instructions on the l................
19 You can usually get goods cheaper if you buy them in an open-air m................
20 If you have a student identity card, some shops may give you a d................
21 Fruit and vegetables in a supermarket aren't as fresh as at a g................
22 You can spread the payments over twelve months by buying something on h..... p.....
23 You can get almost anything you want in a big d................ s................ but some people prefer to buy things by m................ o................
24 If something is too heavy for you to carry home yourself, the shop can d................ it.
25 Personally speaking, I'd say that going shopping is ....

2

C Work in groups or pairs. Imagine that you have to do some shopping BUT there is no department store or supermarket in the area. What sort of shops can you buy these items in? The first is done for you as an example:

1 *half a dozen bananas and a newspaper*
   Greengrocer's or fruit shop AND a newsagent's or kiosk 杂货
2 *a street plan of your town or city and a guidebook about your country*
3 *a litre of milk — and a glass to drink it from*
4 *a kilo of tomatoes — and a knife to cut them with*
5 *some sausages for dinner — and a frying pan to cook them in*
6 *a bottle of white wine — and a corkscrew to open it with*
7 *a personal stereo — and some cassettes to play on it*
8 *a loaf of bread and some butter to spread on it*
9 *a notebook and a pen to write in it with*
10 *a tube of toothpaste and a new toothbrush*
11 *a picture postcard to send to a friend abroad — and a stamp to stick on it*

D Continue working in groups or pairs. Look at each other's CLOTHES. What are you all wearing at the moment? Make sure you can describe each item of clothing in English and its colour or pattern. What would you be wearing if it was much colder today? What do you wear if you want to look extra smart?

1.2 Enter a different world
Reading

A Harrods is a famous department store in London. Before you read the passage on the next page, look at these statements and see if you can guess which are true (**T**) and which are false (**F**). The first is done as an example:

1 Everyone who visits London goes to Harrods. False — but many people do
2 Harrods is one of the sights of London.
3 Harrods sells five million different products.
4 The only thing you can't buy at Harrods is an elephant.
5 Some of the Queen's food is bought at Harrods.
6 Harrods' new warehouse will be the largest in Europe.

Now read the text to find out if you guessed right.

Harrods

HARRODS LIMITED

Knightsbridge London SW1X 7XL

Telephone 01-730 1234   Telegrams Harrods London Telex   Telex 24 319

REGISTERED IN LONDON NO. 30205   REGISTERED OFFICE 87/135 BROMPTON ROAD LONDON SW1X 7XL

ENTER A DIFFERENT WORLD

Welcome to Harrods – a different world for a million reasons. Harrods is the largest store in Europe with goods displayed in 60 windows and 5½ hectares of selling space. In one year over 14 million purchases are made in the 214 departments where you can buy anything from a pin to an elephant – if you can convince the manager of the Pet Department that you are a suitable elephant owner, that is! It is Harrods' policy to stock a wide and exciting range of merchandise in every department to give the customer a choice of goods which is unique in its variety and which no other store can match: Harrods stocks 100 different whiskies, including 57 single malts, 450 different cheeses, 500 types of shirts and 9,000 ties to go with them, 8,000 dresses and 150 different pianos.

Harrods also offers a number of special services to its customers including a bank, an insurance department, a travel agency, London's last circulating library, a theatre ticket agency and a funeral service. £40 million worth of goods are exported annually from Harrods and the Export Department can deal with any customer purchase or order and will pack and send goods to any address in the world. Recently, for example, six bread rolls were sent to New York, a handkerchief to Los Angeles, a pound of sausages to a yacht anchored in the Mediterranean, a Persian carpet to Iran and a £5,000 chess set to Australia. Harrods has a world-wide reputation for first-class service. It has a staff of 4,000, rising to 6,000 at Christmas time.

Harrods sells 5 million different products, not all of which are actually kept in stock in the store itself. To handle this enormous range, a new computerised warehouse is being built. It will be the largest warehouse in Britain and the second largest in Europe and will deal with a wider range of goods than any other distribution centre in the world. Thanks to its modern technology a customer will be able to order any product (for example, a dining table or a dishwasher) from any assistant in the store. The assistant will be able to check its availability immediately on a computer screen, decide with the customer on a suitable delivery date and time and then pass the order directly to the warehouse through the computer. The time of delivery will be guaranteed to within one hour.

For many of London's visitors Harrods is an important stop on their sightseeing programme. Henry Charles Harrod's first shop was opened in 1849, but the building as it stands today was started in 1901 and it has become one of London's landmarks. It has many items of architectural interest: the plaster ceilings are original, as is the famous Meat Hall with its Victorian wall tiles, and the light fittings on the ground floor date back to the 1930s. A morning spent strolling round Harrods is guaranteed to give any shopper an appetite, and to feed its customers Harrods has six restaurants, ranging from the Circle self-service restaurants offering delicious food at reasonable prices to the famous Harrods Restaurant, where queues form every afternoon for the 'Grand Buffet Tea', which for a fixed price allows you to eat as many cream cakes and gateaux as your greed will allow while waitresses serve you with India or China tea. If you feel like a drink you can choose between the pub atmosphere of the Green Man Tavern and the sophistication of the Cocktail Lounge. Harrods truly is a different world.

B   Decide whether the following statements are true (**T**) or false (**F**), according to the passage. Find and underline the words in the text that help you to answer each question.

 1 The Pet Department will sell an elephant to any customer who can afford one.
 2 Other stores are unable to match Harrods' range of merchandise.
 3 There are 500 shirts for sale in Harrods.
 4 Harrods stocks 100 different brands of malt whisky.
 5 You can borrow books from Harrods.
 6 You can arrange for a dead body to be buried by Harrods.
 7 A customer once asked to have a handkerchief sent to the USA.
 8 Harrods exports over £3 million worth of goods a month.
 9 Harrods employs 6,000 regular staff.
10 A greater variety of products will go through the new warehouse than any other in the world.
11 To obtain a product that isn't in the store, a customer has to go to the warehouse.
12 When the new computerised system is operating, any product will be delivered an hour after you have placed the order.
13 The wall tiles in the Meat Hall were made in 1849.
14 The restaurants at Harrods are good but very expensive.
15 You can eat as much as you like at the 'Grand Buffet Tea' for a fixed price.

When you have finished, compare your answers with a partner's. If you disagree about any of the answers, look again at the text to check who was right.

C   Work in groups and discuss these questions.

1 What are the **advantages** and **disadvantages** of shopping in a department store? Make a list, considering the following points:
     price   choice   service   quality   convenience
2 What would you personally **never** buy in a department store – and why?
3 What products can you **not** buy in department stores in your town or city? Where would you buy these items instead?

■ The grammar sections in *Progress to First Certificate* are meant to help you to REVISE grammar points you have probably studied before. The examples and exercises cover the main difficulties that students at your level have with English grammar – but ~~more elementary and more advanced points are not covered~~.

A   These examples show the most common uses of present tenses in English. Fill the gaps with more examples, using your own ideas. The first is done for you as an example:

Permanent or regular actions and situations:

I always have two cups of coffee for breakfast.   PRESENT SIMPLE
Where do you live?   (= What is your permanent address?)
After lunch I sometimes *have a cup of black coffee.*   .
I never ....
Every evening I ....

Temporary, developing or changing actions and situations:

I'm trying to concentrate, so please don't interrupt.   PRESENT PROGRESSIVE
Where are you living?   (= What is your temporary address?)
At the moment I ....
I .... a First Certificate course this year.

Actions or situations begun in the past and still true now or continuing now:

Someone has eaten all the cakes.   PRESENT PERFECT SIMPLE
I've never smoked a cigar in my life.
We .... hours on this unit so far.

We've been waiting for twenty minutes.   PRESENT PERFECT PROGRESSIVE
What have you been doing since we last met?
I .... English for .... years.

■ Remember that FOR is used with a period of time and SINCE is used with a point of time. For example:
for two years   for a long time   for a few minutes   for the last three days
(NOT: since two years ✗)
since 1988   since yesterday   since 5 o'clock   since lunchtime   since April

B   Some verbs (STATIVE VERBS) are not normally used in the progressive form, because they usually refer to permanent states or situations.

How much does this cost?   NOT: How much is this costing? ✗
She has owned a car for two years.   NOT: She has been owning a car ... ✗

Write a sentence using each of these ~~stative~~ verbs in NEGATIVE sentences. The first three are done for you as examples:

believe   contain   cost   deserve   fit   know   like   look like   love
matter   owe   realise   remember   seem   smell   suit   understand

I used to believe that shopping was fun, but now I don't believe that any more.
This yogurt doesn't contain any sugar.
A dictionary doesn't cost very much to buy.

C Decide which adverbs from the list below fit into the gaps in these sentences. The first two are done for you as examples:

1 She's looking for a new summer ~~outfit~~ in Harrods ....
2 He .... buys his clothes at Harrods.
3 He goes shopping ....
4 She has been feeling unwell ....

all day *4*	always *2*		
at the moment	generally	once in a while	usually
from time to time	often	today	frequently
occasionally	this morning	for a week	now
sometimes	for a long time	never	since Tuesday
every week	hardly ever	rarely	

D Six of these sentences contain errors and two are correct. Find the errors and correct them. The first is done for you as an example:

1 This packet ~~is containing~~ *contains* 500 grams of coffee.
2 At the moment I read a fascinating book.
3 I'm sometimes buying clothes in the market.
4 I've been waiting for them to arrive since 12 o'clock.
5 My mother prefer to buy fruit in the market.
6 I am waiting since 9 o'clock.
7 This CD is costing £10.99.
8 How are you feeling today? Better I hope!

E Complete the unfinished sentences in this dialogue. The first one is done for you as an example:

Assistant: Good morning. Have ~~you been waiting long~~ ....?
Customer: No, only for a few moments. Could you help me, please?
Assistant: Certainly. What ....?
Customer: I'm looking for a pair of jeans in my size.
Assistant: What *size do you take?* ....?
Customer: I take a size 30, normally. *(lɪʃˈeɪz) サイズです*
Assistant: Thirty. Well, we have these ~~Levis on special offer~~.
            Do *you like the look of these* ....?
Customer: Oh, very nice, yes, I like that style very much.
Assistant: You can try them on in the changing room over there.
Customer: Oh, right, thanks. I'll just see if they fit.
(The customer tries them on.)
Assistant: Do *they fit?* ....?
Customer: Yes, they fit perfectly. How much ....?
Assistant: £16.99. Is there anything else you'd like to see?
Customer: Yes, have *got any jacket to match* ....?
Assistant: I'm afraid we're out of stock of the matching jackets at the
            moment, but ~~we'll be getting some more in~~ soon.
Customer: When ....?
Assistant: We're expecting a delivery at the end of the week.
            If you like, I'll ~~put one aside for~~ you when they come in.

Customer: Oh, thanks very much. And I think I'll keep these jeans on now.
            Do ....?
Assistant: Yes, we take all major credit cards.
Customer: Good, here you are.
Assistant: Thanks. Let me just cut off the label ... there we are! And if you
            could just sign here ...

1.4   I had to go to the shops . . .   *Listening*

A   ⊟   Before you hear the recording read these statements through.
Then listen to the recording and decide whether they are true (**T**) or false
(**F**), according to the conversation. The first is done as an example. Listen
to the recording more than once to get all the information, if necessary.

1 Tim is late because he has been shopping. **T**
2 There would be no time for Tim to go shopping in the evening.
3 Tim didn't use the 'fast' checkout because there was a longer queue
   there.
4 Tim enjoys shopping for food.
5 Ann likes buying presents for people.
6 Tim likes buying presents for people.
7 Both Tim and Ann like looking for bargains in the sales.
8 Ann hates shopping at Christmas.
9 Both Tim and Ann like small shops.
10 Tim agrees that supermarket prices are lower.
11 Ann likes mail order shopping.
12 Tim looks forward to automated shopping by computer.

B   Match these products to the containers in which they're sold. How do
they fit into this sentence:
    Could you get me a .... of ...., please?

CONTAINERS   bottle   box   can   carton   jar   bar   packet   tin   tube
PRODUCTS   biscuits   chocolate   Coke   honey   matches   milk
             mineral water   peas   toothpaste

1.5   Abbreviations and numbers   *Word study*

A   Work in pairs. Look at these common abbreviations and write down
what each one stands for. The first is done for you as an example:

approx. *approximately*
c/o   intro.   RSVP
cont'd   max.   VAT
GMT   min.   VIP
incl.   misc.   vocab.
info.   PTO   Xmas

B Write these numbers out in full. The first is done as an example:

333 three hundred and thirty-three

144   850,000 $\frac{7}{8}$

113   5.75 $1\frac{1}{4} + 2\frac{2}{3} = 3.9167$

227   1,992 $4\frac{3}{4} - 2\frac{1}{2} = 2.25$

When you've finished, compare your answers with a partner.

C   Listen to the recording and write down the numbers you hear. The first six are telephone numbers, and the rest are different kinds of numbers. The first is done for you as an example:

1   'Five one eight O four double seven'   5180477

When you've finished, compare your answers with a partner. If necessary, listen to the recording again to check your answers.

D   Work in pairs. One of you should look at Activity 1 (on page 209), the other at Activity 10 (on page 212). You'll each have some names, addresses and phone numbers that you must dictate to your partner. Write down all the information that your partner gives you.

1.6   Advertisements
Speaking and listening

A   Look at this advertisement. Imagine that you want to describe it to a friend who hasn't seen it.

- What would you tell them about it?
- What do you find amusing or interesting about the product advertised?

B 🎬 Work in pairs. One of you should look at Activity 13, the other at 20. You'll each see an advertisement that you will have to describe to your partner.

C 📼 You'll hear five authentic radio commercials. Listen to the recording and fill the gaps in these sentences, using the information given.

1 HARRODS is open on August 29th (Bank Holiday Monday) from .... a.m. to .... p.m.
2 FILIPPO BERIO is a brand of ....
   'Filippo Berio .... – the .... choice.'
3 HEATBUSTERS can help to make your office .... in .... weather. Heatbusters supply .... air .... on hire.
   'Call Freefone Heatbusters – no ....'
4 CITRUS SPRING is a sparkling blend of .... water and .... juice.
   'Citrus Spring, the .... fruity drink.'
5 Lucy persuaded Dirk Studebaker to get out of his car by cooking him a meal.
   'I cooked him dinner: frankfurters and ....,
   with two .... and for a surprise,
   we had some gammon with a .... ring,
   that's what I cooked him.' 'Did you miss ....?' 'Don't think so.'
   'Was the .... on the side of his plate?'
   'It was Heinz, it was Heinz on his plate.'
   'Give me ...., give me .... of that Heinz ketchup taste.
   Eat it all, eat it all, 'cause it's too good to ....'
   'Are you seeing Dirk again tonight, Lucy?' 'You betcha !!*'
   'Heinz is the ketchup so .... and so ....,
   Heinz is the ketchup for .... for two.'   * Yes, definitely!!

When you've finished, compare your answers with a partner. Which of the products would YOU buy and/or not buy?

D Work in groups. Look at some more magazine or newspaper advertisements. IF POSSIBLE, CUT SOME INTERESTING ADVERTISEMENTS OUT OF MAGAZINES AND BRING THEM TO CLASS TO DISCUSS.

• Which is the most attractive and the least attractive? Why?
• Which is the most amusing? Why?
• Which is the most effective and the least effective? Why?

E Describe your favourite AND most hated TV commercials to your partners.

1.7   Which gift?   *Problem solving*

The problem-solving sections in *Progress to First Certificate* will help you to deal with the last question in the Use of English paper. In this part of the exam you will have to extract information from a text, advertisement, picture or diagram and then rewrite some of it in your own words.

A   Work in small groups. Ask your partners these questions:
- What points do you consider when buying a present for a friend or relation?
- What kind of gifts do you like to receive?

B   Read about these products and note down the MAIN ATTRACTION of each one. Which of them (if any) would YOU like to receive as a gift?

Voice Over Could you be a pop star? Like to sing? If so, this is for you. Using this little unit with your personal or home hi-fi you can sing over your favourite tape and record the result at studio quality. The mixer unit includes echo effect, stereo headphones/microphone, a tape of popular backing tracks and a booklet of lyrics. You can sing solo or with a friend. The Voice Over can also be used with any electronic instrument.

£39.95

The Alarm Wallet It looks like a high-quality leather wallet made of soft leather. Inside, there are special pockets for credit cards, loose change, tickets and stamps – as well as two full length pockets for notes.

It would be a shame to lose such an attractive, practical wallet – but you won't, because under the gold-coloured plate on the front is a light-sensitive cell. When you put the wallet into your pocket, slide the plate to the left. If anyone removes the wallet from the darkness of your pocket or handbag (or if it just falls out) a loud electronic alarm will sound. With the Alarm Wallet, you'll never lose your wallet again!

£14.95 (incl. battery)

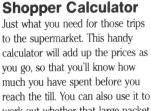

Shopper Calculator
Just what you need for those trips to the supermarket. This handy calculator will add up the prices as you go, so that you'll know how much you have spent before you reach the till. You can also use it to work out whether that large packet is really cheaper than two smaller ones. Complete with trolley attachment and neck cord.

£5.95 (white or black)

Beach Chair The only companion you need for a day in the sun. Made from strong yellow nylon with a lightweight steel frame, the Beach Chair is easy to carry but has masses of room in its insulated cool bag to hold refreshments, sun-tan oil etc., keeping them cool and out of the heat. There's even space for a magazine or sunshade.

Unfolded, it's a comfortable chair for sunbathing or just relaxing with a good book. Just what you need for holidays or weekends. **£14.95**

C Imagine that your two friends, Chris and Jo, have birthdays very soon:

CHRIS is a student, a person who likes being out of doors, enjoys playing sports and also watching sport on TV. Chris also likes learning languages and enjoys shopping – especially in supermarkets! Next summer Chris hopes to go to the USA to work in a summer vacation camp for children to earn enough money to spend two weeks travelling round the country.

JO is a student who likes reading, going to the cinema and listening to music – and also plays the guitar and likes singing. Jo also enjoys swimming and lives near the sea and in the summer holidays often spends the day at the beach. The other members of Jo's family all work, so Jo is the one who has to do all the shopping for the family.

1 Work in pairs or groups. From the items shown in B, choose a gift for Chris and a gift for Jo. Decide first if they are male or female friends – this isn't clear from their names. If a price seems too high, you could share the cost with your partners. MAKE NOTES of the reasons:
   - why each friend would appreciate the gift you have chosen
   - what uses he or she would find for it
   - AND why the other products would be less suitable.

2 Look at Activity 4, where you will see some model notes.

D Now write two paragraphs, explaining which of the gifts you would buy for Chris and Jo. Here are some structures you could use:

As Jo likes ...., the ideal gift would be ...
Jo enjoys .... and ...., so ...
.... would be a suitable gift for Jo because ...

When you've finished, compare your written work with a partner's work. Then look at Activity 27, where you will see two model paragraphs.

1.8 Using prepositions – Revision   *Use of English*

about   at   by   down   for   in   of   off
on   out of   over   to   under   up   with

This exercise gives you a chance to TEST YOUR KNOWLEDGE of some prepositions and adverbs that you should already know.
   Fill the gaps in these sentences with a suitable preposition from the list above. The first is done for you as an example:

1 A is ....for.... apple.
2 Chris is a very good friend .... mine.
3 We both share a love .... music.
4 It's warm .... the time of year.
5 I've been waiting .... an hour.
6 I'm looking for a book .... animals.
7 Why have you got that funny hat .... ?

12

8 Our arrangement for tomorrow is ....
9 Hamlet was written .... Shakespeare.
10 I've read the works .... Shakespeare.
11 We'll discuss this .... lunch.   *at, over,*
12 When does the train .... London leave?
13 Part-time workers are paid .... the hour.
14 When will she be .... hospital?
15 I can't see because the lights are ....
16 The shops are closed .... Sundays.
17 On Monday I'm taking the day ....
18 The bill must be paid .... Monday.
19 When you leave, make sure the gas is ....
20 I bought it .... £3 in a second-hand shop.
21 I opened the can .... a can opener.
22 This pullover is a bargain .... £13.99.
23 I was .... to go out when the phone rang.
24 Liverpool won .... 3 goals .... 0.
25 Harrods is a famous store .... London.
26 Ships are made .... steel.
27 I'm just .... to town to do some shopping.
28 Cambridge is 100 km north .... London.
29 My brother is very good .... maths.
30 Now, I think all our problems are ....
31 He gave me a pat .... the back.
32 The total cost is .... £100.
33 He was wearing a coat .... a torn sleeve.

When you've finished, compare your answers with a partner.

1.9 Buying a camera   *Listening*

A   Before you listen to the recording, look at these instructions. From
your own knowledge of photography, note down in the gaps any
information that you expect will be given. Use a pencil.

ACME INSTAMATIC CAMERA £29.95

SPECIAL OFFER £19.95

INSTRUCTIONS

1 Load film cassette.
2 Set film speed to .... or ....
3 Press WIND lever till .... appears in
   the small ....
4 Set focus to symbol of .... for close-ups
   or .... for landscapes.
5 Press shutter very ....
   If .... light appears, shoot picture.
   If .... light appears, switch to ....
6 Wind film on for next shot.

B 🔊 Listen to the recording and fill the gaps in the instructions on the previous page.

When you've finished, compare your answers with a partner. If you had to leave any gaps, or if you disagree about any of the information, listen to the recording again.

C 🎬 The class is divided into an even number of pairs or groups. Half the groups should look at Activity 16, the others at 23. You'll be discussing what advice you'd give to someone on buying something they haven't bought before.

1.10 Starting out ...   *Composition*

A Even a good composition looks bad if it contains too many spelling mistakes. There are sixteen typical mistakes in these sentences. Find the errors and correct them. The first is done for you as an example:

> _address_
> Please let me know your ~~adress~~.
> My brother is ninteen years old.
> One day he's hopping to go to Amerika.
> It was a realy wonderfull meal!

> I recieved your letter this morning.
> He want to improve his knoledge of english.
> Concorde flys accross the Atlantic in 4 ours.
> Some people find speling especialy dificult.

★ Most spelling errors can be avoided if you use a dictionary to look up any words you're unsure of – and if you check your written work carefully.

B Another problem is punctuation: especially the use of commas and apostrophes. Here is another student's work. Find the punctuation mistakes and correct them. The first is done as an example:

> _London's_
> Harrods is ~~Londons~~ most famous department store, You can buy
> almost anything there and its one of the Landmark's of London?
> people come to eat at it's Restaurants and look round its' 214
> Departments But not everyone comes to buy many of the people
> who go there are just having a look at the enormous range of
> goods on display and at the other customers

C This paragraph has no punctuation at all! Rewrite it, adding any punctuation necessary.

```
Every Tuesday Friday and Saturday in our part of the city
theres an open-air market in the main square which everyone
goes to Farmers come in from the countryside to sell their
fresh vegetables and fruit Other stalls sell all kinds of
things cheese jeans fish and even second-hand furniture Its
almost impossible to carry on a conversation above the noise
and shouting as customers push their way to the front trying
to attract the stall-holders attention and demanding the
ripest freshest fruit or the lowest prices
```

You'll find a corrected version of this paragraph in Activity 37.

14

D Work in small groups or pairs and discuss these questions:
- What is your favourite shop or store?
- What facts do you know about it?
- What is it like to be there? What impression does a foreigner get?
- What do you like and dislike about it?

E Write two paragraphs about the shop or store you have discussed.
  In the first paragraph, describe the shop:
    its location, what it sells, why it's well-known, etc.
  In the second paragraph, give your impressions of it:
    what you like and perhaps dislike about it.

1 MAKE NOTES before you start writing.
2 Write the two paragraphs.
3 When you have finished, look through your work and correct any SPELLING or PUNCTUATION mistakes.
4 Show your work to another student and ask for comments. Make any changes you think are necessary before handing your work in to your teacher.
5 Your teacher will mark your work and give you some advice on how your writing could be improved.

1.11 *Look* and *see*   *Verbs and idioms*

A Fill the gaps in these sentences with a suitable verb from the list – in some, more than one verb can be used. The first is done for you as an example:

see look watch notice recognise observe gaze

1 It's quite amusing to .**observe**. the behaviour of people while they're shopping.
2 We .... them playing football.
3 He .... at her admiringly.
4 I waved at you, but you didn't .... me.
5 I didn't .... you in your new glasses.
6 He tried to get to his seat without being ....
7 I usually .... TV on Fridays.
8 Have you .... that new film yet?
9 I'll .... what I can do to help you.
10 This exercise .... difficult.

B Replace the underlined words with a suitable phrasal verb with LOOK or SEE, using the word on the right. The first two are done as examples:

1 Their aunt cared for them after their mother's death. **looked after**   AFTER
2 They said goodbye to me at the airport. **saw me off**   OFF
3 What are you trying to find?   FOR
4 Be careful! There's a car coming.   OUT
5 All the pupils respect their teacher.   *look* UP TO *(respect)*

15

6 Leave it to me! I'll <u>take care of</u> all the arrangements. 为心.注意
7 The police are <u>investigating</u> a case of shoplifting.
8 He said he was innocent but they <u>realised</u> his story was untrue.
9 If you don't know the meaning, <u>find</u> the word in a dictionary.
10 Next time you're in town, why don't you <u>pay us a call</u> and say hello.
11 Before you <u>hand</u> your work <u>in</u>, <u>check</u> it carefully.
12 I'm <u>thinking about</u> my next holiday <u>with pleasure</u>.

TO
INTO
~~THROUGH~~ See
UP
~~IN~~ look 顺便看望
THROUGH
FORWARD TO

★ There are four types of phrasal verb. Notice the structures in these examples:

1 LOOK AFTER (= care for) – the same as a verb + preposition
I looked after someone ✔ I looked after him ✔ He was looked after ✔
 BUT NOT: I looked someone after ✗ I looked him after ✗

2 LOOK OUT (= be careful) – ~~intransitive~~ phrasal verbs (no object)
You must look out! ✔
 BUT NOT: You were looked out ✗

3 LOOK UP (= find information) – 'separable' phrasal verbs
I looked up a word ✔ I looked a word up ✔ I looked it up ✔
The word was looked up ✔
 BUT NOT: I looked up it ✗

4 ~~LOOK UP TO (= respect)~~ – 'inseparable' phrasal verbs
~~I look up to someone~~ ✔ I look up to her ✔ She was looked up to by everyone ✔
 BUT NOT: I look someone up to ✗ I look her up to ✗

★ Unfortunately, idiomatic phrasal verbs ARE difficult – the only thing to do is to learn them by heart. Moreover, many phrasal verbs have more than one meaning. In the Verbs and idioms exercises in *Progress to First Certificate* you'll only meet the more common, useful meanings.

'I'll take them!'

2 Leisure activities

2.1　Entertainment and sport

Vocabulary

A　Work in small groups. Ask your partners these questions:
- What are your hobbies?
- What kinds of entertainment do you enjoy most?
- What kinds of sport do you enjoy playing? And watching?
- If you weren't here in class, what would you like to be doing?

B　Find the missing words to fill the gaps in these sentences. The first is done for you as an example:

1　Leisure activities are things you do in your s*pare　time.*
2　I've got so much work to do that I don't have much time for r...........
3　Her hobbies are c............ stamps and t............photographs.
4　A TV show, film or play that makes you laugh is called a c............
5　I sat biting my nails during the film because it was such an exciting th............
6　The story isn't very good – in other words, it has a weak p.*lot*.
7　The person who tells the actors what to do is called the d............
8　In a cinema it's cheaper to sit close to the s............, but in a theatre it costs more to sit close to the s............
9　That film got extremely good r*eview*...in the newspapers.
10　The magician asked for two volunteers from the a............
11　I like an entertaining show, which is why I enjoy a good m............
12　We had a drink during the i............ between the two acts of the play and discussed the p............
13　Fewer people go to the cinema but instead they watch films at home on v............
14　I didn't like the hero or heroine – I preferred the wicked v............! *Villain 反面人物*
15　If you don't like the programme on BBC1, you can switch to another ch............
16　I enjoy listening to music on my ....
17　My favourite kinds of music are .... and ....
18　Did you see England play Brazil on TV? It was a very exciting m............
19　At the end of the game, when the r............ blew his w............, there was loud a............ from the ....
20　Liverpool is the football t............ that he s............
21　The winner of the competition received a silver c............ and a p............ of $300.
22　The result of the game was a d*raw*............: the final s............ was 4 – 4 (four all). *打成平局,不分胜负*
23　Tennis is played on a tennis c*ourt* and golf is played on a golf c*ourse*.
24　My favourite sports are .... and ....

>>>→

17

C   Work in small groups and find out about each other's favourite summer and winter sports. Using a dictionary, write down the words you need to describe:

- The PLACE each sport is played (in a stadium, on a pitch, in a pool, etc.)
- The EQUIPMENT needed (goals, a racket, skates, etc.)
- The PEOPLE involved in each game (players, referee, linesmen, etc.) 巡 边员
- The system of SCORING (3–nil, 15–love, etc.)

2.2   Fitness or fun?   *Reading*

A   Before you read this magazine article, look at these questions and see if you can guess the answers. Then find the answers in the text.

1 The most popular sporting activity in Britain is ....
2 More money is spent on .... than any other leisure-related activity.
3 Over the past 15 years 1,500 private .... have been built in Britain.
4 Over the past 15 years 1,500 public .... have been built in Britain.

Fitness *or fun?*

THE BRITISH as a nation do all kinds of things in their spare time: we go shopping or jogging, we play darts or football, we collect records or stamps, we go to church or to the pub. Some of these activities, like visiting relatives or taking driving lessons, may not be fun, but whatever we do, the way we spend our free time is probably providing someone with work. More people work in the sports industry than in the coal industry and the number of employees in restaurants, pubs and shops is rising all the time.

According to a recent survey, the number one leisure expenses are alcohol and smoking: every person in Britain spends £150 a year on beer, £140 on spirits and wine and £110 on cigarettes. Spending on sports is £60 per head and we each spend £20 gambling on sports. Do-it-yourself goods cost each person £50 per year and we each spend £40 on newspapers and magazines and £15 on cassettes, records and CDs. Cinema-going now accounts for only £2.50 per head and many families prefer to sit at home watching the same films on video. We still each spend £25 on our pets, and taking the dog for a walk provides good exercise for the dog and its owner.

In fact, walking is the most popular sport of all: out of a total population of around 55 million people, 9.5 million regularly walk two miles or more. More energetic sports are keep fit, including aerobics and yoga (1.2 million), and football, squash and golf each have 1.2 million regular players. Less actively, 4.7 million play snooker or pool and 1.7 million go fishing.

Watching other people playing is also a popular leisure activity: the favourite sports among TV viewers are horse-racing, football, snooker, cricket and tennis. Although 11 million watched the F.A. Cup Final on TV in May, only 1.3 million regularly go to watch professional and amateur football matches. 'New' TV sports like American football, basketball and even yachting are attracting more and more loyal armchair experts.

The fitness boom of the eighties led to a big rise in the numbers of people participating in

18

sports. To cater for this boom and provide the up-to-date facilities people want, over 1,500 private health and fitness clubs and the same number of public sports and leisure centres have been built during the past fifteen years. These modern centres, with their swimming pools, squash courts, gyms and indoor courts for tennis and other sports are competing with discos, pubs and cinemas as places for people to go to spend their leisure time – and their money. Now practically every town has a leisure pool with a wave machine, water slides and tropical plants. Four million people regularly swim in an indoor pool and now families can spend their holidays at huge indoor water parks, where they can play or relax all day long in warmth and comfort without worrying about the weather outside, though four million do swim in the sea at least once a year. One problem with this is that we may be becoming a nation of splashers not swimmers. The big question fitness experts are asking is: should sport be something you take seriously or should it just be fun?

B   Fill the gaps in these charts with information you'll find in the article:

Annual expenditure per head of population:

Motor vehicles	£180
Beer	£ ....
Spirits & wine	£ ....
Smoking	£ ....
Electricity	£90
Gas	£75
Bread	£75
Sports	£ ....
DIY goods	£ ....
Newspapers & magazines	£ ....
Pets	£ ....
Gambling	£ ....
Bingo	£5
Cinema	£ ....

Number of people who regularly take part in leisure activities:
(total population of UK 55 million)

Walking	....
Snooker & pool	....
Indoor swimming	....
Outdoor swimming	....
Darts	3.8 million
Fishing	....
Going to football matches	1.3 million
Keep fit, aerobics & yoga	....
Football	....
Squash	....
Golf	....

C   Work in small groups. Ask your partners these questions:
• What sports and entertainments are most popular in your own country?
• What are the differences between your country and Britain?

2.3   Articles   *Grammar*

A   Remember that these common English nouns are 'UNCOUNTABLE':
furniture   information   weather   advice   hair   progress   news
We can't say: *a good news* ✗ or *a furniture* ✗
So we say: *a piece of good news* or *some good news* or *a piece of furniture*

■ Most nouns are 'countable', which means that we can use them in the plural.
We can say: *a car, some cars, many cars*
Some nouns are 'uncountable', which means that they can't be used in the plural.
We can say: *petrol, some petrol, much petrol*, BUT NOT: *a petrol* ✗ or *many petrols* ✗

Other uncountable nouns are: *wine   freedom   safety   water*

Which of these nouns are 'countable' and which are 'uncountable' – and which could be either, depending on their meaning?

bread butter food blood glass fire milk salt money suitcase luggage room accommodation mathematics lesson education health

B Look at these examples and fill the gaps with suitable words. The first is done for you as an example:

THE is used in these cases:
- Referring to things that are UNIQUE:

  I'm worried about the future.   The most popular sport in Britain ...

  The Queen of England ...   The sea is too rough to swim in.

  .... best football team in the world ... What time does .... rise?

  (BUT: See the notes on planets, mountains, parks, etc. below.)
- When it's obvious which one you mean:

  We're going to the pub.   I'm taking the dog for a walk.

  How many students are there in ....?

  We are taking .... exam in ....
- When we mean a particular person or thing:

  The actor who played the villain ...

  The big question fitness experts are asking ...

  .... of the film *Psycho* was Alfred Hitchcock.
- Oceans, seas and rivers:

  the Atlantic, the Aegean, the Thames, ..., ...
- Plural mountain groups, island groups and countries:

  the Andes, the Canary Islands, the Netherlands, ..., ...
- Hotels, cinemas, theatres, museums:

  the Ritz, the Gaumont, the Playhouse, the National Gallery, ..., ...

A or AN is used in these cases:
- Referring to a single thing or person:

  There's a cinema opposite the bank (one of many cinemas in the town).

  It's a difficult exercise.   A leisure pool usually has ....
- A friend of mine ...   She's .... of Peter's.   (BUT: He's one of my friends.)
- It was quite an interesting story.   She's such .... person.
- Professions or jobs:

  He's an actor.   She's an engineer.   My father's ....   My mother's ....
- Generalisations:

  An actor performs in front of an audience.   .... has to be a good leader.

0 – the 'zero article' is used in these cases:
- Generalisations about plural ideas, people or things:

  New cars are expensive.   Bicycles are pollution-free.

  .... are useful.   .... are noisy.
- She went to school in England.   You mustn't smoke in class.   We go to church.
- Planets, continents, countries, states:

  Jupiter, Europe, Britain, Holland, California, ..., ...

  (BUT: the Earth, the Sun, the Moon, the Soviet Union, the United Kingdom)
- Languages: English, Dutch, ..., ...
- Mountains and lakes: Mount Fuji, Lake Geneva, ..., ...
- Streets, roads and squares:

  Oxford Street, Fifth Avenue, Trafalgar Square, ..., ..., ...

20

- Parks, stations and public buildings:
  Central Park, Victoria Station, Gatwick Airport, ..., ..., ...
- Referring to things and ideas that are uncountable:
  shopping, freedom, knowledge, pollution, liberty, democracy, history, music, tennis, stamp-collecting, watching television, swimming

C   Each of these sentences contains two (✗✗) or three (✗✗✗) errors. Find the mistakes and correct them. The first is done for you as an example:

1 *I'm attending the class A4, which is preparing for exam in June.* ✗✗
   I'm attending class A4, which is preparing for the exam in June.
2 *I'm looking for an accommodation with a English family.* ✗✗
3 *More women are involved in the politics in Britain than in the other countries.* ✗✗
4 *The most people agree that the women can do the same work as the men.* ✗✗✗
5 *To get to the library, go along the Elizabeth Road and take first right.* ✗✗
6 *The violence is very great problem in the world today.* ✗✗

D   Fill the gaps in this story, using *a*, *an*, *some*, *a lot of*, *lots of* or *the* – or a 'zero article' (∅). The first two are done for you as examples:

Last week I went to ...*an*... exhibition of ...*∅*... paintings at .... Tate Gallery in London. I'm not really .... great art lover but I'd read .... good reviews of .... exhibition and I was keen to see it. When I arrived, there were already .... people waiting outside for .... doors to open. I joined .... queue and in .... end .... doors opened and we went inside to see .... show.
   Now, I must be honest and admit that many of .... paintings disappointed me. Although I spent .... time looking carefully at .... each one, I had difficulty in understanding what .... artist was getting at. Finally, as I was looking rather stupidly at one of .... paintings and trying to decide if it was .... right way up or not, ... old gentleman came up behind me and started to explain .... whole thing to me. He kindly answered all of .... my questions and we talked for over .... hour. Then he said he had .... appointment and had to go, so we shook hands and said goodbye. I went round .... gallery once more and now I found that all .... paintings seemed really beautiful.
   It was only as I was leaving .... gallery that I found out who .... old man was – his self-portrait was on .... posters advertising .... exhibition!

E   Write these notes and headlines out in full. More than one version is possible in some cases, and you'll have to change the tenses. The first is done as an example:

1 *Class 4 need information about exam in December.*
   Class 4 need more information about the exam in December.
2 *Please don't send results of exam to address in UK.*
3 *Bring example of good and bad advertisement to class tomorrow.*
4 **President of France and Queen open Channel Tunnel**
5 **GROUP OF TAXI-DRIVERS WIN £1 MILLION IN LOTTERY**
6 **Man finds valuable painting in garden shed**

2.4 What sort of films do you enjoy?

A 📼 You'll hear part of a conversation between two friends who are planning to go to the cinema. They're trying to agree what film to go and see.

Mark with a tick (✓) in the appropriate column the films each of them likes, and with a cross (✗) the ones they dislike.

	BOB	SUSAN		BOB	SUSAN
Thrillers			Harrison Ford		
Action films					
Horror films			Clint Eastwood		
Love stories					
Films with subtitles			Sylvester Stallone		
Comedies			Robert Redford		
Cartoons					
Black and white films			Eddie Murphy		

Compare your answers with a partner and, if necessary, listen to the recording again to settle any disagreement.

B 📼 Now you'll hear the message they heard when they phoned the local multi-screen cinema to find out what was on. Fill the gaps below.

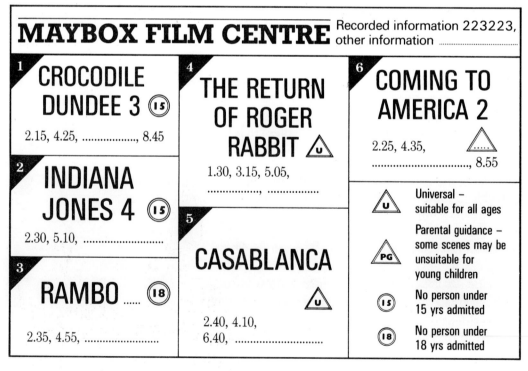

MAYBOX FILM CENTRE   Recorded information 223223, other information ....

1 CROCODILE DUNDEE 3 (15)
2.15, 4.25, ..., 8.45

2 INDIANA JONES 4 (15)
2.30, 5.10, ...

3 RAMBO ..... (18)
2.35, 4.55, ...

4 THE RETURN OF ROGER RABBIT ⚠U
1.30, 3.15, 5.05, ..., ...

5 CASABLANCA ⚠U
2.40, 4.10, 6.40, ...

6 COMING TO AMERICA 2
2.25, 4.35, ⚠ ...., 8.55

⚠U	Universal – suitable for all ages
⚠PG	Parental guidance – some scenes may be unsuitable for young children
(15)	No person under 15 yrs admitted
(18)	No person under 18 yrs admitted

- Which of the films did they decide to go to, do you think?

2.5 Using prefixes *Word study*

A Look at these examples and add more of your own, using the root words below with one of the prefixes in this list.

co   co-chairman co-worker ....
mid   midnight midair midweek ....
over   overact overpaid overdone ....
under undercharged underpaid ....
re   rebuild reappear redone ....
self   self-help self-contained ....
sub   subnormal subway ....
un   untie undo ....

afternoon arrange button charge control done driver excited
fold marry morning screw service standard way winter wrap

B Fill the gaps in these sentences, using a prefix with the correct form of the root word on the right. The first is done for you as an example:

1 I was late because I ...*underestimated*... how much time I'd need.   ESTIMATE
2 He wrote the book alone, so he doesn't have a ....   AUTHOR
3 Even if you're good at a game, you shouldn't be ....   CONFIDENT
4 It is very rude to interrupt someone in ....   SENTENCE
5 Many buildings were .... after the earthquake in 1980.   BUILD
6 Most people who work feel that they are ....   PAY
7 She's having a rest because she has been ....   WORK
8 I'd lost my key so I couldn't .... the door when I got home.   LOCK
9 We have .... temperatures every night in ....   ZERO WINTER *sub-zero*
10 People who .... often become ....   EAT WEIGHT

23

2.6 Safety at sea *Listening*

A   You'll hear part of a radio broadcast. Before you listen to the recording look at the questions below and try to predict what the answers might be.

B 📼 Listen to the recording and answer the questions.
   Compare your answers with a partner and, if necessary, listen to the recording again to settle any disagreements.

The skin diver

A   B   C

The water skier

D   E   F   G

1 Match the signals illustrated above to these meanings:
   a) 'I am OK.'
   b) 'I need assistance.'
   c) 'I have a diver down. Keep clear and proceed at slow speed.'
   d) 'Faster!'
   e) 'Slower!'
   f) 'Speed OK.'
   g) 'Back to jetty.'

2 Instead of using the Faster signal, you can ....
3 Instead of using the Slower signal, you can ....

4 Advice to the water skier:
   a) There should be two people in the boat: one to .... and the other to..............
   b) Before starting, your ski-tips must be ....
   c) Give a clear signal to the helmsman of the boat when you are ready to ....
   d) If you are falling forwards you should ....
   e) If you fall sideways, you should ....
   f) If you fall, recover the skis at once because ....

2.7 The Month in View

A Imagine that you are in Britain in November – an ideal month for TV viewing! Which days would you stay at home and watch television if you were interested in the following subjects? The first is done as an example:

1 crime stories   Nov 16
2 France   ....
3 inventions   ....
4 nuclear disarmament   ....

5 painting   ....
6 recent history   ....
7 women in society   ....

DO NOT study the text. Don't use a dictionary to look up unfamiliar words. Just search for the answers to the questions. It is not necessary to understand every word of the article.

THE MONTH IN VIEW

■ Nov 4. **Eureka** (BBC2)
Children's programme in which one of the liveliest of the new television presenters, Jeremy Beadle, tells us who invented what, & how; this week, the ballpoint pen, safety pin, can opener & zipper.

■ Nov 4. **Tom Keating on Painters** (C4)
The master forger of Samuel Palmer's paintings, & much else, tells how he does it. Keating is fascinated by technique. He copies for the joy of it, not in order to mislead, & his descriptions of the Venetians, Constable & Degas are wonderful to hear.

■ Nov 5. **Sorry** (BBC1)
A new series with Ronnie Corbett trying to escape from home.

■ Nov 5. **Ballroom of Romance** (BBC2)
A simple story, beautifully told, about the people at a dance evening in a small Irish village. This kind of gentle story-telling is something that television can do better than any other medium, & *Ballroom* is exceptionally good of its kind; with Cyril Cusack & Brenda Fricker.

■ Nov 5. **The Other 'Arf** (ITV)
The new series starts with Charles Latimer (John Standing) about to leave the Tories & join the SDP. Also with glorious cockney Lorraine Chase & James Villiers.

■ Nov 7. **Nicholas Nickleby** (C4)
The Royal Shakespeare Company production of Dickens's sprawling adventure was one of the theatrical hits of recent years. This four-part, nine-hour TV version, filmed in the theatre, should recapture all the magic of the performances (notably Roger Rees as Nicholas, David Threlfall as Smike & Edward Petherbridge as Newman Noggs) & much of the rapid-fire action as well.

■ Nov 9 **Intensive Care** (BBC1)
A typical Alan Bennett play, keenly observed & extracting humour from situations that, to many people, don't seem funny at all. Alan Bennett, as the remorseful son, sits with his aunt (Thora Hird) in a hospital waiting room, getting to know the staff (including Julie Walters), & other patients.

■ Nov 10. **The Barchester Chronicles** (BBC2)
A welcome seven-part adaptation by Alan Plater of Trollope's story of clerical intrigue & secular romance; the cast has Nigel Hawthorne, Geraldine McEwan, Clive Swift & Susan Hampshire.

■ Nov 10. **Year of the French** (BBC2)
Twice-weekly documentary series showing the lives of 12 French people. Tonight's film is about singer/song-writer Marie-Paule Belle; Friday's programme looks at Bernard Capdérey, a skiing gendarme in the Pyrenees.

■ Nov 11. **Yes, Prime Minister** (BBC2)
Paul Eddington & Nigel Hawthorne return for a third series of this all-too-accurate Whitehall comedy.

■ Nov 12. **Our Winnie** (BBC2)
The first of five shortish plays by Alan Bennett, all on BBC2, to complement his *Play for Today* on BBC1.

■ Nov 16. **The Manhood of Edward Robinson** (ITV)
This engaging story of a spoof burglary is a lovely vignette of Bright Young Things & their parties in the mid 1930s; sadly, it ends Thames's series of Agatha Christie plays.

■ Nov 18. **The Life & Times of Rosie the Riveter** (C4)
A marvellous, if loosely made, film in which US wartime propaganda about the necessity of women working in factories is contrasted with the women's own views. Most wrenching is how at the end of the war the women were summarily sacked & told to go home to look after the men.

■ Nov 23. **The Bomb** (ITV)
John Pilger, one of TV's (& Fleet Street's) most aggressive investigators, shows how western governments & the media are trying to accustom us to the idea of a limited nuclear war.

■ Nov 26. **The Sixties** (C4)
The best-loved decade since the war? The last of the good times or the beginning of the crack up? This six-part series remembers the Beatles (via an interview with their generous press agent, Derek Taylor), explains why the BMC Mini never made money, & offers an analysis of the economic problems & the emergence of political radicalism.

■ Nov 30. **Stuntman Challenge** (ITV)
Film stuntmen challenge each other to a series of stunts & tricks; an odd mix of bravery & lunacy.

B   Decide which of the following statements are true (**T**) or false (**F**), according to the text. Find the relevant programme and check the information given – you don't need to understand every word. The first is done for you as an example:

1 The presenter of *Eureka* is a well-known old inventor. **F**
2 Tom Keating is famous for his own style of painting.
3 *Sorry* is about a criminal in prison.
4 *Ballroom of Romance* is a story about people in Ireland.
5 Each episode of *Nicholas Nickleby* lasts over two hours.
6 *Intensive Care* is a tragic play about people in hospital.
7 *The Barchester Chronicles* is a serial based on a story by Trollope.
8 *Year of the French* can be seen once a fortnight.
9 *Yes, Prime Minister* is a popular funny programme.
10 According to John Pilger in *The Bomb*, some governments want us to agree that nuclear weapons can be used in a small war.

C   Work in small groups. Out of all the programmes listed, which would you like to see? Which would you definitely NOT watch? Note down your reasons.

   If there are no programmes that interest you among those listed, discuss what's *really* on TV (or at the cinema) this week.

★   In the Directed Writing section of the Use of English paper you'll have to write 3–4 paragraphs based on an information-gathering task. These problem-solving sections will help you to develop your paragraph-writing skills.

D   Write two paragraphs:
1 Explain which of the programmes listed in The Month in View (or TV programmes or films that are really on this week) you would like to see and give your reasons.
2 Explain which of the programmes (or films) you would NOT like to see.

Show your completed paragraphs to a partner and ask for his or her comments.

2.8   Position and direction   *Prepositions*

A   Take a pen or pencil and use it to DEMONSTRATE the meaning of these prepositions and prepositional phrases:

I'm holding it above my desk and now I'm going to put it behind me . . .

above
behind
underneath
on top of
in the top left-hand corner of
at the back of
beside
in the middle of
on the left/right of

at the bottom of	at the top of
between	opposite
next to	on the edge of
on the other side of	in the bottom right-hand corner of

B Look at this rectangle and add the letters B to F in the places described. The first (B) is done for you as an example:

1 B is half-way between A and the right-hand edge of the rectangle.
2 C is half-way between A and B.
3 D is about 1 centimetre above C.
4 E is underneath B.
5 F is in the top left-hand corner of the rectangle.

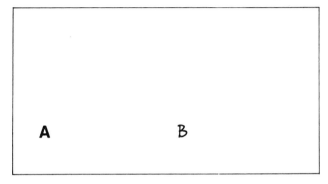

C Work in pairs. One of you should tell the other where to put letters G to K, the other should tell the other where to put letters L to P.

D 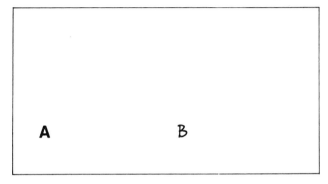 Work in pairs. One of you should look at Activity 32, the other at 40. You'll each have to explain to your partner the 'route' your partner's pencil should take between, past, above and below the letters and numbers in this grid to draw the picture in your activity. Begin like this: 'First of all draw a round spot beside the top right-hand part of R. Now draw another spot just above and to the left of S. OK? Now start drawing a line from ...'

A	B	C	D	E	F	G	H
I	J	K	L	M	N	O	P
Q	R	S	T	U	V	W	X
Y	Z	1	2	3	4	5	6
7	8	9	10	11	12	13	14
15	16	17	18	19	20	21	22

2.9 The jogger's wallet

Before you listen to the recording, look at these pictures and see if you can guess what happened to the man in the story.

Listen to the story and number the pictures to show the correct order.

2.10 Telling a story

A   Work in groups. Discuss these questions:
- What kinds of stories do you enjoy listening to or reading?
- Why are some people better at telling stories than others?
- Which of these things should a storyteller do?
    - get the events in the right sequence
    - add personal feelings and reactions
    - add dialogue
    - think of your audience: put yourself in their shoes

B   Look again at the pictures illustrating 'The jogger's wallet' story above. As a class, decide how you would tell the story as if it had happened to a friend of a friend of yours. (The same kind of event could have happened in a train, bus or lift, so you might decide to change the setting.)

Here are some questions that a listener or reader might ask:

> *What happened before that?*   *What happened next?*
> *What did you/he/she do after that?*   *How did you/she/he feel?*
> *What did you/she/he say?*   *Why did she/he/you do that?*

C   ⚇   Work in groups of three. Student A should look at Activity 17, student B at 24 and C at 46. You'll each see some scenes from a film and will have to work out the story of that film.

2.11   Writing a narrative   *Composition*

One of the topics in the Composition Paper of the exam is a narrative-writing question. When writing a narrative, you should consider how the reader will react to your story – will he or she be bored or interested?

A   Work in small groups. Look at this narrative and decide together:
1   What is wrong with the way it's written (the style)?
2   How can it be improved? What could be ADDED or CHANGED to make it more interesting to the reader? The first improvement is made for you as an example.

I'll never forget the night...   We were on our way home after a marvellous evening out with some friends.

```
I'll never forget the night our car broke down. We were
9.5 km from home and we had to walk there. It was 12.45
and it started to rain. We arrived home at 02.05. The door
of our house was locked because we had left the front door
key in the car. We broke a window but a policeman came and
we had to explain the situation to him. We went to bed at
3 o'clock.
```

Look at Activity 9, where you will see an improved version of the story.

B   Now decide how this narrative could be improved. What could be ADDED or CHANGED to make it more interesting to the reader?

CASABLANCA, starring Humphrey Bogart and Ingrid Bergman

```
An American (Rick) owned a night club in Casablanca
(Morocco) in the war. A girl (Ilsa) came there with her
husband (Victor Laszlo). Rick and Ilsa had been in love in
Paris before the war. Laszlo was in danger and had to
escape to Lisbon (by plane) but he had no visa. Rick sold
his club and bought two visas on the black market. In the
end Laszlo and Ilsa flew off to freedom. Rick and the chief
of police (Renault) stayed at the airport. The End.
```

Look at Activity 3, where you will see an improved version of the story.

C Write a composition on one of these topics:
1 Tell the story of a film you remember well.
2 Write a story about your own or someone else's experiences beginning:
   'I'll never forget the night …'   *or*   'I'll never forget the day …'
   or   'This may sound incredible but it really happened: …'

D Before handing your story in to be corrected, show it to one or two other students and ask for their comments.
- How could your stories be improved?
- Which of your partners' ideas could you use in your own written work?

2.12 *Make* and *do*   *Verbs and idioms*

A Decide which of the endings below go with these beginnings:

Bill made …
Shirley did …

…Shirley laugh   …Bill a favour   …the washing-up   …his/her duty
…a cake   …a noise   …a mistake   …an arrangement   …the shopping
…a comment   …a decision   …an exercise   …his/her homework
…a good job   …badly in the test   …a good impression   …me an offer
…a promise   …a statement   …her/his best   …very well   …nothing at all

B Fill the gaps with suitable forms of the phrasal verbs below:

do
1 Phew, I'm ever so thirsty, I could ……………… a drink.   *do with 将就 能对付*
                                                          希望得到. 需要
2 They've just finished ……………… their flat and it looks really nice now.
3 She was very angry because her rival had ……………… her ……………… of the reward.
4 He had to ……………… sugar in his coffee, because he was on a diet.
make
5 I can't quite ……………… if that's your sister or you in this photo.
6 As you've arrived late, you'll have to ……………… the time you've lost.
7 We were ……………… the station when the thunderstorm broke.
8 Is this the truth or are you ……………… it ………………?
9 A dog picked up my sandwich in its mouth and ……………… it.

do someone out of   do up   do with   do without
make for   make off with   make out   make up
make up for

3 Nature and the environment

3.1 Plants and animals   *Vocabulary*

A   Add THREE more items to each list. Use a dictionary if necessary. The first is done for you as an example:

1 Cereals: oats, rye, *maize, barley, wheat*
2 Fruit: grape, pear, peach, ...
3 Vegetables: spinach, radish, carrot, ...
4 Trees: pine, olive, oak, ...
5 Flowers: rose, daisy, carnation, ...
6 Wild animals (mammals): rabbit, tiger, whale, ...
7 Domestic animals: turkey, camel, goat, ...
8 Pets: parrot, goldfish, ...
9 Birds: sparrow, eagle, pigeon, ...
10 Young animals: puppy, calf, chick, ...
11 Reptiles: lizard, alligator, ...
12 Insects: butterfly, wasp, ant, ...
13 Fish: salmon, shark, ...
14 Other sea creatures: oyster, octopus, crab, ...

B   Find the missing words to fill the gaps in these sentences. The first one is done for you as an example:

1 Less than 2% of the British labour force is employed on farms in *agriculture.*
2 In the autumn, at h............... time, the c...............s in the fields have to be gathered in and the fruit in the orchards has to be p...............
3 In the Alps, cows are kept indoors in winter and spend the summer in the m...............s.
4 The sport that involves chasing or shooting animals is called h...............
5 P............... is caused when waste products or p...............s contaminate the environment.
6 According to the weather f..............., there will be sunny i...............s this morning.
7 In the early morning there may be thick f............... and motorists should drive slowly.
8 We couldn't see very far from the top of the hill because it was slightly ....y.
9 During the night t............... will fall below freezing and there will be a f...............
10 During the .... many trees were blown down.
11 Although it was really boiling in the sun, there was a light b............... from the sea, which made it feel quite pleasant in the s...............
12 Although the storm passed us by, we could hear the th............... and see the l............... in the distance.
13 It's not going to rain all day, it's just a sh............... . We'll soon be able to go out.
14 The s............... in the north of the country is spectacular with deep v...............s and high snow-capped peaks, but the c............... tends to be cool and wet.
15 The west c............... of the country has high c...............s as well as sandy beaches.

31

3.2 The balance of nature Reading

A Work in small groups. Before you read the passage, ask your partners these questions:
- What kinds of animals would be found in a wood or forest in your country?
- What kinds of plants would be found there?

B Read the passage through to find out what it's about. DO NOT use a dictionary.

All the different plants and animals in a natural community are in a state of balance. This balance is achieved by the plants and animals interacting with each other and with their non-living surroundings. An example of a natural community is a woodland, and a woodland is usually dominated by a particular species of plant, such as the oak 5 tree in an oak wood. The oak tree in this example is therefore called the dominant species but there are also many other types of plants, from brambles, bushes and small trees to mosses, lichens and algae growing on tree trunks and rocks.

The plants of a community are the producers: they use carbon 10 dioxide, oxygen, water and nitrogen to build up their tissues using energy in the form of sunlight. The plant tissues form food for the plant-eating animals (herbivores) which are in turn eaten by the flesh-eating animals (carnivores). Thus plants produce the basic food supply for all the animals of a community. The animals them- 15 selves are the consumers, and are either herbivores or carnivores.

Examples of herbivores in a woodland community are rabbits, deer, mice and snails, and insects such as aphids and caterpillars. The herbivores are sometimes eaten by the carnivores. Woodland carnivores are of all sizes, from insects such as beetles and lacewings to 20 animals such as owls, shrews and foxes. Some carnivores feed on herbivores, some feed on the smaller carnivores, while some feed on both: a tawny owl will eat beetles and shrews as well as voles and mice. These food relationships between the different members of the community are known as food chains or food webs. All food chains 25 start with plants. The links of the chain are formed by the herbivores that eat the plants and the carnivores that feed on the herbivores. There are more organisms at the base of a food chain than at the top; for example, there are many more green plants than carnivores in a community. 30

Another important section of the community is made up of the decomposers. They include the bacteria and fungi that live in the soil and feed on dead animals and plants. By doing this they break down the tissues of the dead organisms and release mineral salts into the soil.

C It would be hard to make sense of the passage without knowing the words in the following list:
1 Find the words in the passage and underline them.
2 Read the sentences before and after each word.
3 Match the words to their definitions below:

natural community (line 1) species (line 5) links (line 26)
woodland (line 4) tissues (line 11) organisms (line 28)
dominated (line 5) flesh (line 14) decomposers (line 32)

a) area covered with growing trees f) one ring in a chain
b) have the most important position g) organisms that feed on dead tissues
c) living things h) type of plant or animal
d) meat i) plants and animals living in one place
e) material making up a living thing

D These words in the passage are less important and it's only necessary to know what KINDS of things they are.
   Match the words to their approximate meanings below.

oak (line 5) trunk (line 9) lacewing (line 20)
bramble (line 8) snail (line 18) shrew (line 21)
moss (line 8) aphid (line 18) vole (line 23)
lichen (line 8) caterpillar (line 18) fungi (line 32)
algae (line 9)

a kind of insect a kind of large plant
a kind of simple plant a kind of small animal
a kind of tree part of a tree

E Decide whether the following statements are true (**T**) or false (**F**), according to the text.

1 All the animals in a wood depend on plants for their food supply.
2 All the plants in a wood are eaten by animals.
3 Some animals eat other animals.
4 Plants depend on the sun to grow.
5 Plants depend on the gases in the atmosphere to grow.
6 Not every food chain starts with plants.
7 The consumers are at the base of a food chain.
8 Some animals eat plant-eating animals and also flesh-eating animals.

F Work in small groups. Ask your partners these questions:
● How does man interfere with the balance of nature?
● What might the consequences of this be?

★ Although it's rarely necessary to understand every single word in a reading passage, some of the unfamiliar words may be KEY WORDS that you must know to understand the meaning of the passage. You can often work out the meaning of such words from their CONTEXT. This is often much easier and quicker to do than using a dictionary, or even asking your teacher.

3.3 The past

A Study these examples. Fill the gaps with suitable words, using the correct form of the word on the right. The first is done as an example:

The SIMPLE PAST is the tense most commonly used to refer to events that happened in the past:

The Second World War started in 1939.

I ...went... to the cinema last week.   GO

I .... a film about animals on TV last Wednesday evening.   SEE

In 1988 I .... my summer holidays in ....   SPEND

The PAST PROGRESSIVE is used to refer to simultaneous events or activities that continued or were interrupted:

We were lying in the sun while she was revising for her exam.

At 7.45 last night it was still raining.

We .... cards when the light went out.   PLAY

As the sun .... we decided to go for a drive.   SHINE

While you .... the bus, we walked all the way here.   WAIT

USED TO emphasises that the activity no longer takes place:

He used to smoke twenty cigarettes a day (but not now).

Before the war, more people .... on the land.   WORK

When I was a child, we .... a dog.   HAVE

The PAST PERFECT is normally used to emphasise that one past event happened before another:

Before we got our cat, we had never had a pet in our family.

It rained all day but I .... to pack an umbrella   FORGET

After I .... the book, I made some notes on it.   READ

They were still friends even though they .... apart for ten years. BE

The PRESENT PERFECT is only used to refer to the past:
– when no definite time in the past is given or known, or
– when the activity began in the past and has not yet finished.

It is often used with:

just   already   never   yet

He has seen that film three times.   Have you done your homework?

I have never seen a lion in the wild.

We .... already .... two units in this book.   STUDY

She .... five phone calls since lunchtime.   MAKE

.... you .... Britain?   VISIT

■ Remember that the PRESENT PERFECT is NOT used to refer to a definite time in the past and is NOT normally used after *When...?*

It is not used with:

last week, in July, on Wednesday, yesterday, a few minutes ago, etc.

I saw that film last week. ✓   NOT: I have seen that film last week. ✗

We did this exercise on Monday. ✓   NOT: We have done this exercise on Monday. ✗

When did you go there? ✓   NOT: When have you gone there? ✗

B   Find and correct the mistakes in these sentences. The first is done for you as an example:

The weather ~~were~~ lovely yesterday   *was*
I have gone to the zoo last weekend.
When have you left school?
Where you went on holiday last year?
She has been born in 1975.
Our family is used to live in a smaller flat when I am younger.
Our broken window wasn't mended yet.
The rain started during they played tennis.

C   Finish the incomplete sentences in such a way that each one means the same as the complete sentence before it. The first is done for you as an example:

1 We had a snack and then we had a look round the shops.
   After we <u>had had a snack, we had a look round the shops</u>.
2 The farmer started his tractor and began to plough the field.
   When ....
3 The rain began to fall during my walk in the country.
   While ....
4 We had lunch and then went for a walk by the river.
   After we ....
5 They don't have a dog any more.
   They used ....
6 I went to the zoo last year and that is where I saw a real tiger for the first time.
   Before I ....

D   Work in pairs. One of you should look at Activity 18, the other at 42. You'll each have a short story to tell, using past tenses.
1 Read the story through to yourself.
2 Make a few notes to help you remember the main points.
3 Tell the story to your partner – as if it really happened to some friends of a friend. Turn the book over while you're telling the story. Don't read it aloud.

'There's a furry thing in here eating cheese. I understand that's your department.'

DONEGAN

35

3.4   The earth at risk Listening

A   You'll hear an interview with a film-maker who has made a series of TV documentaries about the harm being done to the Earth.

Look at the questions below with a partner. Which of them can you answer before you hear the interview?

B   🔲 Listen to the recording and fill the gaps in these sentences.

1   In Africa, the Sahara Desert is *expanding* as people cut down trees for .... and their .... animals eat all the available plants.
2   In the USA intensive agriculture requires a plentiful supply of .... for crops to grow.
3   Growing crops stabilise ....; without them it just blows away.
4   American farmers grow huge quantities of extra ...., ... and soya beans that feed the world.
5   In South America (as in Central Africa and Southern Asia) .... are being cut down at an alarming rate.
6   Forests are cut down so that people can support themselves by growing .... or to create ranches where cattle can be raised for export to .... or .... as tinned meat.
7   The problem is that the soil is so .... that only a couple of harvests are possible before this very thin soil becomes ....
8   Huge numbers of trees are being cut down for export as hardwood to Japan, Europe, and .... to make luxury ....
9   Tropical forests contain ...., which we can use for ....
10   Destroying forests affects the climate of the whole ....
11   Floods in Bangladesh happen because forests in .... and .... have been cut down. Trees would hold .... in their roots.
12   There are three suggested solutions:
   1   National governments have to consider the results of their policies in .... or .... years and all the countries in the world have to work together on an .... basis.
   2   The population has to be .... in some way.
   3   We in the West should use .... instead of tropical ....

> Paper for books and newspapers normally comes from 'tree farms', where new trees are planted to replace the trees that have been cut down. Softwood for furniture and building is produced in the same way.

36

3.5 Using negative prefixes *Word study*

A   Look at these examples and fill each gap with more examples, using the root words below with one of the negative prefixes in this list.

un	unkind untidy	....
in	indirect indecent	....
il	illegal illegible illiterate	
ir	irregular irrelevant	
im	immature impossible immoral	....
dis	disagree dissatisfied	....
mis	misunderstand misbehave	....

accurate   approve   comfortable   convenient   expected   familiar   known like   lucky   obey   patient   personal   popular   probable   pronounce spell   tolerant   visible

B   Fill the gaps in these sentences, using a negative prefix with the correct form of the root word on the right. The first is done for you as an example:

1 Don't depend on him, he's a very _unreliable_ person.   RELY
2 Don't be so ...., we've only been waiting a few minutes.   PATIENT
3 7.30 a.m. on a Saturday is a rather .... time for an appointment. CONVENIENT
4 Please don't be so ...., I can't do all the work by myself.   REASON
5 There are always mistakes because the firm is so ....   EFFICIENT
6 Sorry about the mistake, I .... the instructions you gave me.   UNDERSTAND
7 They've .... my name on this form – the first letter is L not R.   SPELL
8 After I had got to know him better, I .... him intensely.   LIKE

3.6 What's the weather going to be like? *Problem solving*

Work in pairs or small groups for these activities. Imagine three friends of yours are travelling to different parts of the world.

A   [cassette] Listen to three recorded messages from your friends. Note down the places each of them will be this week and their contact phone number in each city.

• What temperatures and weather would these places have in June?

37

B   Look at the weather forecast for this week.

	Today			Outlook*	
		Stockholm	23	London	Thundery showers
Oslo	22	Copenhagen	19	Amsterdam	Sunny spells
Amsterdam	18	London	18	Bonn	Showers then fair
Brussels	18	Bonn	18	Brussels	Warmer, sunny
Paris	24	Vienna	20	Copenhagen	Showers then fair
New York	28	Geneva	22	Geneva	Mostly sunny
Los Angeles	21	Rome	26	Los Angeles	Dry and sunny
Moscow	16			Moscow	Cool, showers
				New York	Rain at times
				Oslo	Rain at times
				Paris	Mostly sunny
				Rome	Warm, sunny
				Stockholm	Showers, cooler
				Vienna	Showers then fair

*For next four days

- Note down the weather that Alan, Betty and Colin can expect on each day, according to the forecast.
- What clothes should they each pack, do you think?

C   Now look at Activity 15, where you will find out if the forecast for the middle of the week was correct or not.
- Which place had the worst weather?
- Which friend was most unlucky with the weather?

D   Read this postcard from Alan and then write two more postcards from Betty and Colin in a similar style, describing the weather in each place.

New York, Wednesday evening, 22 June

Dear Eddie,
It's really boiling here in New York: today has been really hot and sunny with a high of 36°! I was expecting that there would be some rain, but it was sunny at lunchtime when I went for a walk in Central Park. Paris on Tuesday was sunny too, but not as hot as here. London was warmer than I had expected but there was some rain in the afternoon.
See you on Saturday. What's the weather been like where you are?

Best wishes,
Alan

3.7 Compound prepositions

Use of English

Fill the gaps in these sentences with suitable phrases from the list below.
The first is done for you as an example:

1 The flight was cancelled ....**owing to**.... the fog.
2 We had wonderful weather every day .... Sunday.
3 Pollution can only be prevented .... international laws.
4 I love all animals .... dogs.
5 Tropical forests are being destroyed .... the demand for hardwood for furniture.
6 .... the weather forecast, it's going to snow.
7 Just a minute, I'll go .... you and hold the door open.
8 Hello. I'm phoning .... Mr Brown. He asked me to give you a message.
9 People should protect trees .... cutting them down.
10 They have two cats .... four pet rabbits.
11 .... pets, I don't think that people should keep them in small apartments.
12 .... conservation, I believe that the government should impose controls.

according to   ahead of   apart from   as for   as regards   by means of
due to   except for   in addition to/as well as   instead of   on behalf of
owing to ✓

3.8 The Greenhouse Effect

Reading

A   Fill the gaps in this diagram with information from the passage:

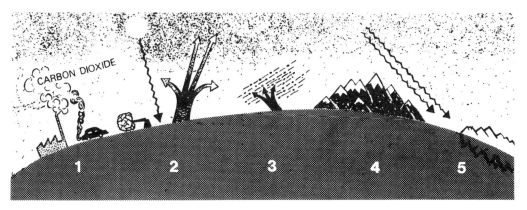

1 The burning of .... (coal, oil and natural gas) and the destruction of .... increase CO_2 in the ....
2 The surface of the Earth radiates .... Some of this escapes into ...., but the rest is .... by the CO_2. The temperature rises.
3 The rise in temperature increases the amount of water .... in the air and this .... more of the Earth's heat.
4 At the poles, snow and ice melt as the .... temperature rises. Because the exposed surface doesn't .... the heat so well, it absorbs more sunlight and more .... is melted.
5 As the oceans .... more heat, they increase the .... effect. The oceans .... and rise as more snow and ice melt.

THE GREENHOUSE EFFECT

In the 1960s Professor Bert Bolin predicted that the 'greenhouse effect', caused by an increase in the amount of carbon dioxide (CO_2) in the atmosphere, would lead to important changes in the Earth's climate. At the time his predictions were regarded as science fiction. But it is now generally agreed that the amount of carbon dioxide in the atmosphere will double from 0.03% to 0.06% in the next 50 years and that temperatures worldwide will rise by 2° Celsius.

Although a temperature rise of 2° may not seem significant, the local effects may be much greater: in polar regions a rise of 10° by 2025 is expected and in Northern Europe a rise of 4°. Indeed the first effects will be felt before the end of the century – perhaps they are already being felt . . .

But how does the 'greenhouse effect' operate and why should such a tiny proportion of CO_2 have such a harmful effect? When living creatures breathe out or when things are burned, CO_2 enters the atmosphere. Until recently all of this was absorbed by plants, which converted it back into oxygen.

However, the balance of nature has been disturbed. In power stations, in factories and in our cars, we are burning more and more fossil fuels (coal, oil and natural gas) and this produces huge quantities of CO_2 – 18 billion tons of it enter the atmosphere every year. Added to this, the destruction of forests means that less CO_2 can be converted into oxygen by plants. So, the amount of CO_2 in the atmosphere is increasing every year.

As sunlight enters the Earth's atmosphere, the surface of the Earth is warmed. Some of this heat escapes back into space, but the rest is trapped by CO_2, which acts like the glass in a greenhouse, allowing sunshine and heat to pass in but not out again. Consequently the temperature rises.

As the temperature rises, the amount of water vapour in the air will increase and this too will absorb more of the Earth's heat. The oceans too will become warmer and store more heat, so that they increase the warming effect.

According to Dr Syukuro Manabe of Princeton University, the polar icecaps will start to melt and the oceans will expand as more snow and ice melt. Because the exposed ground, formerly covered in snow, won't reflect the heat so well it will absorb more sunlight and this will lead to even more snow melting.

It is predicted that the level of the sea will have risen by ½ to 1½ metres by 2050 and this will affect many low-lying areas of the world – millions of people today live less than one metre above sea level.

Some areas may actually benefit: the higher temperatures may allow a longer growing season, for example. For Northern Europeans, the extra warmth may be welcome – but there is also likely to be increased rainfall.

But many areas may suffer: the southern states of the USA can expect hotter summers and less rainfall, leading to worse conditions for agriculture, and the Mediterranean region will probably be much drier and hotter than now.

The experts agree that the 'greenhouse effect' will bring significant changes to the Earth's climate. The inhabitants of this planet will have to get used to living in a hotter world.

B Decide whether the following statements are true (**T**) or false (**F**), according to the text.
1 Professor Bolin's predictions were not taken seriously at first.
2 Only a small proportion of the atmosphere consists of carbon dioxide.
3 No changes in climate will become noticeable for 50 years or more.
4 The rise in temperature will probably be 2° in every part of the world.
5 In the north of Europe, temperatures are likely to rise less than in polar regions.
6 CO_2 is produced naturally when we breathe or burn things.
7 CO_2 is converted naturally into oxygen by plants and trees.
8 Increased temperatures will also affect the amount of rainfall.
9 Countries like Greece and Italy are likely to have more rain.
10 Some parts of the world may become cooler as a result of the 'greenhouse effect'.

3.9 Making notes   *Composition*

The most important key to writing better compositions is deciding what to
write before you put pen to paper – by making notes. Notes help you to:
– organise your thoughts before you begin writing
– remember your ideas after you've started writing a composition.

A   There are several styles of making notes. Which of these examples do
you prefer?

1 RECYCLING
   1 Advantages:
     (a) saving energy
     (b) less need to burn fossil fuels
     (c) reusing resources
   2 Examples:
     (a) paper – save energy + save trees (but much paper produced
       on tree farms in places like Canada and Finland)
     (b) bottles – save energy by making new bottles out of old
       ones, but better to reuse bottles; reusable glass bottles
       better than throw-away plastic
     (c) aluminium cans – aluminium can be recycled, less need
       to mine
     (d) steel – save energy
   3 Drawbacks:
     (a) may be expensive
     (b) may require high technology

2

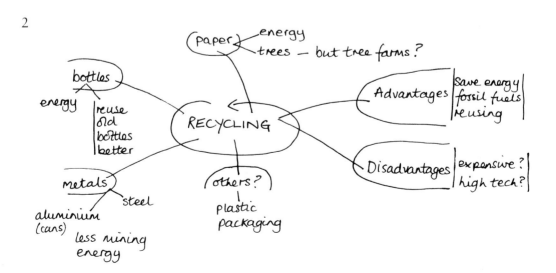

3 *paper – save energy, save trees*
bottles – save energy by making new bottles out of old ones,
    but even more saved by reusing bottles
cans – aluminium can be recycled, less need to mine
steel – save energy
energy saving / reusing resources
expensive / high tech ?

B Work in pairs. Make your own notes, summarising your own views
FOR and AGAINST one of these questions:
1 Save the whales
2 Stop scientific experiments on animals
3 Close all zoos

C Write two paragraphs of about 100 words each, giving reasons why
you agree with and disagree with the question.
    Check your completed work through and correct any errors in spelling
or grammar.

3.10 For or against?

Listening

A You'll hear three topics being discussed. Take notes (in your
own notebook) on the points the speakers make. The first is started for
you as an example here:

Discussion 1 is about: Keeping pets in cities.
Points FOR: Dogs can protect you from thieves and
    intruders.

Points AGAINST:

B Work in small groups. Find out your partners' views on the topics
that were discussed.

3.11 How sweet !?

A Work in pairs. Look at the pictures and write down THREE or FOUR questions that you can ask another pair about each one, or about any related discussion points. Try to think of questions that will lead to INTERESTING, LONG ANSWERS – not just Yes or No.

B Join another pair and ask them your questions. If you get a very short answer, encourage them to say more by prompting them, like this:
- What do you mean exactly?
- Can you give an example?
- I don't quite follow you.
- That's interesting.
- I see, is that what you both think?

C [icon] Work in pairs. One of you should look at Activity 34, the other at 44. You'll each have a different picture. Ask your partner these questions:
- What does your photograph show?
- What do you like and dislike about it?
- What kind of pets did your family have when you were younger?
- How would you feel if you were the person in the picture?

A   Fill each gap with a suitable phrase from the list below.

1 I'm trying to .... my cold.
2 I hope you soon ....
3 I .... after working all night.
4 She .... because her work was unsatisfactory.
5 We ought to go home, it's ....
6 He didn't laugh because he didn't ....
7 I need plenty of time to .... before I go out.
8 I .... after the party.
9 I was so excited that I couldn't ....
10 If you can't do it yourself, you'll have to .... for you.

get better   get ready   get rid of   get someone else to do it   get the joke
get to sleep   get dark   get a headache   get home late   get the sack

B   Fill the gaps in these sentences using the phrasal verbs given below.
The first is done for you as an example:

1 Please ..**get on with**.. your work, I didn't mean to interrupt you.
2 She doesn't .... her younger brother, they're always quarrelling.
3 I hope I'll be able to .... answering the letters this evening.
4 They managed to .... doing the work by pretending to be busy.
5 I tried to .... the point .... to him but he didn't seem to see what I
   was ....
6 This dull weather is so depressing – it's .... me ....
7 However difficult a problem is, there's usually a way to .... it.
8 You don't need two hot meals a day. I'm sure you can .... on one.
9 .... the bus when you get to the railway station.
10 How are you .... with this exercise?
11 I've tried ringing her several times but I haven't been able to ....
12 They decided to .... later in the week for an informal meeting.

get across   get around/round   get at   get by   get down   get off
get on   get on with ✓   get on with   get out of   get round to
get through   get together

'As you can see, we're very humane
in the way we test cosmetics on
animals.'

4 Transport and travel

4.1 On the move
Vocabulary

A Fill the gaps in these sentences with suitable words. The first is done for you as an example:

1 We got on the bus and the c.onductor............. came along to collect our f................s.
2 Some cities have buses, trolley-buses and also t................s.
3 By 1993, there won't just be ferries across the English Channel but also a t................
4 If you're travelling you can get a single or a r................ ticket.
5 Pedestrians are supposed to walk on the p................
6 We were pleased to find there was a f................ so we had a beautiful walk along the cliff top.
7 The lower tax on unleaded p................ is not going to affect many m................s.
8 If you're sitting in the front seat of a car, you're supposed to wear a s................
9 Before you get in the car, put your luggage in the b................
10 Chris started the engine, looked in the m................ and drove ....
11 There was something wrong with the e................ of the car so I looked under the b................
12 In Britain you have to give w................ to traffic from the right on a r................
13 If you're going to turn left at the traffic l................s, get into the left-hand l................
14 On a narrow road it's almost impossible to overtake a car that's towing a c................
15 Take the first left, then the second right and then go s................ on.
16 We drove round the town centre for half an hour looking for a parking s................
17 Jo hates being a passenger in a car because she gets c................ s................
18 The driver swerved to avoid hitting the dog but he crashed into a road s................
19 In Britain, drivers usually stop if you're waiting to cross at a p................ c................
20 When someone is leaving you can say to them, 'Have a nice t................', 'Have a good j................' or 'Have a safe j................!'

B In these sentences, choose the best of the alternatives given to fill the gaps.

1 The quickest way to get from London to the north of England is to take the M1 ....
  by-pass highway main road main street motorway ring road
2 It's quicker to cross London by .... than to drive across.
  bus car foot metro subway tube
3 It's generally cheaper to travel a long distance by .... than to take the train.
  coach hearse limousine plane pullman taxi
4 Go straight down the hill and take the third .... on the left. You can't miss it.
  bend branch corner crossroads junction roundabout turning
5 If you want to stop the car, what you have to do is to put your foot on the ....
  accelerator brake break choke clutch handbrake gas

C   These nouns are all used in connection with travel, to describe different kinds of JOURNEYS. Match each word to its definition on the right. One is done as an example:

cruise   a short pleasure trip with a group
trip   visiting different places, often with a guide
tour   a short journey or a journey made on business
flight   by ship between two ports
crossing   visiting different places by ship
voyage   by air
excursion   a short pleasure trip
outing   a long distance by ship

★   Remember that the noun *travel* is uncountable and only used as a general term. People say 'Travel broadens the mind' but NOT 'Did you have a good travel?'

D   Work in small groups. Ask your partners these questions:
- How do you usually travel to work or school? Why?
- If you have to go to an island, how do you like to travel? Why?
- If you're going away for the weekend, how do you prefer to travel?
- If you have to travel abroad, how do you usually travel?
- When was the last time you ...
  went by train   took a taxi   flew   sailed on a car-ferry   rode a bike

---

4.2   The Orient-Express   *Reading*

A   Read through the text fairly quickly. Indicate with an arrow (↓) on the map where the following meals are eaten during a journey on the Orient-Express:

Lunch (day 1)   Dinner   Breakfast   Lunch (day 2)

46

DEPARTURE INTO LEGEND

The 'Orient-Express' was originally conceived by two men, Georges Nagelmackers and George Mortimer Pullman, and built to standards of outrageous luxury late last century and early this. Many carriages were lost during the war. The remainder gradually fell into disuse and finally, in 1977, the service was discontinued.

The present owners began buying one carriage here, another there and restoring them in a way that has not so much become a legend as recreated one.

Today's passenger's first sight of the train is of the magnificent English 'Pullman' cars waiting grandly at London's Victoria Station for their prompt departure.

Days of Days

Just as you may take any sector of the London-Venice route, so you may, of course, fly in to Venice and take the train in a northerly direction home. The route is exactly the same and in both directions we coincide lunch in all its splendour with the Alpine panoramas in all theirs.

But let us suppose that you are journeying from London south to Venice. Your lunch, as you diddly-dum (and you really do) through the ever-pleasing countryside of Kent, will be a taste of things to come. Exquisite food flawlessly served in surroundings of magnificent opulence.

At Folkestone you will slip aboard the ferry, special accommodation reserved and refreshments available, to bid the white cliffs farewell and savour the prospect of the Continental sector.

At Boulogne the stewards are on the platform to welcome you aboard. Courteous and professional to a fault, they love the train and show it in everything they do.

In your cabin, a private day room till its nightly transformation into a bedroom, you will be greeted by your luggage, yet more dazzling marquetry and period brass fitments that will fascinate you. Unpack. Try the gadgets so carefully demonstrated by your steward. Pen a line home on the cards or writing paper provided. Plot your route on the map.

Because now you are well and truly on your journey.

If you are travelling only to Paris your dinner sitting will be the early one.

But early or late, it will be dinner worth calling dinner — and worth dressing for. Course after tantalising course cooked to perfection by superb French chefs, accompanied by famous wines and formally served in restaurant cars each differently appointed but equally devastating in its Twenties opulence.

Yet not even with the brandy is your evening over. For as you retrace your footsteps live piano music lures you to the Bar-Salon.

A Night to Remember

And so, with your cabin miraculously transformed, top sheet turned down and reading lamp left thoughtfully aglow, to bed.

As the train pauses at daybreak your steward will tiptoe past your cabin to pick up the morning papers and fresh croissants.

Continental breakfast, served in your cabin at the time you arranged, sees you stopping at Zürich before the real ascent begins.

Up and up you climb, the views ever grander as you head for the dizzying Arlberg Pass and its $6\frac{1}{2}$ miles of amazing tunnel, then a brief stop at St Anton before lunch.

Lunch, as we promised is a scenic one. Towering forests, and peaks you have to crane to see, alternate with pretty waterfalls and rushing streams to take your breath away.

Innsbruck, 'Roof Garden of Europe' is yet to come, the colossal Brenner Pass where Austria joins Italy, and then the grand descent through the Dolomites to Verona and across the Venetian Plain to the most romantic city in the world.

Venice the Unforgettable

Few would dispute that the train journey is a difficult act to follow.

Even fewer, however, would dispute that if one city can follow it at all, it is certainly Venice.

Over 200 palazzi line the Grand Canal. 400 picturesque bridges link island to island in a web of secluded squares, narrow streets and tiny gardens.

Venice is a splendid prelude or a grand finale to the world's most romantic adventure.

From Venice you can now travel on to Istanbul, the train's original destination, by sea. Board the mv 'Orient-Express' for a week-long cruise back to Venice calling at Piraeus for Athens and the Parthenon, Istanbul, Kusadasi for Ephesus, Patmos and finally Katakolon for Olympia.

B Decide whether the following statements are true (**T**) or false (**F**), according to the text. Refer back to the text whenever necessary.

1 The Orient-Express has been running continuously for 100 years.
2 You can fly from London to Venice and then return on the Orient-Express.
3 Lunch is taken on board the ferry between England and France.
4 At Boulogne you will be greeted in your cabin by your steward.
5 From Boulogne you travel in a private cabin.
6 Your cabin on the train is converted into a sleeping compartment by night.
7 After dinner you can dance to the music of a band in the Bar-Salon.
8 In the morning, breakfast is served in the restaurant car.
9 After Innsbruck, the train takes you on to Verona and Venice.
10 From Venice you can sail to Piraeus and Istanbul.

C Now underline FIVE phrases used in the passage that help to create an impression of luxury, elegance, wonder and excitement (for example: *built to standards of outrageous luxury*).

D Work in small groups. Describe to your partners a journey you regularly make (e.g. to work, to school, to a holiday destination, etc.). Try to make it sound as attractive, exciting and interesting as possible!

4.3 Revision of modal verbs
Grammar

A These examples revise the main uses of modal verbs, most of which you should be familiar with. The forms given on the right are the past tense forms. Fill the gaps with suitable words, using your own ideas.

Ability: can / is able to   was able to / managed to
Inability: can't / be unable to / not be able to couldn't / wasn't able to
Questions about ability: Can he?   Was he able to?
  Alex can't swim. Tony can speak Spanish very well.
  Anne was able to do the research, but she couldn't write the report.
  I know you're a good swimmer, but how well .... on your back?
  I .... find my pen anywhere – .... you help me to .... it?
  I .... unable .... finish all my work yesterday, but I hope .... it tomorrow.

Possibility: can/may/might/could   may have/could have/might have
Certainty (or near certainty): must   must have
Impossibility: can't/couldn't   can't have/couldn't have
Questions about possibility: Could/Might it ...?
  It could/may/might rain later.
  We may not be able to get on the bus – it may be full up.
  If his name's Spiros, he can't be Italian, he must be Greek.
  Your bus .... been two hours late, surely?
  .... difficult to get a seat at such short notice?
  Jane is always so careful, she .... forgotten to check the timetable – the train .... been delayed.

48

Permission: can/may   was allowed to
Refusing permission: can't/mustn't   couldn't
Questions about permission: Can/Could/May we ...?

You can/may make notes during the talk if you like.
Can/Could/May I finish off this work tomorrow?
We were allowed to visit the church after the service was over.
You .... when you're in a non-smoking seat.
You .... a calculator in the maths test because it was against the rules.

Obligation or responsibility:
must/have to/have got to/should/ought to   had to/should have
Lack of obligation or responsibility:
don't have to/needn't   needn't have
Obligation or responsibility NOT to do something:
can't/mustn't/shouldn't/oughtn't to   wasn't allowed to/shouldn't have
Questions about obligation or responsibility:
Must/Have we got to/Do we have to/Should/Ought we to/Do we need to?
Do I have to hand the work in tomorrow?
You don't have to/needn't book in advance if you're going by rail.
You must/should arrive at 4.30 if you want to get a good seat on the train.
You .... on the bus unless all the seats are occupied.
In the exam .... in pen or are we allowed to use pencils?
You .... so much time listening to music when you .... working.

■ One of the more difficult aspects of the use of modal verbs is that some
different forms have different implications. Look at these examples:
I should have checked my ticket implies that I didn't check it.
I had to check my ticket implies that I did check it.
You shouldn't have used a dictionary implies that you did use one.
We weren't allowed to use dictionaries implies that we didn't use them.
He needn't have said that implies that he said it even though it was unnecessary to.

B   Find the errors in these sentences and correct them:

1 You needn't to worry about meeting me at the station, I'll get a taxi.
2 Do I ought to phone the airport to find out if there might be any delays?
3 Did you able to find the papers you lost?
4 I couldn't have to show my passport to get a rail ticket.
5 I could buy my ticket after queueing for five minutes.
6 You mustn't write anything down unless you want to.
7 I checked the timetable so I can't to be wrong about the departure time!
8 You don't spend as much time as you must on your homework.
9 May you tell me where I can catch a bus to the railway station?

C   Change these sentences so that their meaning remains the same, using a modal verb.

1   In Japan you aren't supposed to eat food as you walk down the street.   You ...
2   It was a mistake for me to spend so much money on records.   I shouldn't ...
3   Is it necessary for me to pay for my ticket now?   Do ...?
4   Please tell me how much luggage I am allowed to take on the plane.   Can ...?
5   It isn't possible that her car has broken down again.   Her car ...
6   If you have a reserved seat it isn't necessary to stand on the train.   You ...
7   I'm sure that you made a mistake when you added up the total.   You ...
8   Can you manage to get to the airport at 6.30 a.m.?   Will ...?
9   Why did you travel first class? It wasn't necessary, you know.   You ...
10   The ticket inspector didn't let us go onto the platform.   We ...

D   In this short story, all the auxiliaries (will, did, do, have, etc.) and modal verbs are missing. Fill the gaps using the words listed below. Some of them are needed more than once.

1 .... you ever driven a van? I 2 .... once. It 3 .... just after I left college and I 4 .... got myself a temporary job as a delivery man. When I accepted the job I thought I 5 .... have to sit beside a driver, chat to him and help him to carry things from the van to the houses, but no, I 6 .... on my own and I 7 .... to drive the van and carry everything by myself. It 8 .... have been very strenuous but after no more than a week I 9 .... got used to it and I 10 .... able to relax and enjoy the driving. But I 11 .... say that I 12 .... very glad when I 13 .... finished after six weeks. It 14 .... have been rather boring in the long run. I 15 .... imagine that someone who 16 .... to do that kind of job permanently 17 ....n't mind getting held up in traffic hold-ups as much as I 18 ...., but something really 19 .... to be done to improve road conditions: it 20 .... be so frustrating having to spend half your working life sitting in traffic jams. If you 21 .... read a book or something it 22 ....n't be too bad, but of course that 23 .... impossible. All you 24 .... do is listen to the radio and smoke too much!

can   could   did   do   does   had   has   have   is   might   must
ought   was   would

'It's for you.'

50

4.4 Getting the message

A Before you hear the recordings, study the maps and the questions below.

 Now listen to a loudspeaker announcement being made at Southampton railway station. Note down your answers to the questions.

1 Which platform would you go to for a connecting train to ...
   a) Lyndhurst Road b) Portsmouth   c) Romsey
2 Should you get on the train now if you want to go to ...
   a) Poole   b) Dorchester South c) Christchurch
3 What should you do if you want to go to ...
   a) Parkstone   b) New Milton   c) Millbrook

B   Listen to a recorded telephone report on road conditions. Put a cross (✖) at the four places on the map that drivers should AVOID on Saturday afternoon.

4.5 Using suffixes: Adjectives *Word study*

A Look at these examples and fill the gaps with more examples, using the root words below + one of the suffixes in this list.

-al	regional national	....
-ical	biological geographical	....
-able	acceptable reliable	....
-ful	careful fearful	....
-less	painless thoughtless	....
-ish	childish whitish	....
-y	hairy woolly	....
		....

alphabet break bump care colour comfort draught enjoy
fear fool grammar grey hope mathematics music noise
obtain old pain profession rain rest sleep small smell
success sun tall thought tradition use wash young

★ Remember that these words end in -IBLE not -able:
(in)credible (in)edible (in)flexible (im)possible (ir)responsible
(in)visible eligible horrible indelible negligible terrible

B Fill the gaps in these sentences, using a suffix with the correct form of the root word on the right. The first is done for you as an example:

1 It was very ......**careless**...... of you to break that coffee cup.	CARE
2 Thank you for your postcard, it was very .... of you to send it.	THOUGHT
3 She's quite ....: she plays the flute and the piano.	MUSIC
4 It was rather .... of him to cry when he did badly in the test.	CHILD
5 We started our trip on a beautiful .... morning.	SUN
6 I enjoyed the book very much because it was so	READ
7 His .... knowledge is very poor – he thinks Paris is in Italy.	GEOGRAPHY
8 Her hair is ...., not bright red.	RED
9 A very old car is usually an un............ car.	RELY
10 I'll always remember that journey – it was an un............ experience.	FORGET

4.6 *Come* and *go* *Verbs and idioms*

A Fill the gaps in these sentences with a suitable form of:
bring carry come deliver fetch go take

1 Will you be able to .... and see us next weekend?
2 Will you be able to .... and see them in London?
3 I'm certainly going to .... a swimsuit with me when I go to the coast.
4 .... round to my house tonight and .... a friend with you, if you like.
5 It was very kind of you to .... my suitcase for me.
6 The goods were .... to the factory in a van.
7 I'm just going to my room to .... my glasses – I'll be back in a minute.

52

B Replace the underlined words with a phrasal verb with COME or GO.

1 While I was going through my drawers I <u>found</u> these old love letters.   ACROSS
2 We <u>were faced with</u> several problems.   UP AGAINST
3 I don't understand how these difficulties <u>happened</u>.   ABOUT
4 You shouldn't wear those red socks, they don't <u>match</u> your grey suit.   WITH
5 The beach is washed clean by the sea when the tide <u>rises</u> and you can see the rocks sticking out of the water when the tide <u>falls</u>.   IN   OUT
6 Bob has been Mary's <u>boyfriend</u> for a year.   OUT WITH
7 The date on this yogurt is May 1: it must have <u>gone bad</u> by now.   OFF
8 A bomb <u>has exploded</u> and several people have been hurt.   OFF
9 She <u>left</u> at 7 a.m. and we never saw her again.   OFF
10 He <u>entered</u> the competition and won a Caribbean cruise.   IN FOR
11 <u>Hurry up!</u> We have to be at the station in half an hour.   ON
12 Before we <u>continue</u>, let's <u>examine</u> the correct answers to this exercise.   ON   OVER

4.7   Avoid the queues   *Reading and discussion*

A Look at the advertisement and then answer these questions:

1 How many Qs are missing in the advertisement?
2 Which flights depart from Terminal 4 at Heathrow?
3 Why does Terminal 4 seem so calm?
4 What features make Terminal 4 so convenient for motorists?
5 Where do British Airways domestic flights depart from?
6 How can British Airways passengers get from Terminal 1 to Terminal 4?

uiet,

uick,

tran uil.

You'll miss the Q's when you fly through Terminal 4.)

Right on cue, Terminal 4 at Heathrow opened on April 12th.

If you're flying with British Airways to Paris or Amsterdam, or any intercontinental destination, you'll find it uite different from other terminals.

First there's the sheer size of the place: 64 Check-In desks mean less congestion, and less ueueing.

This uni ue uality of calm continues all the way through to boarding.

Avoiding lifts, stairs and escalators you can uickly wheel your trolley direct from car to plane.

There's easy access by road, parking for 3,200 cars, a brand new Underground station and our own fast, fre uent bus service from Terminal 1 for passengers connecting from domestic flights.

In fact everything's organised to help you fly through Terminal 4 in double- uick time.

Any uestions?

BRITISH AIRWAYS
The world's favourite airline

B   Work in small groups. Find out about your partners' experiences of airports and long distance travel by land, sea and air. Ask these questions:
- What do you like and dislike about airports and flying?
  If you've flown, tell us about your most recent experience.
  Describe the last time you saw someone off or met someone at an airport.
- What do you enjoy and hate about travelling by sea?
  Have you ever been on a ferry? Tell us about it.
- What are the advantages and disadvantages of travelling by car?
- What do you like and dislike about travelling by coach or train?
- What was the most UNUSUAL journey you've ever experienced?
- What was the WORST journey by land, sea or air you've ever experienced?

4.8   InterCity services   *Problem solving*

A   Work in pairs. Imagine that three friends of yours (Alain, Bobby and Conny) are in Britain for the first time. Each of them has to make a different journey.

Using the map and timetables decide what advice you'd give them:
- What trains should they catch?
- When will they arrive at their final destination?
- How long will the journey take?
- What should they do if there is a slight delay and they miss the first train?

(They should allow at least 40 minutes to travel between London stations by Underground, preferably longer.)

MAKE NOTES on the times and routes you have chosen.

ALAIN is arriving by ferry at Portsmouth at 07.30. He has to get to Glasgow as soon as possible. There is a free bus from the Ferry Port to Portsmouth Station (journey time 15 mins). How can he get to Glasgow and when will he arrive there?

Portsmouth – London

Portsmouth	0755	0855	0955	1055	1155	1255
London Waterloo	0919	1019	1120	1218	1322	1418

London – Scotland

London Euston	1030	—	—	1300	1400
London Kings Cross	—	1100	1135	—	—
Glasgow Central	1544	—	—	1830	2009
Edinburgh	—	1556	1652	—	—
Glasgow Queen Street	—	1718*	1821*	—	—

*change at Edinburgh

London Heathrow – Glasgow

London Heathrow*	0715	0815	then flights every hour until	2015
Glasgow Airport†	0825	0925		2125

*Underground from Central London to Heathrow – journey time 55 minutes
†Express coach from Airport to Glasgow City Centre every 30 minutes – journey time 20 minutes

BOBBY is flying in to London, Gatwick from Dallas, Texas at 09.55. How can he get to Manchester and when will he arrive there?

Gatwick Airport – The Northwest (direct trains)

Gatwick Airport	1017	1347	1857
Clapham Junction	1049	1419	1939
Kensington Olympia	1057	1427	1953
Manchester Piccadilly	1405	1805	0010

Gatwick Express: London – Gatwick Airport

Gatwick Airport	0620	0635	0650	then trains every	2250
London Victoria	0650	0705	0720	15 minutes until	2320

London – Manchester

London Euston	1020	1150	1250	1420	1520	1600	1700
Manchester Piccadilly	1258	1436	1525	1659	1805	1833	1936

CONNY has been staying in Bristol for a few weeks and on Monday she has an interview in York. The interview is at 12.30.

Bristol – London

Bristol Temple Meads	0620	0700	0740	0813	0925	1008
Bath Spa	0632	0712	—	0825	0937	1047
London Paddington	0801	0839	0906	0940	1058	1213

London – York

London Kings Cross	0900	0935	1000	1025	1100	1135	1200
York	1110	1154	1211	1224	1307	1354	1401

Bristol – Midlands – The North

Bristol Temple Meads	0617	0848	0959	1135
Birmingham New Street	0755	1029	1129	1256
York	1046	1325*	1338	1513

*change at Leeds

B   Now look at Activity 12 for some more information about Alain, Bobby and Conny and discuss this with your partner. Make notes on your decisions.

C   Using the notes you have made, write three postcards or short letters – one to each friend. Include the advice you would give if they start their journeys on time AND the advice you'd give if they are delayed (as explained in Activity 12). Here are some expressions you can use:

> *When you get to …, you should …*   *The best train to take is the …*
> *If you miss the connection in …, you should …*   *If you're late, you should …*
> *If all goes well, you'll arrive in … at …*   *Have a good journey!*

4.9 How do I get there?

Listening

A 📼 You'll hear a telephone conversation. The man wants to get from Trumpington Street (marked with a ✱ on the map) to an office in St Mary's Street (marked with another ✱). Unfortunately, because of the one-way system he can't just drive straight there, so he phones the office for directions.

Mark the route he has to take with arrows (→→) on the map.

★ Warning: At one point his route takes him off the edge of the map!

B   Work in pairs. Using the map of Cambridge, take it in turns to tell each other how to get on foot:
- from St Mary's Street to the Bus Station
- from the Bus Station to Bridge Street
- from Bridge Street to St Mary's Street
- from St Mary's Street to the station

Here are some useful expressions:

> *Excuse me. Could you tell me how to get to …?*
>
> *Go straight on until you get to the … and then cross the road.*
> *Bear right at the junction and the … is about 5 minutes' walk.*
> *Go past the … and take the first turning on the left.*
> *You'll see the … on your right. You can't miss it.*

4.10   Layout of letters, directions   *Composition*

A   In the two letters which follow, Jan is writing to a friend from abroad who is coming to stay for a few days and needs to be told how to get from the airport to 12A Pine Road.

Work in pairs or small groups:
- Which letter do you prefer?
- Looking at both letters, decide which parts of each are more helpful and which parts are less helpful.

12A Pine Road
Greenwood GD12 5OK

6th June 19 - -

Dear Alex,
  I'm afraid I won't be able to meet you when you arrive at the airport as I'll be at work. Unfortunately, there's no easy way of getting here apart from taking a taxi, which would be very expensive.
  So, if you haven't got too much luggage, I'd suggest taking the underground. You'll have to change twice to get to the nearest station (GREENWOOD). When you come out of the station, turn left and walk along the main road past Sainsburys supermarket and take the first left (South Road). Pine Road is on the right and 12A is on the first floor. My mother will be there to welcome you!
  But if you don't mind a slower journey there is a direct bus (No. 108) which will take you all the way from the airport – there's a stop opposite Greenwood Station. Ask the driver to tell you when to get off.
  Looking forward to seeing you on friday evening.

  Jan

P.S. If you get lost or if you're delayed, phone me at work (071 4418 extension 679).

12A Pine Road
Greenwood GD12 5OK

6 June 19--

Dear Alex,
　　　　Sorry I won't be able to meet you. Here's a quick
note on how to get here from the airport. There are three
alternatives :
1/ TAXI : This would be very expensive, so unless you
have a lot of luggage not advisable.
2/ BUS : There is a direct bus (number 108), which is
cheap, but slow. Ask the driver to tell you when he gets
to Greenwood Station.
3/ UNDERGROUND: This is quick but you'd have to change
twice, which could be tricky if you have loads of luggage.
Looking forward to seeing you.

　　　　　　　Jan

P.S. I enclose a map to help you find your way to our flat
in Greenwood.

B　　How do you get from the airport (or main station) in YOUR city or
town to YOUR home?
1　Write an informal letter to a friend who has never visited your country
　before, giving advice on how to get to your home when he or she
　arrives.
2　Make notes before you start.
3　Check your completed letter through afterwards and correct any
　mistakes you notice.
4　Show your completed letter to another student and ask for comments.

'Excuse me, those seats are taken.'

4.11 Using prepositions – 1 *Use of English*

This is the first of three exercises on prepositions used after certain verbs, adjectives and nouns.

Fill the gaps with a suitable preposition from the list below:

1 Everyone **admires** him .... his wisdom and common sense.
2 I **agree** .... you .... the need to improve public transport services.
3 Dick **apologised** .... not sending us a thank you letter.
4 I don't **approve** .... travelling first class on trains or planes.
5 We all started to **argue** .... him .... his political ideas.
6 I **believe** .... government support for public transport services.
7 Everyone can **benefit** .... a better road system.
8 You can't **blame** me .... your own mistakes.
9 Peter's always **boasting** .... his own achievements.
10 Would you like to **borrow** a pen .... me?
11 Max is **capable** .... doing much better work than this.
12 We would like to **congratulate** you .... getting engaged.
13 Water **consists** .... hydrogen and oxygen.
14 The salesman tried to **convince** me .... the advantages of buying the car.
15 There is no simple **cure** .... hay fever.

about   for   from   in   of   on   with

4.12 Transport in the future *Communication activity*

What changes will there be to transport systems in the future?

1 Work alone. Begin by making a few notes on this subject.

2 ▐▆▌ Work in groups of three. One of you should look at Activity 2, another at 8 and the other at 28. You'll each have different ideas to consider about transport in the future. Study the notes for a few moments.

3 Ask your partners for their views on transport in the future. DON'T read word-for-word from the notes.

Here are some useful expressions:

> *I'm quite sure that in the future ...*   *It seems to me that ...*
> *Perhaps one day in the future we'll ...*   *Do you think that ... ?*
> *I don't agree that ...*   *Why do you think that ... ?*

5 Somewhere to live

5.1 Make yourself at home!
Vocabulary

A Work in small groups. Ask your partners these questions:
- In your own home, where do you work or study? How is this room furnished?
- When you're working, do you need complete silence or is it easy to concentrate?

B Fill the gaps in these sentences with suitable words:

1 If I could build my own house I'd make sure it had a ....
2 Our n .... s are always complaining about the noise we make.
3 My friends live in a small .... house in a street where all the houses look alike.
4 The block of flats she lives in has five s .... s and she lives on the top f ....
5 In the city centre, inexpensive a .... is hard to find because it is scarce.
6 Many new estates are being built on the o .... s of the city and in the s .... s.
7 I'd love to m .... to the country and live in an old ....
8 If someone borrows money to buy their home, they have to repay the m ....
9 If someone else owns your house or flat, you have to pay r .... to a l ....
10 Modern flats often don't have enough .... to store things in.
11 Books are usually kept in a b .... or on s .... s.
12 Even though their house has c .... h .... there is a fireplace in the l ....
13 In a bedroom, clothes are kept in a ....
14 The most important thing about a house or flat is that it should be ....

C Choose the best alternative to fill the gaps in these sentences:

1 Some houses have a basement room where things are stored called a(n) ....
   attic   cave   cellar   grave   loft
2 Some rooms don't have curtains at the windows, they have .... instead.
   blinds   carpets   glass   stores   wallpaper
3 We haven't got a garage, so we leave our car outside the house in the ....
   drive   garden   parking   patio   pavement   porch
4 He keeps all his tools and do-it-yourself equipment in a .... in the back garden.
   barn   bungalow   hut   shack   shed   stable
5 In your own garden, you can sunbathe on the .... in the summer.
   field   flowerbed   lawn   meadow   pasture

D Work in small groups. Draw a floor plan of your own homes.
- Explain to your partners what FURNITURE and equipment is in each room.
- Find out about your partners' homes and the area or district they live in.
- How are your homes different from each other's?
- If they had the choice, where would your partners most like to live?

5.2 Different places
Listening and speaking

A 🔲 Listen to the conversation and answer these questions:

1 Where exactly does Charles live?
2 Where exactly does Ruth live?
3 What does Ruth like about where she lives?
4 What does Charles like about where he lives?
5 What does Charles dislike about it?
6 What does Ruth dislike about it?
7 Where would Charles prefer to live?
8 Where would Ruth prefer to live?

B Work in groups. Ask your partners these questions about the photographs:
- What would it be like to live in each place? (Or what is it like to live there?)
- What would be the attractions of living there?
- What would be the disadvantages of living there?
- If you had to choose between the two, which would you prefer and why?
- How is the place you live in different from these places? How is it similar?

5.3   The future

A   The examples below show the ways in which we can refer to the future. Fill the gaps with suitable words, using your own ideas.

PREDICTIONS + GENERAL FUTURE: *will/will be doing/will have done*
   In the future the Earth will be hotter.   I expect it will rain tomorrow.
   By the end of this year I'll have taken my exam.
   While I'm studying, my younger sister will be enjoying herself.
   I'm sure the weather .... towards the end of the week.
   She is very clever, so I expect that she .... her exams next summer.
   If you don't hurry up, the bus .... before we get to the bus stop!

■   Remember that *will* and *'ll* are NOT normally used in a clause following
a time conjunction: *when   if   until   before   after   while   by the time*
   If you do your work tonight, you'll be able to go out tomorrow.
   We'll tidy up our rooms before she arrives.
   After he has done the housework, he'll have to start cooking the dinner.
   If you ...., you'll find it easier to remember the new words.
   When my friend ...., I'll tell her all about my plans.
   By the time our guests ...., all the food will have been eaten.

The short form *'ll* is normally only used after pronouns:
   I'll do it.   It'll rain tomorrow.
But in writing, or for emphasis, the full form is often used:
   I will do it.   It will rain tomorrow.

FUTURE EVENTS that we can 'see coming':   *going to*
   One day there's going to be a terrible accident on that road.
   My wife's going to have a baby.
   Look out! That dog .... bite you!
   Look at those black clouds – it .... soon.

INTENTIONS and PLANS: *going to*
   I'm going to leave now.   We're going to visit Spain next year.
   I .... the work later, when I've got more time.
   Your room is in a terrible mess – when ....?

ARRANGEMENTS: PRESENT CONTINUOUS
   I'm seeing the dentist at 2.30.   I'm meeting my friend this afternoon.
   I can't meet you this evening because ....
   Mr and Mrs Jones .... to dinner tomorrow.

FIXED EVENTS on a timetable or calendar: PRESENT SIMPLE
   The exam takes place on June 13th and 14th. (= it's in the calendar)
   The plane from London .... at 9.30.
   Tomorrow, according to my diary, the sun .... at 5.09.

■   *Going to* can be used instead of *will* or a present tense. In conversation,
going to is more common than *will*, but in writing *will* is more often used.
A rule of thumb for conversation is: 'If in doubt, use *going to*' – except if
you're making a promise, offer or suggestion (when *going to* may sound
like a threat).

I'll pay for lunch if you help me with my work.   I'll help you tomorrow.
Give me your suitcase and .... in the boot of the car for you.
I .... the money you lent me next Friday.

■ Normally, in modern English, *shall* is only used when making
suggestions:

Shall I help you? ✓   NOT: Will I help you? ✗
Shall we take a break now? ✓   NOT: Will we take a break now? ✗
and NOT in these cases:

He shan't arrive on time. ✗   They shall be late. ✗
He won't arrive on time. ✓   They'll (will) be late. ✓

B   Find the errors in these sentences and correct them.

1 If the telephone will ring, I'll answer it.
2 After the floor will have been cleaned, I'll polish the furniture.
3 This evening I tidy my room.
4 By the time you get home we will finish dinner.
5 We'll be waiting for you when your plane is going to land at the airport.
6 Elizabeth has a baby next month.
7 The new by-pass shall be finished in the spring.
8 You won't be able to unlock the door if you won't remember your key.

C   Rewrite this 'telegram' as an informal letter – add any necessary
grammatical words but NO extra information. Each line of the 'telegram'
should become a complete sentence, as the examples show.

Dear Jan,
1 WE NOT SEE / YOU / SUCH A LONG TIME.
   We haven't seen you for such a long time.
2 OUR LATEST NEWS BE / NEXT WEEK / WE MOVE HOUSE!
   Our latest news is that ...
3 NEW FLAT BE / OUTSKIRTS / CITY.
4 FLAT NOT BE LARGER / BUT WE BE ABLE GROW / VEGETABLES / GARDEN.
5 WE HOPE / NO PROBLEMS / NOISY AND NOSY NEIGHBOURS AS / NOW.
6 WE BE GLAD / ESCAPE / NOISE AND TRAFFIC / CITY CENTRE.
7 MY JOURNEY TO WORK TAKE LONGER / BUT / ENJOY / FRESH AIR AND
   PRIVACY.
8 WE / TAKE / DOG / WALK / ACROSS FIELDS EVERY EVENING.
9 SUNDAY 14TH / WE HAVE / FLAT-WARMING PARTY.
10 YOU BE ABLE / COME?
11 WE LOOK FORWARD / SEE YOU / ANY TIME AFTER 7 P.M.
   Best wishes from Terry and Jo
12 P.S. YOU NOT FIND / NEW FLAT / WITHOUT DIRECTIONS.
13 IF YOU PHONE ME / I TELL YOU / HOW / GET THERE.

5.4   A nice place to live

A   Decide which of these statements are true (**T**) or false (**F**), according to the newspaper article.

1 Swansea was the second politest place in the country.
2 The British Polite Society tested Norwich by visiting the city.
3 The British Polite Society's secretary has not personally visited Norwich yet.
4 The healthiest town in Britain is now Shrewsbury.
5 The rudest place in Britain is not named by Mr Gregory.
6 The British Polite Society has received complaints about doctors.
7 Both bar staff and bar customers are rude to each other.
8 According to Julian Roux there is one place nicer than Norwich.
9 In 1988 Norwich was named the most pleasant place in Europe.
10 Norwich's public relations officer says nowhere is as nice as Norwich.

Norwich is pleased to pull off a nice one

David Sharrock

IF you're reading this in Norwich, the chances are that you got out of bed on the right side this morning, that the newsagent smiled and said thank you as he took your money, that your bus queue is orderly and well-behaved, and that all is peace and harmony.

That's because the British Polite Society has just named the good people of Norwich as the "courteous community of the year".

The society's secretary, the Reverend Ian Gregory, said Norwich received the most recommendations from members this year, beating Swansea, Northampton and Portsmouth, and squeezing Alresford, Hampshire, into second place.

Polite Society agents tested the city's reputation, and returned with nothing but praise for the manners of its hoteliers, shopkeepers and publicans.

"We found Norwich to be a city with a smile," says Mr Gregory, who will visit the town for the first time this week. "Last year Shrewsbury won the award, and I hear they've just been placed top of a list for healthy living."

Could he name the rudest place in Britain? "No, we don't do that sort of thing," recalling the commitment to good manners. What about a clue, then? "Well, we did have a problem with doctors' receptionists about six months ago, and we get a lot of complaints about bar staff. But then, we also get complaints from bar staff about the customers."

None of this, needless to say, concerns Norwich. Julian Roux, landlord of the Louis Marchesi pub, swears he knows not a single unpleasant person, and rates only Lowestoft, his birthplace, as a nicer place. "The people here are very relaxed, which a Londoner would probably mistake for stupidity. If you played poker here, you'd discover we can be very cunning."

Probably none of this will come as a surprise to the citizens because in 1986 the EEC decided that Norwich possessed the most pleasant environment in Europe.

It fell to Norwich council's public relations officer, Mr Tim Anderson, to offer the only consolation non-Norwich residents can expect. "We're reasonably nice to each other, but I'm sure that many other towns are equally as nice." Now isn't that nice of him to say so?

B Find the word or phrase in each paragraph of the passage that means the same as these words and phrases. There are nine paragraphs: the numbers show which paragraph you should look at. The first is done for you as an example:

1 were in a good mood – *got out of bed on the right side*
2 polite   5 prize   8 people
3 pushing   6 behaviour   9 comfort or reassurance
4 representatives   7 of course

C Work in small groups. Ask each other these questions:
- How polite are people in different parts of your own country?
- Which place would win the 'most courteous community' award in your country?
- Which nation would win the 'most courteous nation award'?
- Why are people sometimes rude or unpleasant to each other?
- What kind of behaviour would you describe as 'nice' and 'polite'?

5.5 High-rise buildings
Listening

A [cassette] You'll hear a radio programme in which an expert is being interviewed about skyscrapers and high-rise apartment blocks. Make notes in the spaces below:

NOTES

Where and when was the first skyscraper built?
....

Why was it built? 1 ....
                        2 ....
                        3 ....
Where is the world's tallest apartment block?
....

Where is the tallest in the UK?
....

How do people who live in tower blocks feel?
....

What kind of flats are vandalised?
....

How can vandalism be prevented?
    1 ....
    2 ....
    3 ....
    4 ....

B Work in small groups. Find out about your partners' experiences of living in high-rise flats. Is vandalism a problem in their area or their city?

5.6   Using prepositions – 2

Fill the gaps in these sentences with a suitable preposition:

  1 How are we going to **deal** .... this problem?
  2 There's no such thing as a perfect home – it all **depends** .... the individual.
  3 Bill was **engaged** .... Liz for two years and then got **married** .... Jane!
  4 I'll never **forgive** Bill .... the way he treated his fiancée.
  5 Our new sofa was uncomfortable so we **exchanged** it .... a different one.
  6 I said I could move the furniture by myself, but she **insisted** .... helping me.
  7 I hope that our plans don't **interfere** .... your own arrangements.
  8 Helen, I'd like to **introduce** you .... George, our next-door neighbour.
  9 George is **involved** .... politics: he's our local councillor.
10 Now that George has been elected we all **hope** .... better things in the future.
11 Are you **interested** .... local politics, by any chance?
12 Many residents don't have much **confidence** .... our new mayor.
13 Some of the tenants are angry about the **lack** .... car parking spaces in the area.
14 She's **longing** .... the day when they can move out of the city.

5.7   Spelling and pronunciation: Vowels

A   One of the main difficulties of English spelling is that some words are spelt differently and have different meanings but are pronounced the same. Can you think of words pronounced the same as each of these, but spelt differently?

guessed ....   brake ....   whole ....   steel ....   threw ....

B   Work in small groups. Add the words on the next page to the appropriate lists below, according to their pronunciation. The first is done for you as an example:

æ	**bad** damage	*scandal* *marry*	
e	**bed** pleasure leisure lent/leant	....	....
	....		
aɪ	**bite** height guide eye/I	....	....
aː	**calm** heart	....	
ɔː	**bored**/board warm caught/court	....	....
	....		
ɜː	**bird** worm	....	
aʊ	**now** crowd	....	
ɔɪ	**boy** point	....	
eə	**there**/their scarce where/wear	....	....
ɪə	**here**/hear steer	....	....
eɪ	**make** sale/sail break/brake	....	....
əʊ	**note** joke whole/hole	....	....
iː	**sheep** piece/peace	....	....
	....		
ɪ	**ship** sink mystery	....	....

ɒ	**pot**	what	yacht	....	....	....	....
uː	**boot**	truly	threw/through	....	....	....	....
ʊ	**put**	should	wood/would	....	....	....	....
ʌ	**cut**	worry	money	....	....	....	....

....

plough   allowed/aloud   •   not/knot   knowledge   quality   wander
•   ceiling/sealing   seize/seas   weak/week   receive   meat/meet
seen/scene   •   cleared   atmosphere   sincere   •   wore/war
shore/sure   source/sauce   walk   warn/worn   raw/roar   •   cushion
butcher   pull   push   •   scandal   marry   •   destroy   employer   •
bury/berry   weather/whether   guessed/guest   merry   check/cheque   •
stares/stairs   fare/fair   pair/pear   •   guilty   business   witch/which
mist/missed   •   paint   wait/weight   male/mail   waste/waist   •
turn   work   •   soup   blue/blew   root/route   new/knew   •
folk   soap   nose/knows   •   laugh   castle   half   guard   •   blood
tongue   country   one/won   thorough   wonder   •   climb it/climate
right/write   by/buy/'bye   [cassette icon]

★ Note that in American English and in regional accents of British
English, several of these 'rules' of pronunciation and spelling don't apply.
For example, *caught* and *court* are pronounced differently in many accents.

C   Find the THREE spelling mistakes in each of these sentences and
correct them:

1 I am quite shore that this weak is going too be wonderful.
2 We are truely sorry that you had to weight so long four the delivery.
3 He has dredful manners – he paws tomato source on all his food.
4 They couldn't get thier new armchare threw the door.
5 Witch of these too alternatives is the write one?
6 He lent the ladder agenst the wall and climed onto the roof.
7 The cieling and walls of this room need peinting ergently.

D   [cassette icon]   Now listen to the tape and write down the missing word in
each of these sentences. The first is done for you as an example:

1 I'm afraid that I might ....**break**.... this glass.
2 What's the matter with him I ....?
3 They .... across the park hand in hand.
4 What is the .... of this wall?
5 In some cities, apartment blocks have ....
6 I don't really have any .... of this subject.
7 I find that .... to work keeps me fit.
8 It's no fun if you're .... in a downpour.
9 I'll pay for any .... I have caused.
10 Let me know when you .... the package.

5.8 Finding a flat

Listening and problem solving

Imagine that Jill and John are two English friends of yours who are looking for a flat to live in when they get married in the spring. They have been looking at flats in Greenwood, where Jill works. John works in the city, about half an hour by train from Greenwood station.

A First look at these advertisements for three flats they have decided are worth viewing.
- Which of these properties would YOU prefer?
- What is not mentioned in the ads that you would only find out by viewing them?

room, 2 bedrooms, bath room. Quiet cul-de-sac position. Immediate possession. £70,000

13A Balmoral Way

Superb 2-bedroom apartment, overlooking Queen's Park. 3 mins Greenwood Station. Newly decorated living room and bedrooms. Compact modern kitchen. Bathroom with shower. Extensive views over nearby countryside. £65,000

St Matthews St

A spacious and well maintained house in an exc~"

~~u), shower ro rooms, bathroom. tral heating. Integr. garage. £179,000

44C Sandringham Gardens

Ideal first home. Delightful south-facing living room with balcony. 1 good-sized bedroom. Kitchen and bathroom. £40,000

Halewood Lane

A spacious semi-detached house with la· gara~

~~uom. Gas central heat ing. Two parking spaces. Small garden. £72,500

7B Windsor Avenue

Charming ground-floor flat with secluded garden. Living room. 1 bedroom. Spacious kitchen. Shower room. £45,000

Lovell Road

A spacious older style semidetached house needing ~rovement. Hall ~ 7 di·

B [cassette] You'll hear Jill and John discussing the three flats after viewing them.
- Listen to their discussion and MAKE NOTES on the pros and cons of each flat.
- Which of the three did they like best of all, do you think? Did they both agree on this?

C Write three paragraphs, describing your friends' feelings about each of the flats they viewed, beginning as follows:
Jill and John might have chosen 7B Windsor Avenue because ...
They might have decided against 44C Sandringham Gardens because ...
They might have rejected 13A Balmoral Way because ...

D Work in small groups. Design your own ideal home. Draw a simple plan and make a list of the features you would have.
When you're ready, describe your dream house to the rest of the class.

A   Read the passage through and then answer the questions on the next page.

G __ is a delightfully unspoilt village surrounded by fields and woods at the mouth of a river. Yet it's only a short bus ride from the old city of H __ with its factories, industry and heavy traffic.

The countryside around the village is incredibly green, with fertile fields, olive groves and eucalyptus and cypress trees. Through the village flows a wide, clear river, along the banks of which are moored a fleet of fishing boats. Upstream the river is broader and shallower and is the home of a multitude of birds and other wildlife. Along the banks of the river you can glimpse wild duck peeping shyly from the undergrowth.

If you're a nature-lover the walk through the countryside to Lake K __ is wonderful and as it takes less than an hour is well worth the effort. This big inland lake which is fed by the melting winter snow off the mountains is lovely for swimming. The fishing is said to be excellent too, though I've no personal experience of this.

In the centre of G __ is the village square. Like many of the 'roads' in G __, the square is unpaved but rock hard from centuries of foot traffic. Dominating the square are a couple of silver-barked eucalyptus trees which in the spring are alive with nesting birds. Between the trees are a statue and a fountain. Around the square are a few inexpensive restaurants, a couple of bars and some little shops. Right in the middle of the square, in the way of what little traffic there is, is a small kiosk run by an old lady, who sells everything from razor blades to chewing gum. Locals and visitors alike sit for hours over a drink in one of the bars, watching nothing much happen.

From the village square a dirt track

leads you down through eucalyptus trees to the beach in a few minutes. This is a magnificent stretch of pale yellow sand, overlooked by bamboos and a few trees, which stretches away to the horizon. There's just one bar on the beach which serves light lunches and drinks.

The local people are farmers or fishermen, though more and more are now building extra rooms on their property, which they let to visitors in the summer. However, so far there are no large hotels and the village has avoided the effects of mass tourism and kept its character and charm.

If you're looking for peace and quiet and a lovely rural environment, then G __ is the place to escape to – before everyone else discovers it!

Welcome to G __!

1 From G— to the nearest town it is ...
  a long way   not far
2 At its mouth the river is ...
  shallow   deep
3 From G—, Lake K— is ...
  under an hour's walk   over an hour's walk
4 G—'s village square is ...
  lively   sleepy
5 From the village square to the beach is ...
  a short walk   a long walk
6 For their income the local people ...
  depend on tourism   don't depend on tourism
7 As more visitors come to G—, they have ...
  changed its atmosphere   not changed its atmosphere
8 The writer refers to the village as 'G—' because he or she ...
  wants to keep it a secret   doesn't remember its name

B   Work in small groups. Ask your partners these questions:
- Would you like to live in a place like G— ?
- What are the advantages and disadvantages of living in a village like G— ?
- What are the benefits and drawbacks of living in a large city?
- If you could choose, would you rather live in a city or in the country? Why?

5.10   Starting and ending well   *Composition*

A good piece of writing requires:
- an INTRODUCTION that will catch the reader's attention
  and
- an ENDING that will leave the reader satisfied.
The first and the last sentence are particularly important.

A   Which of these sentences could be used in place of the opening sentence of the description of G— in 5.9:
  'G— is a delightfully unspoilt village surrounded by fields and woods at the mouth of a river.'

1 ... is a village I know very well.
2 One of the most interesting developments of recent years is ...
3 The village of ... is set on a scenic river mouth.
4 The other day, I was talking with some friends about ...
5 I'll never forget the day that I first went to ...
6 One thing we tend to take for granted nowadays is ...
7 Recently everyone has been talking about ...
8 ... is a subject that is on everyone's mind these days.
9 I'm going to tell you something about a place I know, called ...
10 I'd just like to say a few words about ...

B   Which of these sentences could be used instead of the closing sentence:

'Welcome to G__!'

1 Looking forward to seeing you in ... before too long.
2 You can imagine how we felt!
3 You can catch a bus back to the city from the village square.
4 So that's about all there is to say about it.
5 One thing is certain: a solution must be found before it is too late.
6 You'll find that ... is surprisingly easy to make and delicious too!
7 So, goodbye from ...!
8 It is quite different from other places you may have visited.
9 So I hope you'll be able to come with me to ... soon.
10 I can't think of anything else to write.

C   Work in pairs. Look back through all the previous reading pasages in Units 1 to 5 and pick your two favourite opening sentences and your two favourite closing sentences.

Look at your own recent compositions. Can you or your partner improve on the opening and closing sentences you wrote?

D   Write a description of:

the district, town or village you live in OR your own home.

Imagine that you're writing to a foreign friend and you want to persuade him or her to come and visit you.

● MAKE NOTES before you start writing and decide what your opening and closing sentences will be.
● Check your work through afterwards.

5.11   Grammar revision

This exercise revises some of the grammar points that you have studied in the first five units. In the exam, you'll have to do an exercise very like this one.

Finish each incomplete sentence in such a way that it means the same as the complete sentence before it. The first is done for you as an example:

1 We have known each other since 1987.   We first ...
   We first met in 1987.
2 We lived in the country during my childhood   When ...
3 We moved into this district eight years ago.   We have ...
4 The chairs and tables have to be moved from this room.   The furniture ...
5 We'll redecorate our flat after our summer holiday.   After we ...
6 I'm sure that someone forgot to lock the door.   Someone must ...
7 We finished spring-cleaning and then went out for a meal. After we ...
8 During our meal, we discussed what to do at the weekend. While ...
9 This room has been painted since the last time I was here. You hadn't ...
10 It wasn't a good idea to paint the walls pink.   You ...

6 Science and technology

6.1 Talking about science

Vocabulary

A Work in small groups. Ask your partners these questions:
- What aspects of science or technology have a direct effect on your life?
- What is the purpose of scientific research?
- What is the purpose of studying the stars and other planets?
- Is it worth spending huge amounts of money on space travel and exploration?

B Fill the gaps in these sentences with suitable words.

1 A single __molecule__ of water (H_2O) consists of two a................s of hydrogen and one of oxygen.
2 The most common e................ in the air we breathe is nitrogen (N).
3 Salt (sodium chloride – NaCl) is a c................ of sodium and chlorine.
4 Plutonium and uranium are r................ substances used in nuclear power stations.
5 The three main branches of science are: ch................ (the study of the elements that make up the universe), ph................ (the study of matter and natural forces) and b................ (the study of living things).
6 Einstein's famous f................ $E = mc^2$ (where E = energy, m = mass and c = the speed of light), is part of his theory of relativity.
7 Scientists can find out if a theory is true by carrying out e................s.
8 An experimental scientist does much of his or her work in a l................
9 The inventor made a working model of his invention in his w................ and then invited the press to watch a d................
10 An idea may sound as if it works in theory, but it may not work in p................
11 In mathematics, a theorem (e.g. 'the sum of the angles in any triangle is 180°') is a concept or idea that can be p................ by logical reasoning.
12 Technology is the activity of using scientific knowledge for p................ purposes.
13 An expert method or skill used in doing something (e.g. playing a musical instrument or taking exams) is called a t................
14 Computers, radios and TV are all e................ equipment.
15 A computer and the equipment used with it are known as the ....ware and the programs that tell it what to do are known as ....ware.
16 The data (information) produced on a computer is stored on a ....
17 To find out how something works and how to operate it you must read the ....
18 Some video recorders have a remote control: you just have to press a .... to pause or to rewind the tape.
19 You can .... the volume on the TV by turning this knob.
20 Any complicated piece of equipment needs to be .... regularly, otherwise it ma .... unexpectedly at any time and it may be expensive to have it ....
21 In a modern car factory, some of the work is done by r................s, not people.

22 Two of the ....s of a car are the tyres and the engine.
23 Some common tools used by a .... are a hammer, a saw and a ....
24 To make a piece of furniture you need some wood, ... and some ....
25 If you're not sure what something is called you can call it a ~~watchamacallit~~ or a ~~thingumajig~~ or a whatnot or a ....

C Work in small groups. Think of some gadgets or equipment that you use at home or at work (e.g. bicycle, hairdryer, electric shaver, cassette player, etc.). Without getting too technical (and without opening them up to find out what's inside!), list the important controls, parts and components. Use a dictionary if necessary. Tell the other groups what you have found out.

6.2 For a pint, just add water

Reading

A Before you read the article, find out if anyone in the class knows how beer is brewed – what are the ingredients and how do they become beer?

B Read the newspaper article and answer the questions on the next page.

For a pint, just add water

STRASBOURG: Fischer, the third largest brewery in France, has developed a new product that it hopes will put some life back into the beer market – a beer concentrate.

The thick brown liquid is the latest product to emerge from Fischer's laboratory. When mixed with six parts of carbonated water, the reconstituted beer is indistinguishable from the real stuff even to experts, the brewery's president Mr Michel Debus said.

Mr Debus said it took 30 years to develop a method of removing water from beer without sacrificing its original flavour or fragrance.

Fischer uses a new process called "inverted osmosis". The beer is forced at high pressure through a molecular sieve which separates water and alcohol from the brew.

A similar process is used in some Arab countries to desalinate seawater. Fischer has patented the process but has added a secret technique to preserve the beer's taste.

Beer concentrate, Mr Debus said, "is the dream of brewers all over the world." In the beer brewing business, he said, increasing capacity meant building new, costly breweries. With the concentrate, "one plant can supply bottlers anywhere on earth."

Fischer has sent samples of the concentrate to dozens of countries, offering an impressive variety of flavours, sweet for the United States, bitter for Japan, non-alcoholic for Muslim countries.

The initial response, Mr Debus said, was very encouraging. Fischer hopes to sign its first big contract in September for the distribution of reconstituted beer in Japan, and is negotiating deals with West German and Swiss firms.

Mr Debus said Fischer is likely to do most business with countries in the Far East and North Africa where brewing beer is either not well established or impractical. He wants to break into the US market with the non-alcoholic version, to be called Energy.

The concentrate, Mr Debus said, will be sold only to bottling companies, not directly to consumers, and bottlers will be required to use water specified by Fischer but may add alcohol and choose the trade name.

Fischer hopes to corner 2 per cent of the 26 billion gallon world beer market.

»»→

1 This article is about ...
    a) a new kind of beer that contains no alcohol
    b) a new kind of beer that is more tasty than traditional beers
    c) a new liquid that can be mixed with water to make beer
2 According to Mr Debus ...
    a) Only the most expert tasters can tell that the concentrate is not real beer.
    b) No one can taste the difference between the concentrate and real beer.
    c) The average consumer cannot taste the difference.
3 The process used by Fischer is similar to ...
    a) freezing   b) removing salt from seawater   c) filtering coffee
4 The advantage of the new process is that beer ...
    a) will be cheaper
    b) can be bottled more cheaply
    c) will be more tasty all over the world
5 Mr Debus thinks the most promising market will be ...
    a) the USA   b) Europe   c) Asia and North Africa
6 Fischer will supply ...
    a) one flavour   b) a wide range of flavours   c) three flavours
7 Mr Debus hopes to sell the product in America as ...
    a) a drink for active people
    b) an old-fashioned European beer
    c) a non-alcoholic drink
8 The new product will be on sale to consumers ...
    a) as a concentrate
    b) under the 'Fischer' brand name
    c) under various brand names

6.3 Using the passive   *Grammar*

A   Study these rules and examples of the main uses of the passive.

The passive is used when the person responsible for an action is not known or is not important:
    The beer **is forced** at high pressure through a sieve.
    A similar process **is used** in some Arab countries.
    I **was given** a watch for my birthday.
    These problems **will have to be solved** before we can go ahead.

The passive is also used when we want to avoid mentioning the person responsible for an action:
    You **were asked** to arrive at 8 a.m.   (less 'personal' than: I asked you to arrive.)
    This composition **must be handed in** next Monday.

***By* is often used with the passive to show who was responsible for an action:**
    Penicillin **was discovered by** Alexander Fleming.
    The first landing on the moon **was made** in 1969 **by** the Americans.
    The research **is being done by** a team of European scientists.

■ Often there is no great difference in meaning between a passive and an active sentence when the person who performed the action is unimportant. The passive can be used to give variety to the style of a passage, as in these examples:

Seventeen muscles **are used** when you smile but 43 **are used** when you frown.

You use seventeen muscles when you smile but you use 43 when you frown.

Fischer has sent samples to dozens of countries.

Samples **have been sent** to dozens of countries.

The committee will announce the names of the Nobel Prize winners in May.

The names of the Nobel Prize winners **will be announced** in May.

(But NOT: I'll meet you tomorrow. / You will be met tomorrow.)

B Fill the gaps in this table, which shows the basic structures used in the passive. The first two are done for you as examples:

ACTIVE		PASSIVE
They often do it.	→	It is often done.
They are doing it now.	→	It is being done now.
They did it yesterday.	→	It ....
They were doing it last week.	→	It ....
They have already done it.	→	It ....
They will soon do it.	→	It ....
They will soon have done it.	→	It ....
They had done it earlier.	→	It ....
They have to do it at once.	→	It ....
They may not have done it yet.	→	It ....

C Finish the incomplete sentences in such a way that each one means the same as the complete sentence before it.

1 Fischer has patented the process.   The process ...
2 Fischer will only sell the concentrate to bottling companies.   The concentrate ...
3 Fischer will require bottlers to use water that Fischer specifies.   Bottlers ...
4 The bottlers can choose the trade name.   The trade name ...
5 You can only see these particles through a microscope.   These particles ...
6 Charles Townes produced the first laser in 1960.   The first ...
7 People are using computers in all kinds of work.   Computers ...
8 You have to keep dangerous chemicals in a safe place.   Dangerous ...
9 You shouldn't have left the laboratory unlocked.   The laboratory ...
10 We are unlikely to discover intelligent life on other planets.   Intelligent life ...

D Work in small groups. Can you decide which of these inventions or discoveries were made in which year?

Write a sentence beginning with *If* ... about each of them. One is done for you as an example below.

bicycle   computer   jet engine   laser   margarine   printing press   Scotch tape
telephone   television   thermometer
1455   1593   1840   1869   1876   1926   1930   1937   1943   1960   1971

'I think the thermometer was invented in 1593.'

If the thermometer hadn't been invented, we wouldn't be able to measure temperature.

[serən'dipiti] 易奇像的运气

6.4 Serendipity

Listening

> **serendipity** /serəndɪpəti/ is the natural talent that some people have for finding interesting or valuable things by chance.

A   You'll hear part of a broadcast about some important discoveries which happened by accident. Answer the multiple-choice questions below.

1 Penicillin was discovered when Alexander Fleming found some mould growing on a laboratory dish he had left ...
   a) beside the window   b) in a dark corner   c) above the window
2 Antibiotic drugs based on penicillin have helped to ...
   a) cure every disease   b) stop bacteria spreading
   c) reduce the number of deaths from disease
3 Radar is now used ...
   a) by military scientists   b) by motorists   c) by ships and aircraft
4 Radar was discovered while scientists were looking for a new ...
   a) form of radio communication   b) type of weapon
   c) way of increasing safety at sea
5 Teflon was discovered while chemists were doing research on ...
   a) cooling systems   b) plastic   c) poisonous gases
6 Teflon is now used in ...
   a) computers   b) refrigerators   c) spacecraft
7 Artificial sweeteners were discovered when scientists ...
   a) tasted a substance they had produced in the laboratory
   b) were doing experiments with sweet substances
   c) were looking for patterns in substances
8 Chewing gum was discovered while scientists were doing research into ...
   a) artificial sweeteners   b) materials to use instead of rubber
   c) trees in Mexico
9 'Post-It Notes' were invented after a researcher discovered a substance that ...
   a) could be used instead of sticky tape   b) would stick for ever
   c) wouldn't stick properly
10 The 'useless' adhesive ...
   a) left a mark on some surfaces   b) became less sticky after a while
   c) could be easily removed later
11 On Sundays the 3M researcher ...
   a) did research into adhesives   b) sang in a church   c) wrote songs
12 'Post-it Notes' are now used ...
   a) by choirs in churches   b) to leave messages for people
   c) to send messages by mail

B   Work in small groups. Find out your partners' views on luck by asking these questions:
● Do you believe in good luck and bad luck?
● What part has 'good luck' played in your life?
● What lucky accidents have happened to you?
● Are some people born lucky and others born unlucky?

A The passage below describes a simple experiment that you can carry out with different people to test the speed of their reactions. Read the passage before you listen to the recording.

A SIMPLE REACTION TIMER

Quick reactions are important if you're an airline pilot, a motorist, or even a cyclist – and of course in sports, fast reactions are especially valuable. This simple but effective Reaction Timer makes use of the principle that, if we ignore the effects of air resistance, all objects fall with the same acceleration.

Equipment required:
a 30 cm ruler, sticky tape, paper, scissors and a pen.

Procedure:
1 Cut out a piece of paper the same size as this page.
2 You will see along the side of the page a scale with divisions marked on it. Each division shows a time interval. These represent fractions of a second.
3 Copy the scale carefully onto the side of the piece of paper you have cut out and then tightly wrap it round the ruler so that the scale is visible. The bottom end of the scale should be at the bottom end of the ruler. Fix it securely with sticky tape.
4 While you hold the ruler at the point marked 'HOLD HERE', get the person to place his or her thumb and forefinger on either side of the zero line on the scale. Tell them to catch the ruler as soon as it begins to fall. If they grip the ruler *before* it begins to fall, this result is not counted.
5 Without letting the person know when you are about to drop it, release the ruler. The time that it took the person to react is shown in seconds on the scale at the point they caught it.
6 Repeat the experiment several times with each person and record the results in a chart.

B 🔲 Listen to the first part of the recording. You'll hear the first paragraph read aloud. Why is this reading difficult to understand?

C 🔊 Now you'll hear a better version of the instructions. As you listen, mark the PAUSES that the reader makes, using a vertical line (|), on the passage on the previous page. The first paragraph is done as an example:

Quick reactions are important if you're an airline pilot, | a motorist, or even a cyclist | – and of course in sports, | fast reactions are especially valuable. | This simple but effective Reaction Timer | makes use of the principle that, | if we ignore the effects of air resistance, | all objects fall with the same acceleration. |

D 🔊 Now listen to the recording again. This time, mark the syllables that are STRESSED in each sentence in the text. Again, the first paragraph is done for you as an example:

Quíck reáctions are impórtant íf you're an aírline pílot, a mótorist, or éven a cýclist – ánd of cóurse in spórts, fást reáctions are espécially váluable. Thís símple but efféctive Reáction Tímer mákes úse of the prínciple that, íf we ignóre the effécts of aír resístance, áll óbjects fáll with the sáme accelerátion.

When you have finished, compare your version with a partner and then look at the completed version in Activity 11.

E Now read the passage aloud yourself. If you're working with a partner, take it in turns to read alternate paragraphs and comment on each other's reading.
- Did you find it easy to understand your partner?
- How could he or she read more clearly?

6.6 Reaction times   *Directed writing*

A Work in small groups. Imagine that you have carried out the Reaction Timer experiment (in 6.5) with the other members of your group. You have recorded the results in this table:

RESULTS OF OUR GROUP AFTER 6 ATTEMPTS

Try no.	1st	2nd	3rd	4th	5th	6th	Average (mean)	
Hand.	RIGHT	LEFT	RIGHT	LEFT	RIGHT	LEFT	RIGHT	LEFT
ANNE	0.14	0.19	0.15	0.20	0.13	0.20	0.14	0.20
BILL	0.19	0.20	0.18	0.10	0.18	0.09	0.18	0.13
CHRIS	0.11	0.11	0.12	missed	0.12	0.10	0.12	0.10
ME	missed	0.19	0.17	0.04	0.16	0.13	0.16	0.12

Which person had the fastest and slowest reactions?
- taking each one's average (mean) score
- taking only their best efforts
- taking only their worst efforts

B   Write three paragraphs:

1 Imagine that you carried out the Reaction Timer experiment and
   summarise the PROCEDURE (see 6.5), beginning like this:
      'An experiment was carried out in which ...'

2 Imagine that you carried out the experiment and describe the RESULTS
   (see A above), beginning like this:
      'We found that ...'

3 Explain how you would feel if you really had to carry out the
   experiment, beginning like this:
      'I think carrying out the experiment would ...'
   OR, if you really have carried out the experiment:
      'We thought that the experiment was ...'

6.7   Using prepositions – 3   *Use of English*

Fill the gaps in these sentences with suitable prepositions.

1 Sarah **quarrelled** .... Louise .... the **preparations** .... the party.
2 Eric **reminds** me .... Paul McCartney, but they aren't **related** .... each
   other.
3 You can never **rely** .... Anna to **provide** you .... information.
4 The staff are **responsible** .... their boss .... the decisions they make.
5 You can only **succeed** .... passing an exam if you **revise** carefully .... it.
6 I've got plenty of sandwiches, would you like to **share** them .... me?
7 The police suspected that the goods had been **stolen** .... the shop, but the
   receipt proved that they had been **paid** ....
8 Kate is **suffering** .... a bad cold and she wants you to **sympathise** .... her.
9 At the end of the party, we **thanked** our host and hostess .... inviting us.
10 I'm **tired** .... waiting .... Jim to arrive. **I object** .... his unpunctuality.
11 On behalf of the students and staff, I'd like to **welcome** you .... our school.
12 Helen **worked** .... ACME plc for a year and then she **resigned** .... the job.

A   This article comes from a consumer magazine. When you've read it, answer the questions on the next page.

WHAT DOES THE CHIP MEAN FOR YOU?

Massive and unreliable, the first computers of thirty years ago are as dead as the dinosaur. Today, computers which are 30,000 times smaller and 10,000 times cheaper can beat them hollow. High-speed, low-cost computing power has begun to convert science fiction into reality.   1

In this report, we use the words **chip** or **microchip** when we're referring to the chips themselves. Where we're dealing with the wider subject of chips in use – eg in computers, communication systems, and the like – we use the words **microelectronics**, or **micros**, for short.   2

A LOOK TO THE FUTURE

What will the world of the future be like? Here are some ideas to consider: 3

● **a divided society?** The coming of the micro will benefit many people: others may be left behind. People at risk are those who can't afford to use new technology, or who can't understand it. Something can be done for both groups –public viewdata terminals can give free access to information, and new machines (including computers) can be made easy to use, provided time, money and care is spent in programming them.   4

● **variety or uniformity?** Will we be surrounded by an enormous variety of products? Or will the result of micros be cheap uniformity? Either of these is possible. The main factor is the cost of writing programs. If the cost remains high, products will have to be made in large quantities – in order to spread the cost. To get variety, programming costs need to come down. There are signs that this may happen: some manufacturers are now using relatively unsophisticated chips, which can be cheaply programmed for simple functions.   5

● **goodbye humans?** If people work at home and do their banking and shopping at home, the result could be an inward-looking and immobile society, as families retreat into a private world of video games and computer holograms. On the other hand, people seem to need human contact, and to enjoy the social aspects of office life and escaping from their homes.   6

● **beyond the human brain.** A simple electronic calculator goes far beyond the human brain in speed and accuracy – but only in a very closely defined field. In the future, computers will surpass humans in more and more ways. It's predicted by some people (and hotly disputed by others) that the intellectual capabilities of the human brain will be overtaken in the early years of the next century. When (or if) this happens, we will no longer be the most intelligent entities on the planet. No-one knows how we would cope with this wounding loss of status.   7

CONCLUSIONS

The microchip revolution is based on size and cost. Microchips give us cheap computing power in a tiny space. As the cost of microchips continues to fall, it becomes economically worthwhile to use them in more and more ways.   8

We have to accept the microchip, or face the alternative of opting out of the free world market.   9

Accepting the microchip brings benefits and problems. The benefits include greater efficiency in finding and using information; the possibility of higher living standards through increased productivity; greater control over pollution and the use of natural resources; help for the sick and the disabled; and a whole range of 'smart' machines to inform, entertain and serve us.   10

We can guard against some of the problems. We can, for example, be alive to the danger of the misuse of information held on computer files.   11

There is the problem of alienation: people who cannot find a place in the technological world of the future. To guard against this problem, we need education and training schemes, and machines which are easy to use. Finally, there's the problem of people whose skills are made redundant by machines. Again, there's a need for education and retraining. The wealth needed to pay for schemes like these is more likely to appear if we use the microchip.   12

1 In the article the word 'micros' refers to ...
   a) all kinds of computers   b) microchips   c) microchips and their uses
2 The new machines will be easier to use ...
   a) because we will all be familiar with them
   b) only if the programs are user-friendly
   c) because the programs will be user-friendly
3 All products are likely to become very similar to each other unless ...
   a) production costs fall
   b) programming costs fall   c) the public demands variety
4 Microchips are not used everywhere at present because they are still too ...
   a) complicated   b) expensive   c) small   d) specialised
5 According to the article, the average person ...
   a) likes going to work
   b) dislikes going to work   c) enjoys working at home
6 A computer that is more intelligent than a person will be developed after 2000 ...
   a) according to all the experts
   b) according to some of the experts   c) according to the article
7 Retraining people who lose their jobs because of computers will be ...
   a) cheap   b) easy   c) expensive   d) impossible
8 On the whole, the article suggests that ...
   a) there are more problems than benefits
   b) there are fewer problems than benefits   c) the problems match the benefits

B   Find words in the text that have the following meanings. The numbers
show which paragraph you should look at. The first is done as an example:
very large (1) massive
change (1)   do better than (7)
bring advantages for (4)   painful (7)
in danger (4)   not taking part in (9)
lack of differences (5)   intelligent (10)
simple (5)   feeling of not belonging (12)

C   Work in small groups. Ask your partners these questions:
- Which parts of the article do you agree with
  and which do you disagree with?
- What do you see as the main benefits of
  computers?
- What are the main disadvantages of
  computers and electronic equipment?
- Do you enjoy using a computer – or do you
  find it unpleasant or difficult?
- What have you used a computer for? What
  will you use one for in the future?
- To what extent are computers over- or
  underused nowadays in your country?

'When we split up, James got the
hardware and I got the software.'

6.9 I'd better explain how it works

🔲 Listen to the instructions that Annie is being given. Decide which of these photos show the 'right way' to load and operate the dishwasher.

6.10 How does it work?

👥 The class is divided into an even number of pairs.

Half the pairs should look at Activity 39, the other half at 47.

Study the explanations there. Later you'll have to explain to another pair how soap or a cassette works.

★ Normally, you write things so that someone else can read them – so try to imagine how your reader will react. Put yourself in your reader's place as you write.

You can assume that the 'general reader' (or the average examiner!) knows something about the subjects you know about – but he or she may not be an expert. Bear this in mind as you look at the extracts below.

A   Decide what is 'GOOD' and 'BAD' about these paragraphs:

> Soap is made up of molecules. Each one has a tail and this sticks to the dirt and it pulls away from the cloth, making the cloth clean.

> The cassette consists of a plastic case, containing the recording tape. The two halves of the case are sometimes screwed together but may also be glued permanently together. The tape travels between the spools across tiny rollers and behind a small opening. When the recorder is going, the tape leaves the first spool and is wound onto the second. As it travels behind the opening in the case the tape head pushes against the tape, so that it remains in contact as it winds past it.

B   Write an explanation of how another everyday process works – for example, a telephone, an LP record or compact disc, a microwave oven, etc.

(If you are not a technically-minded person, you may prefer to describe one of the processes shown in Activity 39 or 47 – but the information contained within the diagrams must be given in words.)

First of all, make notes of the main points you want to make in the composition. If possible, discuss your notes with another student before you start writing.

★ When you check your work afterwards, look systematically for mistakes you may have made in each of these areas:

Spelling
>   What was the affect of this ? x

Prepositions
>   I'm interested for science.   x

Verb forms and endings
>   I was gave it. x   If I would be rich ... x   She live in London. x

Articles
>   I'm interested in the science. x

6.12 *Keep* and *take*   *Verbs and idioms*

A   Which of the endings below go with these beginnings:

Kim and Chris took ...
Chris and Kim kept ...

some photographs   calm   a holiday together   a long time
house for their father   control of the situation   quiet   action
no notice of each other   their tempers   the engine to pieces   care of the children
their hands in their pockets   listening   an eye on each other

B   Fill the gaps in these sentences with suitable verbs from the list below:

   keep
 1 You're doing very well. Try to .... the good work!
 2 Don't give up. You've got to .... your work until you've finished.
 3 I advise you to .... that machine, it's dangerous.
 4 One member of the audience .... snoring throughout the lecture.
 5 Zoë is such a fast runner that I couldn't .... her.
   take
 6 The magician's trick .... everyone in the audience ....
 7 You need to keep fit. Why don't you .... jogging?
 8 Our new boss was so pleasant that everyone .... her at once.
 9 If you ask David for help, he always wants to .... completely.
10 We had to check in at 3 a.m., but the plane didn't .... till 7.
11 I find that my work .... so much of my time that I don't have any free time.
12 There was simply too much information, I couldn't .... it all ....
13 If you .... 6 .... 21, the answer is 15.
14 His grandfather and father were lazy too. I think he .... both of them!

keep away from   keep on   keep on with   keep up   keep up with
take after   take away from   take in   take in   take off   take over
take to   take up   take up

'No, no – that's E as in Einstein,
M as in Manhattan, C as in cataclysm ...'

7 Good health!

7.1 In sickness and in health   *Vocabulary*

A Fill the gaps with suitable words.

1 If you want to find out someone's temperature, use a .... *clinic*
2 Please don't cough all over everyone! Don't forget that a cold is ....
   As it is a virus, there is no .... for it. *immunization*
3 I hurt my wrist yesterday playing football and today it's .... *swelling*
4 I had to wait three-quarters of an hour in the doctor's ....
5 I went to the doctor about my insomnia and she prescribed some ....
6 The main symptom of hay fever is that you keep ....
7 It was quite a bad cut and it was bleeding a lot, so I put on a .... *plaster*
8 I think he's broken his leg! Quick, someone call an .... *am*
9 If someone is seriously ill they may need to go to hospital to have an ....
10 I hate going to the dentist – I've got to have two .... done.
11 If you want to stay fit, don't eat too much and take plenty of ....
12 Her mother sent her to bed because she had a ....
13 He was ten kilos overweight and was advised to go on a .... *diet*
14 You've eaten too much, that's why you have a pain in your .... *✓*
15 Oh dear, I feel awful. I think I'm going to ....

B Choose the best alternative to fill each of the gaps in the next five sentences.

1 If you want antibiotics, you'll have to ask the doctor for a ....
   medicine   note   prescription   receipt   recipe
2 She was in terrible pain, so the nurse gave her a(n) ....
   injection   scratch   stab   vaccine   wound
3 If you've got measles, your skin is covered in ....
   blots   dots   freckles   spots   stains
4 Why not take up tennis? It'll help you to keep fit and it's a great ....
   amusement   game   match   play   tournament
5 He didn't feel like going to the party because he had a terrible ....
   disease   headache   homesickness   infection   nostalgia

C In the last five sentences THREE of the alternatives are correct and TWO of them are wrong. Choose the three best alternatives for each.

1 If you've got a bad cold, it's no wonder you're feeling ....
   off your food   on form   out of order   out of sorts   under the weather
2 I walked into a door yesterday, which is why I have a .... on my forehead.
   black eye   bruise   bump   cut   hurt

⟫→

85

3 You're less likely to become ill if you are ....
  hygienic   physically fit   living a healthy life   in good shape   running
4 Doctors say that smoking and drinking can both .... your health.
  affect   damage   improve   ruin   wound
5 As I haven't had anything to eat today, I'm feeling a bit ....
  dizzy   faint   funny   silly   unconscious

D   Work in pairs. Draw a rough sketch of the human body at the centre of a blank page and label the parts, starting at the toes or at the fingers. Use a dictionary if necessary.

When you've finished, compare your labelled body with another pair's.

● What can go wrong with each part? Write sentences like this:
  HEAD – She's got a headache.
  WRIST – He's sprained his wrist.

7.2   What to do about flu

Reading

A   Read these sentences. Which do you think are true (**T**) or false (**F**)?
  Then read the leaflet on the next page and find out if you were right, according to the text.

1 One symptom of flu is an aching back.
2 Antibiotics can help you to get better from flu.
3 Flu always lasts several days.
4 It's advisable to drink two to three litres of liquid a day.
5 If you have flu, it's essential to eat three times a day.
6 Flu is not a serious illness for anyone.
7 Flu is infectious – other people can catch it from you.
8 People are more likely to catch flu in a crowded place.
9 Elderly people should tell their doctor if they think they've got flu.
10 If you have flu badly, you should lie in a darkened room.
11 Doctors, nurses and policemen are always vaccinated against flu.
12 One vaccination gives several years' protection against flu.
13 The worst time of year for flu is the autumn.
14 Wash up very thoroughly if someone in your family has flu.
15 You should call the doctor if your flu goes on for longer than a week.

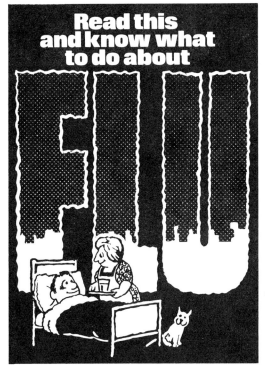

Read this and know what to do about FLU

You've got your own defence system — here's how to make it work.

You're feeling rotten – weak, shivery, with an aching head, back and limbs. Your temperature's up over 38°C (100°F). Probably you're sweating a lot, you've lost your appetite and you feel sick. You've got flu.

So what do you do?

There's no quick cure. Flu – influenza – is caused by a virus. And viruses can't be killed with antibiotics. Only the body's own defence system can get rid of them.

So for most of us there's no point in seeing the doctor when we've got flu. But while a bout of flu lasts, which may be anything from 24 hours to several days,

here's what you should do.

Stay indoors, keep warm, and keep away from other people as much as possible so you don't pass on the infection.

Have plenty of cool drinks – water, fruit drinks, milky drinks. About 2-3 litres a day.

If you feel shivery or feverish, with a temperature over 38°C (100°F) or aches or pains, try taking soluble aspirin every 4 hours during the day. And rest in bed if you can.

Try to have 3 light meals a day. But don't force yourself to eat if you've lost your appetite.

FLU VACCINATION Flu vaccine is usually only given to people who are especially at risk because of their health and to people who cannot miss work, like nurses, doctors, firemen or policemen.
These people may be offered flu vaccination once a year, generally in the autumn before winter epidemics. But even vaccination cannot give complete protection against flu.

REMEMBER Keep flu to yourself. Stay away from other people. Make sure handkerchiefs and also plates, knives, forks etc., are always well washed.
Look after yourself by resting in bed and having lots of cool drinks.
There's no need for the doctor unless the flu persists for more than a few days or gets suddenly worse.

But if you are elderly and in poor health, or if you suffer from a severe chest condition like bronchitis or asthma, then flu can become a more serious illness.
So remember:
❊ When there's flu about, try to avoid crowded places and keep away from anyone who's got flu.
❊ If you think you've caught flu, get in touch with your doctor. Then he can at least keep an eye on you.
❊ In the autumn, ask your doctor if he thinks you should be vaccinated against flu.

B Work in pairs. Imagine that a friend of yours is unwell and may have flu.
• Write down five questions you would ask to find out if he or she has flu.
• What advice would you give, once you're sure he or she has flu?

Role-play the conversation, with one of you playing the role of sick friend.
Look at these expressions before you begin.

> If I were you, I'd ...   The best thing to do is to ...
> I think you should ...   It's best to ...
> You ought to ...

C Now imagine that your friend hasn't got flu, just a BAD COLD. What advice would you give him or her?
Role-play the conversation. This time the *other* person is the sick friend.

7.3 Comparing and contrasting   *Grammar*

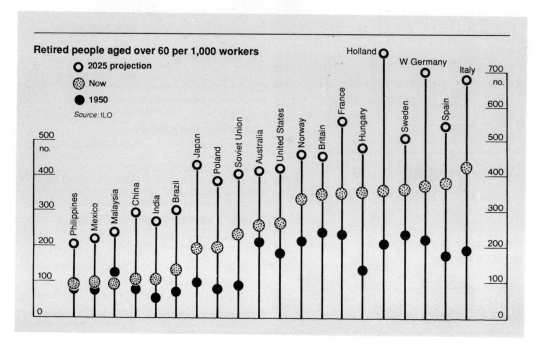

Retired people aged over 60 per 1,000 workers

○ 2025 projection
◉ Now
● 1950

Source: ILO

A These examples show the principal uses of comparatives and superlatives. Notice how similar ideas can be expressed in different ways.

People in Italy live **longer than** anywhere else in the world.
  = There are **more** retired people in Italy **than** anywhere else in the world.
  = Italy has **the oldest** population in the world.
Far more people live to retirement age in Britain **than** in the Philippines.
  = **Not as many** people live to retirement age in the Philippines.
There are **about the same** number of old people in Australia **as** in the USA.
  = The number of old people in Australia is **similar to** the number in the USA.
There are **not as many** old people in Mexico **as** in Japan.
  = There are **fewer** old people in Mexico **than** in Japan.
The population of France is **less young than** the population of Brazil.
  = The population of Brazil is **not as old as** the population of France.
There are about **twice as many** retired people in the USA **as** in Brazil.
  = There are about **half as many** retired people in Brazil **as** in the USA.
Spain has **the second oldest** population.
Throughout the world, people live **much longer** nowadays **than** they used to.
The number of old people in China is **nothing like as** high **as** in Sweden.

B Referring to the statistics in the table, write five sentences comparing 1950 with the present day AND five sentences comparing 2025 with the present day.

88

C Find and correct the errors in these sentences. One of them has *no* errors.

1 Hot, wet weather has a much worse effect on people's health than cool, dry weather.
2 July in Cairo is far more dryer as Athens.
3 The daytime temperature in Tokyo in July is the same than New York.
4 There are much differences between the weather in Cairo and Tokyo.
5 The weather in Athens in July is more warmer than London.
6 New York is more cold in winter as London.

World Weather Guide

| | Average temperature: | | | | Average number of rainy days: | |
| | JULY | | JANUARY | | | |
	day	night	day	night	JULY	JANUARY
Athens	33°	23°	13°	6°	2	16
Buenos Aires	14°	6°	29°	17°	7	8
Cairo	36°	21°	18°	8°	0	1
London	22°	14°	6°	2°	12	15
New York	28°	19°	3°	–4°	12	12
Tokyo	28°	21°	8°	–2°	10	5

D Rewrite each sentence starting with the words on the right, so that its meaning remains the same.

1 Cairo is much hotter than London in July. London isn't …
2 There are fewer rainy days in Buenos Aires than in New York. There aren't …
3 There is less rain in Tokyo than in Athens in January. More rain …
4 In July New York is warmer than Buenos Aires, but wetter. Buenos Aires …
5 The amount of rainfall is similar in London and New York. About the same …
6 Summer nights in Cairo are much warmer than in London. In London …
7 A broken leg is more serious than a sprained wrist. A sprained wrist …
8 No one can imagine a more frightening illness than AIDS. AIDS is …
9 Flu is a more serious illness than a cold. A cold is less …
10 Fewer people die from flu than 50 years ago. Not as …

E Work in small groups. What are the SIMILARITIES and DIFFERENCES between your country and Britain and/or the USA? Consider the following aspects:

size   population   climate   scenery
health care   music   entertainment   TV and radio
family life   science   technology   transport
food and eating habits: breakfast, lunch, dinner, snacks
drinks: hot drinks, non-alcoholic, alcoholic
attitudes to health: illness, drugs, a healthy diet, keeping fit, etc.

Make notes of the most interesting points that are made. Write ten sentences about the major differences between life in the two countries you've discussed.

7.4 Sleep and dreams

A Before you listen to the recording, look at the statements below. Which do you think are true (**T**) or false (**F**)?
   Then listen to the interview and find out if you were right.

1 Our brains require deep sleep, not REM (rapid eye movement) sleep, to restore them.
2 Dreams occur when you are about to wake up.
3 Dreams occur during REM sleep.
4 Dreams only last a few seconds: they happen much more quickly than in real life.
5 Dreams can help sleepers to solve problems in their waking lives.
6 In dreams of falling or being chased, the dreamer is not usually hurt or caught.
7 There are some people who never have dreams.
8 Most people require eight hours' sleep a night.
9 Many successful people need only a few hours' sleep a night.
10 Talking in your sleep only occurs during dreaming sleep.
11 People who take a midday sleep (a siesta) need more hours' sleep in 24 hours.
12 A very short sleep (a nap) has no physical benefits.

B Work in groups. Carry out some 'research' by asking each other these questions:

- How much sleep do you need?
- How do you feel if you have less sleep than normal?
- Are you a light sleeper? What kinds of things wake you up?
- Do you ever suffer from insomnia? What do you do to help you to get to sleep?
- Do you find it easy to go to sleep?
- Do you remember your dreams? Tell us about one of them.
- Have you ever dreamt about anyone in the class?

Report to the rest of the class about your 'research'. Do your findings confirm or contradict the research of the doctor you heard in the recording?

'If diseases were easier to pronounce, Mrs Jarvis, everyone would have them.'

7.5 Using suffixes: Actions and people   *Word study*

A Look at these examples of verbs. Add more of your own, using the root words below with one of the suffixes in this list.

-ise/-ize modernise sterilise ....
-en   widen strengthen harden lengthen ....

-ify   classify clarify ....

central flat individual less loose pure sharp simple soft
summary symbol tight

★ Notice that these verbs don't have a suffix:
↑ raise lift   ↓ lower drop
   heat warm melt   cool chill freeze
   cure heal

B In these examples of personal nouns, the stressed syllables are shown with áccents: emplóyer, employée, etc. Add more examples, using the root words below.

-er   emplóyer (= someone who employs) ríder advíser
      ....
-ee   employée (= someone who is employed) trainée addressée
-or   invéntor condúctor ....
-ant partícipant ímmigrant sérvant ....
-ist chémist bíologist mótorist ....

art assist broadcast clean cycle direct inhabit inspect instruct
manage science sing ski teach type visit

★ Notice that these words all end in -ent:
absent ancient efficient correspondent confident convenient
efficient evident independent frequent resident patient student
violent

C Fill the gaps in these sentences, using the correct form of the root words:

1 If someone faints you should .... their clothing, not
  .... it.   LOOSE   TIGHT
2 The .... needed an .... to help with the experiment. SCIENCE   ASSIST
3 After the road had been .... every .... drove faster. WIDE   MOTOR
4 A good .... pays all his .... well.   EMPLOY   EMPLOY
5 The knife may need .... before it is used.   SHARP
6 Milk can be .... by .... it to boiling point.   STERILE   HOT
7 A motorbike .... can go much faster than a ....   RIDE   CYCLE
8 The city has over a million ....   INHABIT

91

7.6 Welcome to the health farm!

A 📼 You'll hear some newly arrived guests being welcomed to a 'health farm' (a centre where people go to lose weight and become fit). Decide which of these statements are true (**T**) or false (**F**).

1 Guests are not allowed to leave the premises.
2 If you don't lose weight your diet will change.
3 Sports and exercise are optional.
4 The only social activity is a cross-country treasure hunt.
5 Visitors are only permitted before 11 p.m.
6 Breakfast is served at 7.15 a.m.
7 Guests on the intensive one-week course don't get breakfast.
8 Cakes are only served on Sundays.
9 Incoming mail for the guests is opened in case it contains food.
10 Guests with problems are dealt with by Mr O'Hara.

B Work in small groups. Ask your partners these questions:
● What is your reaction to the idea of a 'health farm'? What kind of people pay to starve?
● Have you ever gone on a diet? Describe the experience.
● What do you think are the best ways for an overweight and unfit person to lose weight and to become fit?
● Are spas or health resorts common in your country? What kind of people go to them?

7.7 Suppleness, strength and stamina

A Work in pairs. Read the information below and decide which of the sports described would be most suitable for your partner to take up – and which would be least suitable.

Activity	Suppleness rating	Strength rating	Stamina rating
Cycling (hard)	☆☆	☆☆☆	☆☆☆☆
Dancing	☆☆☆☆	☆	☆☆☆
Football	☆☆☆	☆☆☆	☆☆☆
Golf	☆☆	☆	☆
Gymnastics	☆☆☆☆	☆☆☆	☆☆
Jogging	☆☆	☆☆	☆☆☆☆
Swimming (hard)	☆☆☆☆	☆☆☆☆	☆☆☆☆
Tennis	☆☆☆	☆☆	☆☆
Weight lifting	☆	☆☆☆☆	☆
Yoga	☆☆☆☆	☆	☆

☆ SUPPLENESS is flexibility: being able to move your neck, spine and body easily. The more supple you are, the less likely you are to suffer from stiffness and aches.

☆ STRENGTH is muscle power: being able to lift things and do heavy work. Strong stomach muscles help you take the strain when lifting heavy objects and keep a slim waistline.

☆ STAMINA is endurance: being able to keep going longer without gasping for breath. With stamina you have a slower, more powerful heartbeat.

B Now look at these profiles and decide which of the activities you would recommend to each person.

Make notes of the REASONS for your recommendations.

ANNA is 15 years old. She lives in the city centre but is not allowed to go out on her own in the nearby park. She plays the piano and likes classical music, but not pop. She usually gets out of breath when climbing stairs. She needs to take more exercise. What do you recommend?

RICHARD is 35 years old and slightly overweight. He lives 3 km from the city centre where he runs his own computer business. He always drives to work. He often suffers from stiffness. As he is very busy he hasn't got much free time, so he can't take up anything too time-consuming. What should he do?

ERIC is 55 years old. He is the manager of a seaside hotel, but he can't swim. He used to play football but gave it up 15 years ago. What do you recommend?

C Write three paragraphs (about 50 words each), explaining what advice you would give to each person, beginning as follows:

'My advice to Anna is ...'
'If Richard wants to keep fit ...'
'The best thing for Eric to do would be ...'

AND write a fourth paragraph about yourself:
'What I do / should do to keep fit is ...'

★ In this part of the exam you'll often have to continue a sentence by using a particular structure: you may have to use conditionals or passives, for example. But once the first sentence is completed, you may be able to steer the paragraph back to easier structures!

7.8 A pain in the neck

A Work in small groups. Before you read the article, ask your partners these questions:
- What is stress? What are its symptoms?
- How does it affect you or people like you?

TAKING THE STRAIN

Monday 11.40 BBC1

Every year, one person in six resorts to tranquillisers. In BBC1's series, Noel Edmonds investigates healthier ways of coping with stress. For the next five weeks, **Robert Eagle** offers practical advice on the problem

A pain in the neck

PEOPLE USUALLY think of 'stress' as something the world inflicts on them. Worry and hassle are blamed for all kinds of ailments, from asthma to headaches, from high blood pressure to stomach ulcers. And we often blame other people for making us feel bad: when we call someone a 'pain in the neck', we are describing the physical and psychological effect they have on us.

But although it is tempting to regard stress as some nasty germ attacking us from outside, the truth is that we are largely responsible for what stress does to our bodies. Once we make ourselves aware of how our bodies respond to worry, fear, anger and fatigue (all of which are forms of stress), we can start learning to relax.

Pains in the neck are a very common stress complaint. Some people get a pain in the neck from driving, others from working at an office desk. I suffer from a complaint I call 'typewriter neck', which tends to strike when I am hunched over my typewriter worrying about an approaching deadline. (Arthritis or bone injuries might also give you a pain in the neck, of course,

but I suspect that these are a much less common cause than muscular tension.)

It would be easy to blame these pains on 'bad posture'. Hunching your shoulders up to your ears is certainly not a relaxing way of sitting.

But we should first think about why we adopt this posture. In fact, it is an instinctive way of reacting to a situation which alarms or worries us. It is a defensive stance – and many people find that they tend to make their hands into a fist or grip their steering wheel or the arms of a chair at the same time.

Because it is instinctive, we are often not aware that we are doing it and wonder why we get a pain in the neck. If you find yourself doing it, there are two kinds of relaxation exercise which may help you overcome the habit. You can either exaggerate it: deliberately raise your shoulders as high as they will go, hold the position for a few seconds, then drop your shoulders, and feel the difference. Alternatively, you can exercise the muscles which pull your shoulders in the opposite direction: balance your head on the top of your neck so that it is not dragging your shoulders forward, then draw your shoulders down towards your feet. Stop and feel the difference.

If you are a fist-clencher, try similar routines with your hands. Clench them very tightly, then let go. Or stretch and splay your fingers and thumbs, then stop and feel the difference as they rest on your thighs.

Though simple, these exercises should help you regain control of these parts of your body. ●

Taking the Strain by Robert Eagle (BBC Publications) is available from bookshops.

Karen Daws

94

B   When you've read the article, choose the best alternative to complete each of these sentences:

1 People suffer from stress because ...
   a) modern life is full of worries
   c) they don't know how to relax
   b) other people inflict it on them
   d) they have no time to relax
2 The writer gets a pain in the neck when he ...
   a) is driving
   c) is stuck in a traffic jam
   b) is in a hurry to finish some work
   d) meets annoying people
3 People who sit like the woman in the top picture ...
   a) deny that they do it
   c) don't realise how they're sitting
   b) do it deliberately
   d) find it helps them to sit like that
4 The writer describes altogether ...
   a) one exercise   b) two exercises   c) three exercises   d) four exercises
5 The idea of the exercises recommended by the writer is to help you to ...
   a) become a relaxed person
   c) know what your muscles are doing
   b) feel different
   d) relax for a short while

C   Work in pairs. Help each other to try doing the exercises recommended by the writer. Which seemed the most difficult and the most pleasant?

D   Work in small groups. Ask your partners these questions:
- Do you agree with the ideas expressed in the article?
- What kinds of things cause stress (e.g. living in a city, driving, etc.)?
- How can people reduce or cope with stress or worry (e.g. screaming, yoga, etc.)?

7.9 *At*...   *Prepositional phrases*

Fill the gaps in these sentences with a suitable phrase from the list below:

1 I thought .... that I had flu, but then I realised it was only a cold.
2 There were .... 500 people in the crowd, probably more.
3 Sorry to keep you waiting, I've finished .... !
4 .... it looked like a new car, and I didn't realise it was second-hand.
5 A successful business sells its products .... and not ....
6 For five years the two countries were .... but now they are ....
7 The receptionist only allows one patient to see the doctor ....
8 You can't lose weight just by taking exercise, ... I don't think so.
9 When you receive the report, please pass it on to me ....
10 The twins always speak .... as each other.

at first   at first sight   at last   at least   at a loss   at once   at peace   at a profit
at any rate   at a time   at the same time   at war
~~In~~ any case   simultaneously,
any way,

95

7.10 Staying healthy
Picture conversation

★ The Interview Paper of the exam includes a 'Picture Conversation'. The purpose of this exercise is to give you a topic to talk about – not to force you to describe every detail of the picture at great length.

A   Work in pairs. Write down SIX questions that you can ask another pair about these photos. Questions like these are NOT suitable:
   Is the woman running?   *What kind of packet is this?*
because they'll only lead to very short answers, like these:
   Yes.   *A cigarette packet.*

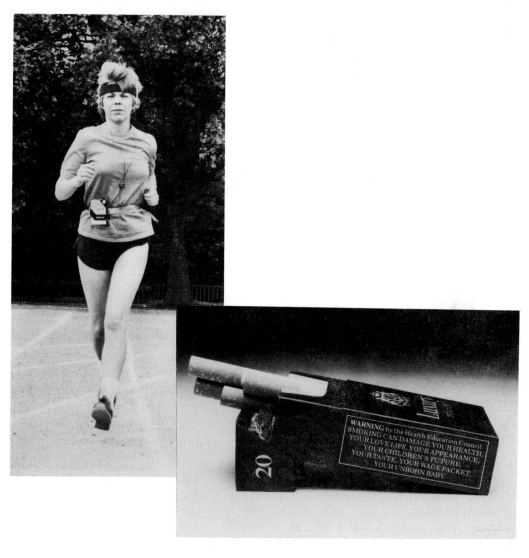

B   Now join another pair and ask them your questions. Don't interrupt, but encourage them to say as much as they like in answer to your questions – even if they seem to be going off the subject.

7.11 Doctor's orders

A   You'll hear a doctor giving some advice to one of her patients, a Mr Brown. Before you listen to the recording, can you guess which of these foods are less healthy, and perhaps likely to be forbidden?

Fresh fish	Bread	Apples	Grapes
Canned fish	Margarine	Bananas	Carrots
Fish and chips	Butter (unsalted)	Potatoes	Crisps
Fresh meat	Tomato ketchup	Sausages	Hamburgers
Salt	Coffee	Tea	Beer

B   Listen to the recording and mark with a tick (✔) the foods Mr Brown can eat and with a cross (✘) the foods that he is not permitted to eat.

C   Compare your ticks and crosses with a partner. Can you work out what is wrong with Mr Brown and how this diet will help him?

D   Complete the unfinished sentences in this dialogue. The first one is done as an example. You'll have to use your imagination to finish it!

Patient: Good morning, doctor.
Doctor: Hallo, Mr Jones, what _seems to be the trouble ?_
Patient: Well, I keep getting these headaches.
Doctor: When ....
Patient: After I get home from work usually.
Doctor: What ....
Patient: I usually take a couple of aspirins and that seems to do the trick.
Doctor: How long ....
Patient: For the past two or three months.
Doctor: Why ....
Patient: Well, it didn't really seem bad enough to be worth troubling you about.
Doctor: Have .... than usual?
Patient: Yes, I suppose so. Since my assistant was made redundant I've been doing his work as well as mine.
Doctor: Have ....
Patient: Yes, but he says that if I can't do the work, I'll lose my job too.
Doctor: What ....
Patient: Can you give me a certificate so that I can be off work for a week – then my boss will have to do my work for a week and he'll see how overworked I am.
Doctor: Would ....
Patient: Oh yes, *two* weeks would be even better.
Doctor: ....
Patient: Thank you very much.
Doctor: ....
Patient: All right, doctor.

7.12   What would you say?   *Composition*

A   In the exam you'll have to write two compositions of 120 to 180 words. Look at the last two or three compositions you've written and count the number of words in them to give you an idea of how much space your own writing takes up. (Count the number of words in 5 or 10 lines and then work out the total, rather than counting every single word!) For the composition exercise in this and in later units, try to keep to about 150 words each time.

★ In the exam don't waste time by counting the *exact* total number of words you have used. If you write too much or too little, this will count against you – so you should get used to writing 150-word compositions!

B   One of the writing tasks you may choose to do in the exam is to write down what you would say in a particular situation.
    Do you remember Dr Lawrence's speech in 7.6? This is how it began:

Good afternoon, everybody. I'm Dr Jane Lawrence, the administrator and medical officer. I hope you're all going to be very happy here. I must explain first that you've got to participate in all the activities we offer and no absences from the premises will be permitted. Every morning everybody has to weigh in and your progress will be monitored. Your diets are adjusted according to the progress you make – that is, how much weight you lose. Now first of all, I'd like to introduce Mr O'Hara, the sports organiser ...

and this is how it ended:

... Let me wish you a pleasant stay here with us and if you have any questions about the course you are on, please come and see me in my office.

C   Work in pairs. Imagine that you are organising a weekly keep-fit course – less strict than Dr Lawrence's! What would you need to tell the course members at the start of the first session? Look at the information about suppleness, strength and stamina in 7.7 for some ideas.
    Make notes on the points you would make – and decide which are the most important ones.

Here are some useful expressions you could include in your speech:

> *Ladies and gentlemen, ...*
> *Could I have your attention for a moment?*
> *I'd just like to say a few words about ...*
> *Does anyone have any questions?*
> *Thank you very much and enjoy the ...*

D   Write the welcome speech. It should be about 150 words long.

E   When you have written your speech, show it to a partner (or perhaps read it out as if you were really making the speech). Ask for comments.

7.13 *Put*   *Verbs and idioms*

Fill the gaps in these sentences, using the phrasal verbs listed below.

 1 It's getting dark, could you _____ the light _____ please?
 2 If you want to stay with us, we can _____ you _____ in our spare room.
 3 I'm trying to concentrate but if you keep whistling you'll _____ me
 4 Don't forget to _____ the lights _____ when you leave the room.
 5 I'm afraid we'll have to _____ our meeting _____ till next month.
 6 Since I last stayed at this hotel, they have _____ their prices _____
 7 He has _____ a lot of weight since I last saw him.
 8 You'll remember the words if you _____ them _____ in your notebook.
 9 If you've finished with the book, would you mind _____ it _____ on the shelf?
10 I _____ the aspirins _____ somewhere safe, but now I can't remember where.
11 At the start of Summer Time we _____ the clocks _____ and at the end we _____ them
12 Mr Green is on the line, shall I _____ him _____ or ask him to ring back?
13 If you've got a cold, you've just got to _____ it.
14 They had planned to go out but they were _____ by the bad weather.

put away   put back   put back   put down   put forward   put off   put off   put off
put on   put on   put out/off   put through   put up   put up   put up with

7.14 **Fill the gaps**   *Exam practice*

Fill the gaps in this newspaper article with suitable prepositions.

HAY FEVER HITS OPERA
The star 1 _of_ the largest scale opera performance ever staged 2 _in_ Britain
pulled out 3 _on_ its opening night 4 _on_ Sunday. Verdi's Aïda is being
performed 5 _at_ London's Earl's Court Arena 6 _with_ a cast of 600 singers,
dancers and actors. American soprano Grace Bumbry 7 _in_ the title role was 女る着
suffering 8 _from_ hay fever, but had promised to be 'all right on the night even if my
nose drips like the Nile'. Half-way 9 _through_ the performance she was unable to
continue and was replaced 10 _during_ mid-performance 11 _by_ Bulgarian
soprano Ghena Dimitrova who was sitting 12 _in_ the audience watching the
show. She was taken 13 _into_ a dressing room where she put on Ms Bumbry's
costume and was made up. She was ready to go 14 _onto_ the stage 15 _after_ a
longer-than-usual interval.
  Tuesday's performance 16 _in_ the presence 17 _of_ the Prince and Princess of
Wales will go ahead 18 _____ Ms Bumbry – her role will be taken 19 _by_ Martina
Arroyo 20 _in_ Italy.
          from

'I'm writing an opera about hay fever.'

8 Holidays

8.1 Getting away from it all *Vocabulary*

A Work in small groups. Ask your partners these questions:
- Where did you spend your holidays last year and the year before?
- What did you enjoy and not enjoy about these holidays?
- What kind of holidays did you have when you were much younger?
- What kind of holidays would you like to have in the future?

B These questions are similar to the ones you'll have to answer in the first part of the Reading Comprehension paper of the exam. Choose the best alternative to complete each sentence. Be careful because some of the alternatives are only slightly wrong!

1 Read all the .... carefully before you decide where to go on holiday.
√brochures   handouts   tickets   prospectuses

2 I'd like to book a room with a(n) .... of the sea.
outlook   scenery   sight   √view

3 And, if possible, I'd like a room with its own ....
√balcony   box   gallery   porch

4 When I'm on holiday, I enjoy ....
getting sunburnt   getting sunstroke   having a sunbathe   √sunbathing

5 The cheapest way to go is to take a charter ....
crossing   √flight   fly   travel

6 I always get nervous on a plane before it ....
lifts off   lifts up   √takes off   takes up

7 And I'm even more worried when it's about to ....
anchor   fall   ground   √land

8 The most popular destinations for .... holidays are Spain, Italy and Greece.
charter   √package   packed   packet

9 When you're abroad, it's useful to be able to speak the language ....
currently   flowingly   √fluently   hesitantly

10 If you can't speak the language it's a good idea to take a(n) .... with you.
guide book   interpreter   language guide   √phrase book   短语集、熟语集

11 If you don't know the language, you may have to use .... language.
hand   gesture   √sign   signal

12 When you're staying at a popular resort, there are plenty of .... to go on.
√excursions   expeditions   pilgrimages   sightseeings

13 One day when I'm rich and famous, I'm going to go on a round-the-world ....
cruise   sail   travel   √trip

14 We brought home a beautiful pottery vase as a .... of our holiday.
memorial   reminder   √souvenir   trophy

15 I wanted to book my summer holiday, so I went to my local travel ....
  ✓agency   bureau   office   service
16 I don't speak Greek very well, but I can make myself ....
  comprehended   heard   listened to   ✓understood
17 We spent a fortnight in the mountains at a winter sports ....
  marina   ✓resort   spa   youth hostel
18 On a winter sports holiday you need warm clothes to .... you from the cold.
  defend   hide   ✓protect   shelter
19 The main attraction of the town is its long sandy ....
  ✓beach   coast   seaside   shore
20 You can save money by choosing a .... holiday.
  do-it-yourself   ✓self-catering   self-study   survival

★ Check through the wrong answers: there's useful vocabulary among them.

C   In these questions there are THREE correct answers and TWO wrong ones.
(These aren't exam-style questions, but they'll help you widen your vocabulary.)

1 In the summer, this little mountain village is full of ....
  beachcombers   day-trippers   globetrotters   holiday-makers   sightseers
2 We stayed in a charming little guest house where we paid £25 a night for ....
  bed and breakfast   breakfast and bed   full board   half board   a pension
3 Some people like to be .... when they're on holiday.
  active   busy   energetic   strenuous   tiring
4 Others prefer a .... holiday.
  dull   lazy   relaxing   restful   tedious
5 Most people like to have a .... of things to do when they're away from home.
  confusion   choice   muddle   range   variety

D   Work in small groups. Find out about each other's experiences of the
items in this list. Which would you enjoy and which would you *not* enjoy?
Give your reasons. Perhaps give each one a mark from 1 to 10 according
to how you feel.

ACCOMMODATION: camping   caravan   villa   apartment
five-star hotel   small hotel   guest house   staying with relations
farmhouse
PLACES: seaside   mountains   countryside   city   at home
ACTIVITIES: studying a language   sunbathing   working (a holiday job)
mountaineering   walking   sightseeing   cycling   winter sports
water sports   other sports   doing nothing   eating and drinking   + ...

E   Make a list of the countries that surround your own country AND the
countries that most visitors from abroad come from. Here are some
examples:

COUNTRY	NATIONALITY	A PERSON	THE PEOPLE	LANGUAGE(S)
France	French	a Frenchman/woman	The French	French
Greece	Greek	a Greek	The Greeks	Greek
England	British/English	an Englishman/woman	The English	English
Scotland	British/Scottish	a Scot	The Scots	English

8.2 Brazilian Contrasts *Reading*

Copacabana Beach

Brazilian Contrasts
Rio de Janeiro: 5 nights
Brasilia: 1 night
Salvador: 3 nights
Sao Paulo: 1 night
Iguacu: 2 nights
plus extension weeks in Rio

Day 1 Wed/London/Rio
Evening departure from Heathrow by scheduled service of Varig Brazilian Airlines to Rio.

Day 2 Thu Rio
Early morning arrival in Rio and transfer to your hotel. In the afternoon an optional tour of the city including cable-car ride up Sugar Loaf mountain, one of this exciting city's most famous landmarks.

Day 3 Fri/Rio/Brasilia
Afternoon departure to Brasilia. This futuristic city was purpose built to become Brazil's new capital in 1960 and its unusual architecture and design sets it apart from all others.

Day 4 Sat Brasilia/Salvador
Late afternoon flight to Salvador. Contrast the unusual designs of Brasilia, with the colour and tradition of Salvador, one of Brazil's oldest cities.

Day 5 Sun and Day 6 Mon Salvador
Two full days to explore this intriguing old city. Rickety old buildings interspersed by narrow, cobbled streets wind up and down the hills on which Salvador was built, providing a fascinating glimpse of the taste and atmosphere of old Brazil.

Day 7 Tue Salvador/Sao Paulo
Early morning departure for Sao Paulo. A million new citizens are added every year to this vibrant city,

a plane lands every minute, a new building goes up every hour and there are more daily newspapers, radio and TV stations than any other city in the world.

Day 8 Wed Sao Paulo/Iguacu
Morning flight to Iguacu. The distant roar of the Falls increases to a deafening crescendo as you approach, announcing your arrival at one of the natural wonders of the world.

Day 9 Thu Iguacu
Full day at leisure to explore this incredible natural phenomenon. Niagara and Victoria Falls pale into insignificance as 275 separate cataracts and falls empty a million gallons of water every second into the foaming Parana river.

Day 10 Fri Iguacu/Rio
An afternoon flight to Rio and transfer to the Continental hotel which is located just 50 yards from Avenida Atlantica and legendary Copacabana Beach.

Day 11 Sat to Day 13 Mon Rio
Three full days at leisure in this exciting city. Visit the statue of Christ the Redeemer on top of Corcovado and enjoy one of the most famous views in the world. In the evening, take the optional Carioca night tour; see the city lights, enjoy dinner at a speciality churrascaria restaurant and then finally on to a samba show, where you'll see some of those fabulous carnival costumes.

Day 14 Tue Rio/London
Final day at leisure before an evening departure by scheduled Varig flight to Heathrow, arriving in the UK

early on Wednesday afternoon. Alternatively, why not extend your stay in Rio and return one week later.

LUXOR CONTINENTAL, RIO
Facts: Rooms: 290 Type of building: high rise. Lifts: four.

Location: Some 50 yards from the Avenida Atlantica and legendary Copacabana Beach, surrounded by cafes, shops, bars, night clubs and the exciting Samba shows.

Facilities: Restaurant, bar and small lounge.

Accommodation: Rooms vary in size and location but all have modern furnishings, central air conditioning, telephone, colour TV, radio, fridge, mini-bar and bathroom with shower only.

Entertainment: It's all around you, so go outside your hotel and discover the night life of the world's most exciting city.

Opinion: An efficiently run hotel. Combining modern accommodation and friendly service with a superb location near Copacabana Beach - excellent value for money.

Rio Carnival
Savour the most famous Carnival in the world by staying in Rio between 04 and 07 February when the main parades and festivities take place. For carnival supplements see price box below.

A   In which places, according to the text, could you find the following?

the atmosphere of old Brazil
historic buildings
a rapidly growing city
a statue of Christ
one of the world's most famous views

a cable car ride
unusual architecture
a samba show
a magnificent waterfall
wonderful costumes

B   Now answer these more detailed questions:

1 Would your flight from London be a charter flight?
2 What time of day would you arrive in Rio on your first day?
3 What are the two optional tours of Rio that you could go on?
4 What is the capital city of Brazil?
5 What are the streets of Salvador like?
6 How quickly is the population of São Paulo growing?
7 How would you know that you were approaching Iguaçu Falls?
8 What time of day would you leave Rio on your last day?
9 When is Carnival in Rio?
10 Would the holiday cost the same if you went during Carnival?

Underline the phrases in the text that led you to choose the answers
(for example, <u>Early morning arrival</u>).

C   Now find the answers to these questions about the hotel in Rio. Again
underline the phrases in the text that provide the answers.

1 What is the name of the hotel?
2 Is it a large hotel?
3 Is the hotel on the beach?
4 Would you get a good view from your hotel room?
5 Would your room have a bath?
6 Is it an old-fashioned hotel?

D   Work in small groups. Ask your partners these questions:
- What would you enjoy most if you went on the Brazilian Contrasts holiday?
- What might be the disadvantages or difficulties you might face in some
  of the places mentioned (e.g. insects, heat, expense, etc.)?
- What difficulties have you (or friends or relations of yours) suffered
  abroad? And on holidays closer to home?

8.3   *If* sentences   *Grammar*

A   *If* sentences are used to describe or imagine the consequences of
events. Study these examples and fill the gaps:

TYPE 1 [*If* + present, followed by *will*] **is used to imagine the
consequences of events that are likely to happen:**

   If our flight lands on time, we'll arrive in time for lunch.
   If you book your summer holiday in December, you'll get a discount.
   If you .... to go to the USA, you .... a visa.

TYPE 2 [*If* + past, followed by *would*] **is used to imagine the consequences of events that are very unlikely to happen or events that cannot possibly happen:**

What would you do if you could go anywhere in the world?
If I was (*or* were) English, I wouldn't need to take this exam.
If I had enough money, I'd go to Brazil.
If you .... £1,000 to spend, where .... on holiday?

In some situations, either Type 2 or Type 1 may be used:

I would go to the USA if I had enough money. (... but I haven't got enough)
I'll go to the USA if I manage to save up enough money. (*more optimistic*)
If I .... abroad next summer, I .... a new passport.

TYPE 3 [*If* + past perfect, followed by *would have*] **is used to imagine the consequences of events that happened or began to happen in the past:**

If I'd known about the delay, I wouldn't have got to the airport early.
If there hadn't been a mix-up with our booking, we'd have had a room with a view.
If you .... me to confirm the booking, I .... you a letter.

We can also 'mix' Types 2 and 3 in the same sentence:

If the weather had been better we would go back there again next year.
If I'd been (had been) born in 1975, I'd be .... today.

■ Remember that **'d** is the short form of *had* and *would*:
If he'd (he had) reminded me I'd have (I would have) arrived on time.

Rewrite each of these sentences with their full forms:

1 They'd have written back by now if they'd received my letter.
2 It'd be better if we travelled light.
3 Who'd have known that it'd be such awful weather in September?
4 I'd have sent you a postcard if I'd remembered your address.

■ Notice the difference in meaning between *if* and the words underlined here:
I'll be in England when the spring comes.
– *but notice we'd say* ... if the weather gets better.
I'll be arriving on Sunday, unless I inform you otherwise. (= if I don't inform you)
I'll wait here at the airport until she arrives.
I'll take an overnight bag in case I have to stay the night.

B Find and correct the errors in these sentences. Two of them contain no errors.

1 If I would have known, I could have helped you.
2 If it's my birthday tomorrow, I'll invite my friends out for a meal.
3 If I were rich, I would buy a villa in the Caribbean.
4 If the weather had been better, we had gone to the beach yesterday.
5 If you will need any help, please let me know.

104

6 We'll enjoy our holiday unless it rains all the time.
7 If I hadn't just been on holiday, I would have had more money now.
8 Where you would go if you can go anywhere in the world?

C   Finish the incomplete sentences in such a way that each one means the same as the complete sentence before it. The first is done for you as an example:

1 My family own a holiday flat and that's why we always go to the same place.
   If my family didn't own a holiday flat, we wouldn't always go to the same place.
2 Go to Britain and you'll be able to speak English all day long.
   If ....
3 You'll get sunburnt by sunbathing all day long.
   If ....
4 I can't go on holiday because I've got a holiday job this summer.
   If ....
5 You won't find any accommodation if you don't book it in advance.
   Unless ....
6 I didn't enjoy my holiday there and so I'm not going back.
   If ....
7 I couldn't get in touch because you didn't tell me where you were staying.
   If ....
8 The evenings may be cool, so pack a jumper to wear after dark.
   .... in case ....
9 Why don't you come on holiday with us – you'll enjoy it.
   If ....

D   Work in pairs. Suppose you had three weeks' holiday starting tomorrow, and £500 each to spend ....
● Where would you go?
● How would you travel?
● What would you do?
When you've decided what you'd do, compare your ideas with another pair.

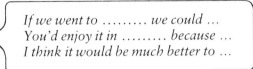

If we went to .... we could ...
You'd enjoy it in .... because ...
I think it would be much better to ...

E   [image] Work in groups of three. Student A should look at Activity 19, student B at 33 and C at 43. You'll each see a different advertisement. Try to persuade your partners how lovely the idea described in your activity **would be**.

8.4 Getting away from it all? *Picture conversation*

A Work in pairs. Ask each other these questions about each picture:
- What does the picture show? What part of the world is it?
- What would it be like to be there on holiday?
- What would you be able to do if you were there on holiday?
- What kind of people take their holidays there?
- In what ways are your own holidays different from the ones shown?
- Which of the places would you most like to be in? Why?

B Bring a few of your own holiday photos to class and tell everyone about them!

C Work in pairs. Ask your partner these questions about the advertisements:
- What would you enjoy about Yugoslavia and Cyprus?
- What kinds of things that *you* enjoy on holiday don't seem to be available in Yugoslavia or Cyprus?
- Which of the advertisements do you prefer and why?

A 🔊 You'll hear a travel agent giving some advice to a customer.
As you listen, make brief notes on the attractions and drawbacks of the
places mentioned.

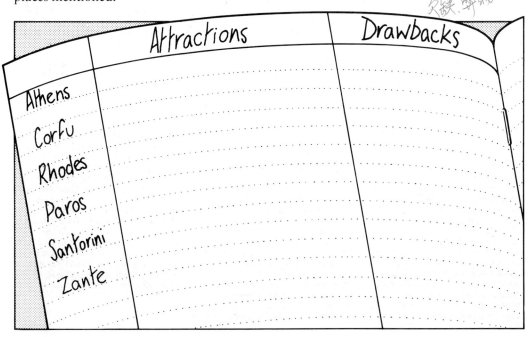

	Attractions	Drawbacks
Athens		
Corfu		
Rhodes		
Paros		
Santorini		
Zante		

B Work in pairs. Imagine that someone wants to visit *your* country or
region for a holiday. What are its attractions and drawbacks? Make a
short list.

Role-play a conversation between a travel agent and a customer and
discuss your own country or region.

8.6 Three more islands!   *Problem solving*

A Work in pairs. Decide which of the islands you would like to visit in August, in April or in October. Why?

MAJORCA

Majorca, largest of the Balearic Islands, lies off the south-eastern coast of Spain. Its wealth of scenery, fine beaches and nightlife have made it one of the most popular holiday areas in the world.

The scenery of this Mediterranean island is particularly beautiful. The majestic mountain ranges of the north contrast with the windmill-dotted plains of the south. Hidden among the folds of the hills are small farming communities which the twentieth century seems almost to have passed by. Yet, on the island's south coast are extensive holiday resorts with many modern hotels, bars, restaurants and two good golf courses.

Contrary to popular belief, not everywhere on Majorca is modern and sophisticated. Wide, tree-lined promenades contrast oddly with dusty cart-tracks. Luxury hotels rub shoulders with modest pensions. You can choose between elegant nightclubs and restaurants or simple bodegas where you'll find fishermen at the neighbouring tables. Majorca caters for all tastes and all budgets.

KOS

Kos is a genuinely unspoilt Paradise of long, white beaches, and almost continual sunshine. It was here that Hippocrates, the father of Greek medicine, founded the first ever School of Medicine – and, centuries later, it is still as peaceful, as relaxing, and as regenerative.

It is a large island, which means that it's easy for you to set off and find yourself a secluded spot to soak up the sun. The almost endless beaches guarantee that you won't suffer from the sort of over-crowding that can ruin a beach holiday.

But, as well as the beaches, Kos offers a great deal to tempt the holiday-maker. The main town of Kos itself is an intriguing blend of narrow back-streets and open, tree-filled squares – with open-air cafés.

The nightlife is excellent, with a wide choice of discos and nightclubs, as sophisticated as you could wish, while the local tavernas provide an ethnic alternative.

It's easy to hire a bicycle, so that you can explore this island fully. A trip through some of the ancient villages will be unforgettable.

MADEIRA

The peaceful island of Madeira, for many years a favourite with British travellers, lies far out in the Atlantic off the north-west coast of Africa. It is a green, fertile island of volcanic origin, with a ridge of great mountains, rising to over 6,000 feet high, running east to west.

Great ravines run down from the mountains and picturesque little fishing villages are usually found where they reach the sea. Miles of levades, old artificial water-courses, carry water from the wild, rugged interior to the closely-settled coastlands where every available patch of land is under cultivation.

The influence of the Gulf Stream gives Madeira a lovely climate. Exotic plants flower throughout the year. Bananas and sugar-cane flourish. And the grapes which produce the world-famous Madeira wine ripen gently in the warm sun.

Miles of unfrequented roads, lined with shrubs and trees, wind through Madeira's varied landscapes on their way to unspoiled fishing villages and to hamlets in the hills. The drive across the island to Porto Moniz on the north coast and to Santana, with its delightful little thatched cottages, is a memorable one. And for those of you interested in walking, Madeira's fantastic scenery is ideally seen on foot.

Close to Funchal, at Cabo Girao, is the world's second-highest sea-cliff and nearby is the fishing village of Camara de Lobos where Winston Churchill loved to paint. At the village of Camacha you will find the centre of the wickerwork industry and throughout the island you will often see women making fine embroidery outside their neat cottages.

YOUR HOLIDAY WEATHER							
	Average daytime temperatures				*Average hours of sunshine daily*		
	London	Majorca	Kos	Madeira	London	Majorca	Kos	Madeira
April	13°	19°	20°	19°	5	7	8	8
May	17°	21°	24°	20°	6	9	9	7
June	19°	25°	28°	22°	7	10	11	7
July	21°	29°	30°	23°	6	11	11	8
August	20°	29°	30°	24°	6	11	12	8
September	18°	26°	26°	24°	5	8	11	7
October	13°	22°	23°	23°	3	6	8	7
November	9°	18°	18°	21°	2	5	4	6

109

B   Work in small groups. Choose one of these roles. If there are four of you, the fourth person can give advice to all three people.

GERRY: **You can only go away during the school holidays. You'd like to find peace and quiet on an unspoilt island.**

KIM: **You love walking and wild flowers. You want to go on holiday in the autumn (September or October) to somewhere warm and sunny.**

SANDY: **You want to go away in the spring (April or May). You like to be active and enjoy scenery, nightlife and hot weather.**

Role-play a conversation between the three friends, and discuss your holiday plans.

C   Write four paragraphs, beginning as follows:

'I'd advise Gerry to ...'
'If I were Kim I'd ...'
'My advice to Sandy would be to ...'
'If I could go to one of the islands ...'

8.7   *By* ...   *Prepositional phrases*

Fill the gaps in these sentences with suitable phrases from the list below:

1   The Mediterranean is .... the most popular holiday area in Europe.
2   I know them both .... but I don't know either of them ....
3   You can cross the Atlantic quickly .... or more slowly ....
4   The only way to remember the words is to learn them ....
5   I didn't tread on your foot on purpose, it happened ....
6   It takes several days to cross Europe .... and even longer ....
7   The weather is very hot .... but it may be quite cool ....
8   The thunderstorm took us .... and we all got wet.
9   We didn't arrange to meet on the beach – we ran into each other ....
10   'Could you fill in this registration form?' 'Yes, ...'
11   Oh, dear, I've put down my old address on the form ....
12   There's no need to send the letter ...., I can deliver it myself ....
13   It's very hard to put sun-cream on your back if you're ....

by accident   by all means   by car
by chance   by day   by far   by hand
by heart   by mistake   by name
by night   by plane   by post   by ship
by sight   by surprise   by train
by yourself

'Why is it we never go on migration?'

Allen

110

8.8　An excursion programme
Listening

A　📼 Imagine that you are in a hotel in Edinburgh having breakfast on the first day of your holiday in Scotland. You'll hear the tour leader announcing some changes to the excursion programme.

Make any necessary alterations to the times and places shown on the programme, according to what the tour leader tells you.

	Depart		Return
Sunday			
Monday	9.00	Braemar Castle and Aberdeen	17.30
Tuesday	8.30	Glencoe and Fort William	17.30
Wednesday	8.00	Inverness and Loch Ness	17.30
Thursday	14.00	Edinburgh city sightseeing tour	16.30
Friday	9.15	Galashiels and the Borders	16.00

B　Work in pairs. If you had to organise a one-day excursion by coach around your own area, what places would you visit? Make brief notes.
● Join another pair and describe your excursion to them.

8.9　Spelling and pronunciation: Consonants
Word study

A　The consonant sounds of English can often be spelt in several ways. Look at these examples first:

p　p ↔ pp
stop　stopped　supposed
b　b ↔ bb
bubble　beach
t　t ↔ tt
bottle　little　capital
d　d ↔ dd
paddle　handled　muddy
k　k ↔ c ↔ cc ↔ ck ↔ qu ↔ ch
climate　accommodation　king
quantity　chemist　lucky
g　g ↔ gg
guard　struggle
dʒ　j ↔ g
jet　germ　jumping
tʃ　ch ↔ ti ↔ tu
church　question　nature

l　l ↔ ll
skilful　silly
n　n ↔ nn
run　running　banana
m　m ↔ mm
image　monument
r　r ↔ rr
wrist　rescue
s　z　s ↔ z ↔ ss
circle　stone　police　zero
ʃ　ʒ　sh ↔ s ↔ ti ↔ c
shirt　sure　leisure　competition　ocean
f　f ↔ ff ↔ ph ↔ gh
affair　photograph　afraid
apostrophe　enough
v　v
vacation

»»→

111

θ ð **th**
thing this truth clothes

w w ↔ u ↔ o
weather/whether quite
once wheel/we'll

j y ↔ u
yacht union Europe

B Listen to the tape and add the words you hear to the appropriate lists above. You'll find the correct spellings in Activity 25.

C Some consonants are written but not pronounced. Here are some examples of these 'silent letters'. Think of more examples to add to these lists.

gh: sigh light caught fought
b: lamb bomb climb combing
t: castle Christmas listen
k: knife knee
l: half walk could
r: beard word *(in some British accents only)*
h: honest hourly

D Work in pairs. One of you should look at Activity 5, the other at 22. You'll each have some more words to dictate to your partner.

8.10 Writing letters

Composition

A In real life, you probably only write letters to people you know to tell them things they don't know. In the exam, you may choose to write a letter to an imaginary person. Here are two typical exam questions:

1 Imagine that you are on holiday, having a wonderful time. Write a letter to the friend who was unable to come with you.

2 Write a letter to a hotel reserving accommodation for your family and yourself. Find out the price you will have to pay and request special arrangements for one member of your family who is a vegetarian.

And here are two students' compositions, both of which contain faults in content and style. What improvements could be made to them both? Add your improvements and corrections to the content and the style.

Villa Don Carlos
Marbella, Spain

August 30th

Dear John,
It is nice here in Spain. The sun is shining and the weather is good. The food is nice, for example yesterday we had a good meal. And the people are friendly, for example the other day we met a man who was very nice.
There are a lot of nice places to visit. On Sunday for example, we went to a town which was very old and interesting.

It's a pity we haven't got a car because the buses are slow. On the other hand it would take a long time to drive here from England because it is a long way. You can hire cars here.
It's a pity you couldn't come with us – perhaps next year. It's lovely here and we like it here.
love,
Jenny and Bill x

London, April 1st

Dear Hotel Romantica,
I want to reserve a room for me and my family for a week from July 7th. We want nice rooms and we want to see the sea from them. How much will they cost? Can you send me a brochure?
My father-in-law is a vegetarian. Is that all right for you? He has a small dog. Do you mind?
See you in July.
Let me know if everything is O.K.
Best wishes,
Alan Green

P.S. Mr Brown told me you weren't a bad hotel. Do you remember him?

B Now look at Activity 41, where you will see better versions of the two compositions. What improvements have been made?

★ If you choose to write a letter in the examination, make sure the style you use is appropriate. A formal letter is laid out differently from a personal letter – as the examples in Activity 41 show.

C Now write your own composition (about 150 words, *not* including the address, date, etc.), choosing from these topics:

1 Write a letter to an English friend from your favourite holiday place. Tell your friend about some of the things you have done during your holiday so far and what else you're going to do.
2 Write a letter on behalf of your family to a hotel to reserve accommodation. Include some special requirements and questions.
3 Write a letter to a tour company complaining about the hotel they sent you to.

MAKE NOTES before you start. If possible, discuss your notes with a partner.

D When you have completed your composition CHECK IT THROUGH and correct any mistakes you have made before handing it in.
  Show your letter to a partner and ask for comments on the content, style, grammar and spelling.

8.11 Duty-free goods *Listening*

You'll hear part of a radio programme in which information is being given about duty-free goods. Fill in the missing details below.

1 Add the prices of duty-free goods to this chart. The first two are done as examples:

```
Airports                      Airlines

Amsterdam                     British Airways  £10.50
Athens                        Air France
Gatwick          £10          Alitalia
Heathrow                      Iberia
Madrid                        JAL
Manchester                    KLM
New York                      Olympic
Paris                         Swissair
Rome                          Varig
Tokyo
Zurich
```

2 The problem with buying duty-free goods on a plane is that ....
3 Abroad, locally-produced wines and spirits are often cheaper if you buy them in ....
4 A bottle of the local drink is a nicer .... than a bottle of whisky.
5 Before making a duty-free purchase, ask yourself two questions:
   • Do I .... ?
   • Is it .... ?
6 'Duty-free prices' are often .... than prices in a .... shop.

8.12 *Break, bring, call, cut* *Verbs and idioms*

A Which of the endings below go with these beginnings?

Kit broke ...   **Lee called** ...
Chris brought ...   **Sandy cut** ...

a doctor   a piece of paper   a window   Jan's heart   Lee to the party
the book to Sandy   the dog Rover   the grass   the ice   the news to us
to see Sandy   himself/herself

B Fill the gaps with a suitable form of the phrasal verbs opposite:

break
1 We had to interrupt our journey because the car had ...*broke down*...
2 He ...*broke off*... in mid-sentence to go and see who was at the door.
3 The children were all happy when their school ...*broke up*... for the holidays.
   bring
4 Can you explain what ...*brought about*... these problems?
5 They were ...*brought up*... by their grandmother after their mother died.
6 My glasses are upstairs, could you .... them ...*down*... for me, please?
7 When you've finished with the books, please .... them ...*back*...

114

call
8 Not enough people booked for the excursion, so it has been ....
9 If you're ever in the area, do .... and see me.
10 They were engaged for six months but they decided to .... it *off*
11 I'll .... you at 7.30 – will you be ready?   *Come and take*
12 I'm very busy at the moment, could you .... me *back* later, please?
    cut
13 I can't give up smoking altogether but I'm trying to ....
14 Do you need a pair of scissors to .... the coupon?
15 During the strike all electricity supplies were ....

break down   break off   break up
bring about   bring back   bring down   bring up
call back   call in   call for   call off   call off
cut down   cut off   cut out

8.13   Fill the gaps   *Use of English*

A   What words are missing in each of these sentences?

1 If you have flu you often have a .... headache.
2 I spent a sleepless .... worrying about my problems.
3 It's safest to .... the street at a pedestrian crossing.
4 We .... arrived after a long journey.
5 .... beach holiday is .... most boring kind of holiday I can imagine.

★ When you're doing this kind of exercise and you're not sure what word fits best,
try to decide if the missing word is an adjective (as 1 above), a noun (as 2 above),
a verb (as 3), an adverb (as 4) or an article (as 5).

B   Fill each gap in this story with one word only. The first is done as an example:

We were late as *1* ..*usual*.. . Michael had insisted on doing his packing by *2* .... ,
and when he discovered that he couldn't manage he'd asked me for help at the last
3 .... So now we had an hour to get to the *4* .... Luckily, there wasn't much
traffic on the *5* .... and we were able to get there just in *6* .... We checked in
and went straight to the departure *7* .... to wait for our *8* .... to be called. We
waited and waited but no announcement was *9* .... We asked at the information
10 .... and the girl there told us that the plane hadn't even arrived yet. In the
11 .... there was another announcement telling us that passengers waiting for Flight
LJ 108 could collect a *12* .... meal voucher and that the plane hadn't left Spain
because of *13* .... problems. We thought that meant that it wasn't safe for the plane
to *14* .... We waited again for *15* .... until late evening when we were asked to
report to the *16* .... desk again. They told us we would be spending the *17* ....
in a hotel at the airline's *18* ....
    The next morning after a sleepless *19* .... because of all the planes taking off and
landing, we reported back to the airport. Guess what had *20* .... while we were
21 .... ! Our plane had arrived and taken off again leaving us *22* .... All the
other *23* .... had been woken up in the night to catch the plane, but for some
24 .... or other we had been forgotten. You can imagine how we felt!

9 Books and reading

9.1 A good read
Vocabulary

A   Work in small groups. Ask your partners these questions:
● What was the last book you read (in your own language)?
● What was it about? What was it like? Would you recommend it?
● How long do you spend reading books, magazines or newspapers per week?
● Which British and American authors can you name?
● What is your favourite kind of book?

B   Fill the gaps in these sentences with suitable words:

1 You can borrow books from a .... or buy them from a ....
2 A writer can also be called an ....
3 I can't afford to buy the book in hardback, so I'll wait till it comes out in ....
4 I can't remember the .... of the book, but I know it had a yellow ....
5 A book that tells somebody's life story is called a ....

C   Choose the best alternative to complete each sentence.

1 *Oliver Twist* is a classic work of English ....
   editions   letters   ✓literature   non-fiction
2 The plot of the novel was exciting, but I didn't find the .... very interesting.
   ✓characters   figures   people   persons
3 Poetry is written in ....
   lines   paragraphs   prose   verse
4 In a poem or a song, the last word in a line often .... with the next.
   matches   ✓rhymes   rhythms   suits
5 You can find out the titles of the units in this book by looking at the ....
   appendix   glossary   supplement   ✓table of contents
6 If you need to find some information in a non-fiction book, look it up in the ....
   atlas   catalogue   diary   ✓index
7 Most novels are divided into several ....
   ✓chapters   units   passages   sections
8 Cambridge University Press is the .... of the book you're reading.
   author   editor   printer   ✓publisher
9 A great novel has a good plot and a ....
   communication   meaning   message   ✓significance
10 The book was marvellously .... and it was a joy to read.
   stylistic   tedious   well-written ✓   wonderful
11 Ernest Hemingway is one of my .... American writers.
   best ✓   favourite   ideal   most popular

thrillers – spy story
Fantasy literature
gripping.
comedy
Accuracy.

116

12 The thriller was so exciting that I couldn't ....
   drop it   pick it up √ put it down   read it
13 I'm not enjoying this book because I haven't been able to .... it yet.
   begin   complete   finish √ get into
14 Even the .... characters in the book are really interesting.
   less   minor √ small   tiny
15 I'd like to .... that book when you've read it.
   √ borrow   hire   lend   loan

D   In these sentences THREE alternatives are correct and TWO are wrong:

1 The .... character in the book is called Oliver.
   central   main   principal   principle   top
2 I enjoy her books because her style is so very ....
   dull   entertaining   readable   tedious   true-to-life
3 I found that the characters in the story were very ....
   amusing   believable   informative   likeable   thrilling
4 There were so many twists in the plot that I didn't really think it was ....
   accurate   convincing   correct   realistic   true-to-life
5 She doesn't read any fiction because she prefers reading ....
   about real life   non-fiction   science fiction   short stories   textbooks
6 I can't .... books like those – they just send me to sleep.
   appreciate   bear   carry   stand   suffer

E   Work in small groups. Ask your partners these questions:
● Who are the most famous writers in your country's literature?
● Who are the most popular writers in your country today?
● Imagine that you are recommending one of their books to a foreign person – what would you tell them about the book and its author?

★ Each year FCE candidates are given a choice of three optional 'prescribed books' to read. If you read one of these you can, if you wish, answer a question on it in the Composition paper and also discuss it in the Interview. Your teacher can tell you more about this, if he or she hasn't already done so.

9.2   Call for the Dead   *Reading*

A   Read the two extracts on the next page, which come from two versions of the same novel: a 'simplified edition' and the original edition of *Call for the Dead* by John Le Carré.

Work in small groups. Ask your partners these questions:
● Which version of the story do you prefer?
● What are the advantages and disadvantages of each version?
● What is added and left out in the simplified version?
● Why do people read simplified editions of famous books?

>>>→

A

He felt safe and warm in the taxi, safe because everything around him seemed unreal. Why was London the only capital in the world that lost its personality at night?

The taxi turned into Cambridge Circus and Smiley sat up suddenly, remembering the reason for the phone call. He could remember every word of the conversation – a skill he had learned years before.

"Smiley. Maston speaking. You interviewed Samuel Arthur Fennan at the Foreign Office on Monday, am I right?"

"Yes . . . yes, I did."

"What was the case?"

"An anonymous letter accusing him of joining the Communist Party while he was a student at Oxford. An ordinary interview, approved by the Director of Security."

(Fennan *can't* have complained, thought Smiley. He knew I'd clear him of the accusation.)

"Were you unfriendly at all? Would he feel that you were attacking him, Smiley? Tell me that."

(Fennan must have complained to the whole Government for Maston to sound so frightened.)

"No. We liked one another, I think. As a matter of fact, I told him not to worry. He was clearly anxious."

"*What* did you tell him?"

"I said that I had no powers and nor had my department, but I could see no reason why we should trouble him further. That's absolutely all."

(He'll never forgive me for making him so dependent on my answers.)

"He says you accused him of disloyalty, that his career at the Foreign Office is in ruins, that people have been paid to give false information against him."

"He must have gone completely mad – he knows he's cleared. What else does he want?"

"Nothing. He's dead. Killed himself at 10.30 this evening. Left a letter to the Foreign Secretary. There's going to be an inquiry."

B

He felt safe in the taxi. Safe and warm. The warmth was contraband, smuggled from his bed and hoarded against the wet January night. Safe because unreal: it was his ghost that ranged the London streets and took note of their unhappy pleasure-seekers, scuttling under commissionaires' umbrellas. It was his ghost, he decided, which had climbed from the well of sleep and stopped the telephone shrieking on the bedside table . . . Oxford Street . . . why was London the only capital in the world that lost its personality at night? Smiley, as he pulled his coat more closely about him, could think of nowhere, from Los Angeles to Berne, which so readily gave up its daily struggle for identity.

The cab turned into Cambridge Circus, and Smiley sat up with a jolt. He remembered why the Duty Officer had rung, and the memory woke him brutally from his dreams. The conversation came back to him word for word – a feat of recollection long ago achieved.

'Duty Officer speaking, Smiley. I have the Adviser on the line . . .'

'Smiley; Maston speaking. You interviewed Samuel Arthur Fennan at the Foreign Office on Monday, am I right?'

'Yes . . . yes I did.'

'What was the case?'

'Anonymous letter alleging Party membership at Oxford. Routine interview, authorized by the Director of Security.'

(Fennan *can't* have complained, thought Smiley; he knew I'd clear him. There was nothing irregular, nothing.)

118

'Did you go for him at all? Was it hostile, Smiley, tell me that?'

(Lord, he does sound frightened. Fennan must have put the whole Cabinet on to us.)

'No. It was a particularly friendly interview; we liked one another, I think. As a matter of fact I exceeded my brief in a way.'

'How, Smiley, how?'

'Well, I more or less told him not to worry.'

'You *what*?'

'I told him not to worry; he was obviously in a bit of a state, and so I told him.'

'*What* did you tell him?'

'I said I had no powers and nor had the Service; but I could see no reason why we should bother him further.'

'Is that all?'

Smiley paused for a second; he had never known Maston like this, never known him so dependent.

'Yes, that's all. Absolutely all.' (He'll never forgive me for this. So much for the studied calm, the cream shirts and silver ties, the smart luncheons with ministers.)

'He says you cast doubts on his loyalty, that his career in the F.O. is ruined, that he is the victim of paid informers.'

'He said *what*? He must have gone stark mad. He knows he's cleared. What else does he want?'

'Nothing. He's dead. Killed himself at 10.30 this evening. Left a letter to the Foreign Secretary. The police rang one of his secretaries and got permission to open the letter. Then they told us. There's going to be an inquiry.'

B Note down your answers to these questions, showing whether you found the answers in version A, version B or in both. The first is done as an example:

1 What time of year did the taxi ride take place? *January – B*
2 Why was Smiley taking this taxi ride?
3 Why was he able to remember the whole of the phone call?
4 Why had Smiley talked to Fennan on Monday?
5 Was the conversation with Fennan friendly or unfriendly?
6 Why did Smiley tell Fennan not to worry?
7 According to Smiley, was Fennan's Foreign Office career ruined?
8 How did Fennan die?

C Work in small groups. Ask your partners these questions:
- How do you decide whether to read a particular book – a friend's recommendation, reading the first page, reading reviews, or what?
- Why do you read or *not* read:
  Spy stories, thrillers, detective stories, poetry, romantic novels, history books, biographies, science fiction, classic works of literature, etc.?
- Do you now want to read more of *Call for the Dead*? Why/Why not?

★ Once you have read a simplified version of a story, it might be worth rereading it in the original version – if you enjoyed it.

9.3 Joining sentences *Grammar*

A   IDENTIFYING RELATIVE CLAUSES identify which person or thing is meant. Notice the lack of commas:

Fennan is the man **who** has killed himself at the beginning of the story.
London was the only capital in the world **that** lost its personality at night.
... it was his ghost **which** had climbed from the well of sleep.
One writer **whose** books I always enjoy is Graham Greene.
I liked the part of the story **where** the car broke down.

When it's the object of the relative clause, the relative pronoun (who, that, which, etc.) can be omitted:

... a skill he had learned years before.
The person I liked best in the story was the father.
Call for the Dead is a book I'm sure you'll enjoy.

■ Notice that *whom* is uncommon in informal writing and in conversation.

Instead of:

The person to whom you spoke was ...
The people with whom I am working ...
The man from whom I received the letter ...

we'd normally say:

The person you spoke to was ...
The people I'm working with ...
The man I got the letter from ...

B   NON-IDENTIFYING RELATIVE CLAUSES give extra information.
They are often used to join sentences and are more common in writing than in speech. *That* is not used in these clauses. Notice the use of commas. Fill the gaps in the last three examples.

Smiley , **who** is the main character in the book , is an ordinary sort of man.
Jupiter's Travels , **which** is about a motorcycle journey , is a fascinating story.
Hamlet , ... is a famous play by Shakespeare , is a tragedy.
Hamlet's father , ... dies before the play begins , appears to Hamlet as a ghost.
Hamlet's mother , ... husband has died , married her husband's brother.

C   Join these pairs of sentences, beginning with the words on the right.
The first is done for you as an example:

1 The detective knew all the answers. He solved the mystery.   The detective ...
    The detective who solved the mystery knew all the answers.
    OR The detective who knew all the answers solved the mystery.
2 New York is a wonderful city. I'd love to visit it one day.   New York...
3 Ms Fortune was a writer. Her body was found in the cellar.   Ms Fortune ...
4 I met an old friend. He told me all about a book he'd just read.   I met ...
5 A car was stolen. It was found at the airport.   The car ...
6 Science fiction books are about the future and space travel. Some
    people love them, others hate them.   Science ...
7 You recommended that book to me. It was very good.   The book ...
8 A simplified edition is easier to read than the original. It's shorter.   A simplified ...

D Look at these examples of CONJUNCTIONS and PREPOSITIONS used to join sentences:

TIME **conjunctions:** and   before   after   while   as
REASON, CAUSE **or** CONSEQUENCE **conjunctions:**
   and   because   as   so that   so ... that   such a(n) ... that
CONTRAST **conjunctions:**   but   although   even though

> I took some books with me **so that** I would have something to do on the beach.
> I read the book **while** I was on holiday.
> The book was **so** exciting **that** I couldn't put it down.
> It was **such a** good book **that** I stayed up all night reading it.
> **Even though** I tried very hard, I didn't manage to finish the book.

TIME **prepositions:**   before   after   during
REASON, CAUSE **or** CONSEQUENCE **prepositions:**   because of   due to
CONTRAST **prepositions:**   in spite of   despite

> It was impossible to concentrate **because of** the noise of the traffic outside.
> I read the book **during** my holiday.
> **In spite of** my efforts I wasn't able to finish the book.

To show PURPOSE, **an infinitive clause can also be used:**

> I used a dictionary **to** / **in order to** / **so as to** look up any unfamiliar words.

We can also join two sentences using these conjunctions:

TIME: Then,   Afterwards,   Beforehand,   Meanwhile,
REASON, CAUSE **or** CONSEQUENCE: Consequently,   Therefore,   That's why ...
CONTRAST: However,   Nevertheless,

> I tried to finish the book. **However,** I didn't manage to.
> We all read the book. **Afterwards,** we discussed it.
> It's a wonderful book. **That's why** I recommended it to you.

E   Rewrite these sentences so that they still mean the same, beginning with the words on the right.

1 The difficulties were enormous but she managed to escape.   In spite of ...
2 It is a wonderful story and I'd recommend it to anyone.   It is such ...
3 I phoned my friends. I wanted them to know when I'd be arriving   As ...
4 I was sitting in bed reading. Meanwhile, my friends were dancing. While ...
5 The book is over 500 pages long. Nevertheless, I'm going to try to
   read it before next week.   Although...
6 I'm going to read the book first. Then I'll go and see the film.   Before ...
7 The heroine escaped from the villain. Then she rescued the hero.   After ...
8 I read a lot of books while I was on holiday in the summer.   During ...

F   Fill the gaps in this story with suitable words. Most of the missing words, but not all, are relative pronouns and conjunctions.

The Captain and the Enemy is a novel 1 .... was written by Graham Greene in 1988. It is a story 2 .... a boy, Victor Baxter, 3 .... father (4 .... he calls 'The Devil') loses him in a game of backgammon to a man 5 .... is only known as the Captain. The Captain, 6 .... real name is never revealed, appears to be some sort 7 .... criminal. 8 .... the boy has been taken away from his boarding school, he is brought 9 .... by a woman called Lisa, 10 .... is the Captain's mistress. From time to 11 .... the Captain returns 12 .... visit them, 13 .... for months on end they are alone together. 14 .... this time a close relationship develops 15 .... them, and Lisa treats Victor as if he is her son. Eventually, the Captain goes to live in Panama, 16 .... tells them that they cannot join him there 17 .... he has made enough money. 18 .... he is eighteen, Victor leaves Lisa and gets his own flat, but 19 .... her death in a road accident he flies to Panama 20 .... meet the Captain ...

9.4   Reading habits   *Listening*

A   Before you hear the recording, look at the questions and see if you can guess what some of the answers are.

🔲 Listen to the recording and fill the gaps with information from the broadcast:

1 According to recent research ..*85*.. % of American adolescents can't read a printed page unless they have an accompanying background of ..*the noise*..
2 The main advantages of printed books over cassettes and computers are that they are relatively .... and very ....
3 To use a book the only equipment you need is a ....
4 Many people only buy .... book(s) a year, which they read in the ...., on the .... and on the ....
5 Books by .... are selling more copies every year.
6 Five best-selling books are mentioned in the broadcast. Match the plots (A to E) to the titles opposite:

A   Five pampered rich women, the wives of powerful mining executives who are battling for control of an international company, travel with their husbands on business to Australia: afterwards they visit a nearby tropical island.

While their husbands visit a copper mine, the women explore the beautiful coast by luxury yacht. On the return trip the yacht breaks down and the women are forced to finish the journey on foot.

As they near the hotel their trip becomes a nightmare when they see their husbands murdered in cold blood by terrorists . . .

B   *One woman's odyssey through a century of turmoil . . .*

St Petersburg: one famous night of violence in the October Revolution shatters the dreams of young Countess Ossupov forever.

Paris: under the shadow of the Great War, émigrés struggle for survival as taxi drivers, seamstresses and ballet dancers. The Countess flees there in poverty . . . and leaves in glory.

America: a glittering world of fast cars and furs in the Roaring Twenties; a world of comfort that would come crashing down without warning.

C   This thrilling new novel is a story of man against the elements, struggling to survive, growing with the land, shaping it, spoiling it, and above all falling under its spell. It is a tale of explorers, Russian and American, fighting their way through this ice-bound world, contesting the colonisation of an increasingly precious territory.

Ranging from pre-history to the present day, this is a classic novel, huge in scope, as vast as the land so richly described – a truly panoramic novel.

D   Jon Darrow, a man with psychic powers, is a man who has played many parts: a shady faith-healer, a naval chaplain, a passionate husband, an awkward father, an Anglo-Catholic monk.

In 1940 Darrow returns to the world he once renounced, but faced with many unforeseen temptations he fails to control his psychic powers. Corruption lies in wait for him, and threatens not only his future as a priest but his happiness with Anne, the young woman he has come to love.

E   Set in Yorkshire, Australia, Hong Kong and America, this remarkable novel continues the story of an unorthodox and fascinating family. As the spirit of Emma Harte lives on in her granddaughter, Paula O'Neill, an engrossing drama is played out in the glamorous arena of the wealthy and privileged, in a cut-throat world of jealousy and treachery.

Paula must act with daring and courage to preserve her formidable grandmother's glittering empire from unscrupulous enemies – so that Emma's precious dream lives on for the next generation . . .

B   Work in small groups. Find out your partners' opinions on these questions:
- Will new technology replace printed books, magazines and newspapers?
- In the future, will students use computers instead of textbooks?

9.5 Using suffixes: Abstract nouns *Word study*

A Nouns from verbs
Add more examples, using the root words below with these suffixes:

-ation* pronunciation qualification ....
-ion prediction description depression ....
-ment arrangement replacement ....
-al arrival refusal ....
-ance performance appearance ....

accept approve assist associate astonish connect demonstrate disappear embarrass encourage improve object propose reflect remove starve survive translate

B Nouns from adjectives and nouns
Look at these examples and add more of your own, using the root words below with one of these suffixes. Use a dictionary to check your spelling, if necessary.

-ness kindness friendliness ....
....
-ce violence permanence ....
-ity* ability possibility ....
-y honesty frequency ....
-ship friendship relationship ....
-hood childhood fatherhood ....

accurate available blind careless cheerful confident efficient fluent intelligent leader member mother owner parent patient photograph probable real sad selfish shy silent sportsman suitable weak

* Notice where the stress falls in these verbs and nouns:
démonstrate demonstrátion quálify qualificátion
áble abílity póssible possibílity réal reálity

Notice the following associated adjectives and nouns:
anxious ↔ anxiety strong ↔ strength delighted ↔ delight
wise ↔ wisdom bored ↔ boredom proud ↔ pride
hungry ↔ hunger thirsty ↔ thirst

C
Fill the gaps in these sentences, using a prefix with the correct form of the root word on the right. The first is done for you as an example:

1 The book describes the ___relationship___ between a mother and her son.   RELATION
2 I've read *War and Peace* – but only in ....   TRANSLATE
3 There was too much .... in the story.   VIOLENT
4 The main .... of the book was the predictable ending.   WEAK
5 There's a lovely .... of the author's early ....   DESCRIBE   CHILD
6 You can't help admiring him for his .... and ....   KIND   HONEST

A   Work in small groups. Which of these books would you choose to read on holiday? Give your reasons.

HILLS OF KALAMATA

It was more or less unwittingly that Sarah Gilmore got herself involved in a plot to kidnap the Greek Charon Drakos – but unfortunately for Sarah he turned the tables and kidnapped her instead. So there she was, borne off to Charon's grim fortress-like home in the most remote, primitive part of Greece, forced into marriage with him. 'Whether you like my kisses or not you're going to have to accept them!' he assured her grimly – and how could Sarah escape him? And yet, when the chance came, she found she did not want to . . .

Like Marco Polo or Clare Francis, Ted Simon made a journey that millions dream of.
He rode 63,000 miles, four years and fifty-four countries round the world.
Spinning through the Sudanese desert, into prison in Brazil, into the Californian commune; through war, revolutions, disasters; into depths of fear, heights of euphoria and a fleeting love affair . . .
Riding the tightrope across vast continents, meeting their peoples, he is seen as a spy, as a glamorous, astonishing stranger and as a deity. And for Ted Simon, Magellan on a motorbike, it became a journey to the centre of his soul.

HE IS SEPARATED FROM HIS PARENTS IN A WORLD AT WAR. TO SURVIVE, HE MUST FIND A STRENGTH GREATER THAN ALL THE EVENTS THAT SURROUND HIM . . .

In EMPIRE OF THE SUN J. G. Ballard has produced a mesmerizing, hypnotically compelling novel of war, of starvation and survival, of internment camps and death marches, which blends searing honesty with an almost hallucinatory vision of a world thrown utterly out of joint. Rooted as it is in the author's own disturbing experience of war in our time, it is one of a handful of novels by which the Twentieth Century will be not only remembered but judged.

'A book of quite astonishing authority and power, one of the very best novels of recent years'
PAUL BAILEY THE STANDARD

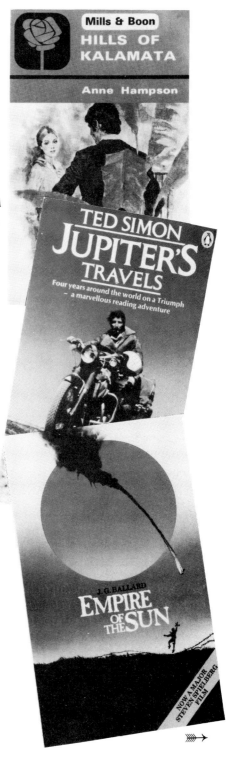

'As fine a novel as he has ever written' –
Observer

A leak is traced to a small sub-section of SIS,
sparking off the inevitable security checks,
tensions and suspicions. The sort of atmosphere,
perhaps, where mistakes could be made?

For Maurice Castle – dull, but brilliant with
files – it is time to retire to live peacefully with his
African wife, Sarah.

To the lonely, isolated, neurotic world of the
Secret Service Graham Greene brings his
brilliance and perception, laying bare the secret
motivations that impel us all.

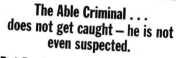

The Able Criminal . . .
does not get caught – he is not
even suspected.

But Professor Krom thinks he has
cornered one. Paul Firman, alias
Oberholzer, is suitably rich,
undeniably shady and obviously
frightened of his academic
persecutor. He agrees to an
interview in his secluded villa on
the French Riviera.

He also plans a few surprises.
Or were they laid on by his master,
the really able criminal?

B   The following people took one of the books on holiday with them,
but each regretted their choice. Why did they NOT enjoy their books and
which book(s) might have suited them better?

ANNA is 13. She chose *Jupiter's Travels* to take with her to read during her
holiday at the seaside with her parents.

BOB is 25 and works as a car mechanic. He chose *The Human Factor* to
read during his walking holiday.

COLIN is 19 and is studying English literature. He chose *Send No More Roses*
to read on the train while he was travelling round Europe.

and YOU took *Hills of Kalamata* with you on YOUR last summer holiday.

C   Write four paragraphs beginning as follows:

'Anna may be rather too young ...'
'*The Human Factor* sounds as if ...'
'Colin's choice of holiday reading was unfortunate because ...'
'I'm sorry I took *Hills of Kalamata* with me because ...'

9.7 *In* ...   *Prepositional phrases*

Fill the gaps in these sentences with suitable phrases from the list below.

1 They get on well with each other because they have so much ....
2 The main character knew she was .... and she managed to escape.
3 She must have been .... because she rushed past me without saying hello.
4 This book contains 224 pages ....
5 .... I like spy stories but I didn't enjoy that particular one.
6 Graham Greene's novels are all good, but I like *The Captain and the Enemy* ....
7 He didn't want anyone else to know, so he told them ....
8 The hero had spent all his money and was ....
9 Let me know if you're .... and I'll see if I can help you at all.
10 He seems charming ...., but .... he's aggressive and disagreeable.
11 If someone says, 'I agree with you ....' it means, ..., that they don't really agree.
12 At the end of the story the heroine was .... because her husband was ....

in a hurry   in a way   in all   in common   in danger   in debt
in difficulties   in general   in other words   in particular   in prison
in private   in public   in secret   in tears

9.8 The Captain and the Enemy   *Reading*

A   Read this passage and then answer the exam-style questions. Be careful because some of the wrong alternatives are only slightly wrong!

1

I am now in my twenty-second year and yet the only
birthday which I can clearly distinguish among all the rest
is my twelfth, for it was on that damp and misty day in
September I met the Captain for the first time. I can still
remember the wetness of the gravel under my gym shoes
and how the blown leaves made the courtyard slippery as
I ran recklessly to escape from my enemies between one
class and the next. I slithered and came to an abrupt halt
while my pursuers went whistling away, because there in
the middle of the courtyard stood our formidable headmaster talking to a tall man in a bowler hat, a rare sight
already at that date, so that he looked a little like an actor
in costume – an impression not so far wrong, for I never
saw him in a bowler hat again. He carried a walking-stick
over his shoulder at the slope like a soldier with a rifle. I
had no idea who he might be, nor, of course, did I know

>>>→

how he had won me the previous night, or so he was to claim, in a backgammon game with my father.

I slid so far that I landed on my knees at the two men's feet, and when I picked myself up the headmaster was glaring at me from under his heavy eyebrows. I heard him say, 'I *think* this is the one you want – Baxter Three. Are you Baxter Three?'

'Yes, sir,' I said.

The man, whom I would never come to know by any more permanent name than the Captain, said, 'What does Three indicate?'

'He is the youngest of three Baxters,' the headmaster said, 'but not one of them is related by blood.'

'That puts me in a bit of a quandary,' the Captain said. 'For which of them is the Baxter I want? The Christian name, unlikely as it may sound, is Victor. Victor Baxter – the names don't pair very well.'

'We have little occasion here for Christian names. Are you called Victor Baxter?' the headmaster inquired of me sharply.

'Yes, sir,' I said after some hesitation, for I was reluctant to admit to a name which I had tried unsuccessfully to conceal from my fellows. I knew very well that Victor for some obscure reason was one of the unacceptable names, like Vincent or Marmaduke.

'Well then, I suppose that this is the Baxter you want, sir. Your face needs washing, boy.'

The stern morality of the school prevented me from telling the headmaster that it had been quite clean until my enemies had splashed it with ink. I saw the Captain regarding me with brown, friendly and what I came to learn later from hearsay, unreliable eyes. He had such deep black hair that it might well have been dyed and a long thin nose which reminded me of a pair of scissors left partly ajar, as though his nose was preparing to trim the military moustache just below it. I thought that he winked at me, but I could hardly believe it. In my experience grown-ups did not wink, except at each other.

(from *The Captain and the Enemy* by Graham Greene)

1 How old was Victor (the narrator) when he first met the Captain?
   a) 11 b) 12 c) 21 d) 22
2 How old is Victor at the time of writing?
   a) 11 b) 12 c) 21 d) 22
3 Victor is called Baxter Three because ...
   a) he has two elder brothers in the school
   b) he has two younger brothers in the school
   c) there are two older boys called Baxter in the school
   d) there are two younger boys called Baxter in the school
4 Victor was running fast because ...
   a) he was playing with some other boys   c) other boys were chasing him
   b) he wanted to meet the Captain   d) the headmaster had called him
5 The Captain said later that Victor's father had ...
   a) asked the Captain to look after Victor
   b) given Victor to him
   c) lost Victor to him in a gambling game
   d) sold Victor to him
6 Victor's fellow pupils ...
   a) did not know his first name   c) liked the name Victor
   b) knew his first name   d) were keen to find out his first name
7 Victor's face was dirty because ...
   a) he had had an accident with some ink   c) he was a careless boy
   b) he hadn't washed that morning   d) the other boys had made it dirty
8 The adults that Victor knew all seemed to him to be ...
   a) kind and generous   c) strict and severe
   b) humorous and friendly   d) unhappy and bad-tempered

Check your answers and, if you made any mistakes, make sure you
understand WHY you were wrong. Did any of the questions seem 'unfair'
to you?

B Find words or phrases in the passage that mean the same as these
words or phrases. Don't use a dictionary – try to work out the meanings
from the context. The first is done for you as an example:

1 stones   *gravel*
2 sports shoes
3 not worrying about the danger
4 slid
5 sudden
6 not knowing what to do
7 unwilling
8 keep secret
9 hard to understand
10 according to what other people said
11 half open
12 cut

C Work in groups. Ask your partners these questions:
- What kind of person does Victor seem to be?
- What would it be like to be a boy like Victor in a tough boarding
  school?
- What are your views on boarding schools?
- What are your views on single-sex schools, as opposed to coeducational
  ones?

9.9 Talking about books

A 🔊 You'll hear a number of people talking about books they have recently read. As you listen to the recording for the first time, match the titles of the books to their authors.

Title	Author
A Taste for Death	Maya Angelou
Boy	Margaret Atwood
Catch 22	Roald Dahl
Cider with Rosie	Joseph Heller
I Know Why the Caged Bird Sings	P. D. James
Surfacing	Laurie Lee

B 🔊 Now listen to the recording again and decide which of these statements are true (**T**) or false (**F**):

1 **David** enjoys thrillers.
2 *A Taste for Death* is about two famous men who are found dead in a church.
3 He liked *A Taste for Death* because it was very amusing.
4 **Jocelyn** enjoys thrillers.
5 The author of *Surfacing* comes from Canada.
6 She enjoyed *Surfacing* because it was more than just funny.
7 **Ken** enjoys books about travel.
8 *Cider with Rosie* is about a period that now seems very long ago.
9 He found some of the descriptions rather dull.
10 **Jill** enjoys reading about people's lives.
11 She enjoyed the simple style of *I Know Why the Caged Bird Sings*.
12 **Blain** likes books that make him laugh.
13 He enjoys *Catch 22* because it is about the author's childhood.
14 **Judy** only likes books that are exciting.
15 She enjoyed the simple style of *Boy*.
16 Some parts of *Boy* are terrifying.

C Complete the unfinished sentences in this dialogue with questions that fit the answers that are given. The first is done for you as an example:

YOU: What *kinds of books do you enjoy reading* ?
Friend: Books that are easy to read and exciting.
YOU: Who .... ?
Friend: Oh, John Le Carré, Len Deighton – writers like that.
YOU: Do .... ?
Friend: No, not only spy stories. I do read other kinds of books too.
YOU: And what .... ?
Friend: At the moment? Well, I'm on the very last chapter of a book by J. G. Ballard.
YOU: What .... ?
Friend: 'Empire of the Sun'.
YOU: What .... ?
Friend: It's about a boy who is separated from his parents during the war.

YOU: Where ....?
Friend: In Shanghai.
YOU: What ....?
Friend: He learns how to survive in spite of all the suffering and
starvation.
YOU: Is ....? It sounds as if it is.
Friend: Yes, parts of it are depressing and even horrifying, I suppose.
YOU: Then what ....?
Friend: Well, it's very exciting and it's really well-written too.
YOU: Would ....?
Friend: Yes, I certainly would. I think you'd enjoy it.
YOU: Will ....?
Friend: Yes, sure. I'll try to remember to bring it along tomorrow.

D   Work in small groups. Find out the same information from your
partners, perhaps using the dialogue in C.

E   Work in small groups. Here are some 'typical questions' you may be
asked about the PRESCRIBED BOOK you're studying if it's a work of fiction
or a play. Ask each other the questions.
   (If you are not studying a prescribed book, leave out this section.)

● What ideas or 'message' is the writer communicating to the reader?
● Who is the most interesting or attractive character in the story? Why?
● Describe the main character in the story.
● Describe one of the minor characters and what happens to him or her in
  the story.
● Tell the story of the book as if you were one of the characters.
● Describe one of the minor characters and the part he or she plays in the
  story.
● What have you found especially interesting about the book?
● What makes the book 'different' from other books you have read?
● Why would you (not) recommend it to a friend who is not taking the
  exam?
● Did you enjoy the book? Why/Why not?

If your prescribed book is non-fiction, what kinds of questions are you
likely to be asked about it?

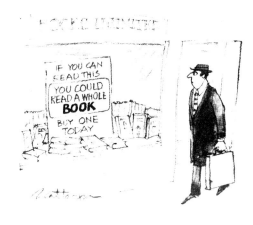

9.10   Writing about a book   *Composition*

★ In the exam, you'll have to write two compositions in 1½ hours – that's
45 minutes per composition, including making notes and checking
afterwards. From now on, whenever you write a composition, time
yourself. Try to finish every composition within 45 minutes (including
planning and checking time).

★ In the exam, you'll need to use your time as efficiently as possible. It
may be best to make notes on BOTH compositions at the beginning, in case
you run out of ideas later. Use a system and routine for making notes and
for checking your work that best suits your way of working.

A   A 150-word composition, like any piece of extended writing, needs to
be divided into PARAGRAPHS. Work in pairs.

1 Look again at the text in 9.8 (*The Captain and the Enemy*) and decide
   WHY the writer chose to start each new paragraph in the place he did.
      If the first paragraph were split into two, where could it be broken?
2 Now look again at the two versions in 9.2. Why does each new
   paragraph start at the place it does?
3 Look at some of the reading passages from previous units – why does
   each paragraph start at the place it does?
4 Look at two of your own previous compositions. Are they divided into
   paragraphs in a suitable way? Ask your partner to comment on them too.

★ In the exam, if you leave three or four blank lines between each
paragraph, there will be room to add an extra sentence later. If your
paragraphs are all squashed up together, you won't be able to do this.

B   Write 120 to 180 words in answer to ONE of these questions, some of
which you may have already discussed in 9.9 E. If your prescribed book is
non-fiction, choose between questions 1 and 7. If you aren't studying a
prescribed book, answer question 8.

1 What lesson or message does the story have for us?
2 Who is the most interesting or attractive character in the story? Why?
3 Describe the main character in the story.
4 Describe one of the minor characters and what happens to him or her in the story.
5 Tell the story of the book from the point of view of one of the minor characters.
6 Describe the setting or background of the story.
7 What have you found especially interesting about the book?
8 Imagine that you're recommending a book you've read to an
   English-speaking friend. Write a letter explaining what it's about and
   why your friend will enjoy it.

Time yourself. Make notes before you start and check your work afterwards.

★ In the exam, you may decide to answer one question on your prescribed
book (if you've read one) OR to answer two of the general questions. This
will depend on whether the Prescribed Book question you get in the exam
is easy or not – this question is always optional.

132

9.11   You know that book I borrowed ...   *Listening*

A   🔊   Listen to the conversation and fill the gaps with the missing information – there's no need to write the *exact* words the speakers use.

1 Jean says Peter borrowed the book ___two months___ ago.
2 Peter says he borrowed it _____ ago.
3 Peter says he left the book in the _____ and it got wet in the rain.
4 Peter admits that he dried the book out on a _____
5 Jean thinks he must have dropped it in the _____
6 Jean points out that the book is now _____
7 Peter offers to _____
8 She accuses him of always losing things and _____
9 The last time he borrowed her bike, he _____
10 She says that in future _____

B   Work in small groups. Discuss these questions with your partners:
• Have you ever been involved in a similar situation?
• How would you have reacted if Peter had damaged your book?
• Imagine that you have borrowed something valuable from a friend and lost it. You know it can't be replaced. What would you do? How would you break the news?

9.12   *Fall* and *hold*   *Verbs and idioms*

Fill the gaps with suitable forms of the phrasal verbs below:

fall
1 In a romantic novel the heroine always ___falls for___ the handsome hero. *be attracted to*
2 She ___fell out with___ him because he was very rude to her. *quarrel*
3 As he wasn't looking where he was going, he tripped and ___fell over___ *fall on the ground*
4 I eventually persuaded everyone to _____ my proposals. *agree*
5 Unfortunately, our plans to spend the weekend away have _____ *fail before completion*

hold
6 The robbers ___held up___ the security van and got away with £200,000. *rob*
7 I tried to get the book from him, but he was ___holding on to___ it so hard *hold tightly*
   that I couldn't get it out of his hand.
8 If you could just _____ a minute, I'll try to find the information you *wait*
   require.
9 All the traffic was _____ because a lorry had overturned on the *delay*
   motorway.
10 As the explorers had eaten all their food, they had to _____ until further *continue in spite of difficulties*
   supplies arrived.

fall for   fall in with   fall out with   fall over   fall through
hold on   hold on to   hold out   hold up   hold up

hang up (put down)

a wee bit

133

10 Food and drink

10.1   Talking about food   *Vocabulary*

A   Work in small groups. Ask your partners these questions:
- What's your favourite dessert?
- What do you normally drink with a meal?
- What did you have for breakfast this morning?
- What did you have for dinner last night?
- What is the worst thing AND the most delicious thing you've ever eaten?

B   Fill the gaps with suitable words or phrases – in some cases there are several possibilities.

1   They love eating at home because they are both fantastic ....
2   Carrots can be steamed and they can also be eaten ....
3   You can save yourself a lot of work in the kitchen if you have a(n) ....
4   Before the onions are fried, they should be finely ....
5   While the sauce is cooking, it should be .... from time to time.
6   Food can be cooked in many ways: bread and cakes are .... in an oven, vegetables can be .... or .... and meat can be .... or ....
7   My sister doesn't eat meat because she's a ....
8   The best way to boil water to make tea is in a ....
9   Before eating an apple some people use a knife to .... it.
10   Mix the flour, eggs and milk together in a large ....
11   Pour the mixture into a baking tin and put it in a preheated ....
12   Most people can't drink pure lemon juice because it's too ....
13   The problem with cooking for a lot of people is the .... afterwards.
14   My favourite sorts of meat are .... and ....
15   We can only recognise four tastes: sweet, ..., ... and ....

C   Choose the best alternative to complete each sentence:

1   I don't really like eating a curry which is very ....
    hot   peppery   sharp   spiced   warm
2   Roast beef is one of my favourite ....
    bowls   courses   dishes   plates   sauces
3   That was absolutely delicious, can you give me the ....?
    formula   instructions   prescription   receipt   recipe
4   Would you like your steak well-done, medium or ....?   半題者知數
    bloody   blue   rare   raw   red
5   A lot of food you buy nowadays contains all sorts of artificial ....
    additions   additives   extras   spices   supplements

6 Waiter, could I see the ...., please?
    card of wines   list of wines   wine card   wine list   wine menu
7 The reason why he always eats so much is simply that he's very............
    eager   greedy   hungry   peckish   starving
8 She liked the dessert so much that she asked for a second ....
    dish   go   helping   plate   serving
9 If you're on a diet there are some foods you have to ....
    avoid   deny   escape   lack   stop
10 You forgot to put the milk in the fridge and it has ....
    gone back   gone down   gone in   gone off   gone out

D   Work in pairs. Make three lists:

10 KINDS OF FRUIT   and   10 KINDS OF VEGETABLES   and   10 DRINKS

Compare your lists with another pair's lists.
Which of the fruit, vegetables and drinks in your lists do you LOVE *or* HATE?

10.2   Eating out   *Reading*

A   Before you read the passage on the next page, look at these questions.
What do you EXPECT the answers to be, from your own experience of eating out?

When you're eating out why should you ...
  1 bother to ring up to cancel a booking?
  2 ring up if you're going to arrive late?
  3 inform the restaurant beforehand if you're bringing a young child with you?
  4 read the menu outside before you go in?
  5 spend plenty of time studying the menu at your table?
  6 ask the staff questions about the dishes on the menu?
  7 worry about your fellow diners?
  8 criticise the way the meal was prepared, if it was poor?
  9 give the waiter a tip even if you had a bad meal?
10 tell your friends about your eating experiences?

B   Read the magazine article and find the answers that the *Good Food
Guide* gives to the questions above. Are they the same as your answers?

C   Work in small groups. Ask your partners these questions:
● How do the *Good Food Guide*'s recommendations differ from your own ideas?
● Which of them would you NOT follow at a restaurant in your own country?
● Which of the recommendations do you try to follow when eating out? Why?
● What advice would you give a foreign visitor about eating out in your country?
● How do you attract a waiter's attention in your country?
● What are 'polite table manners' in your country? Is it bad manners to eat
   chicken with your fingers, put your elbows on the table, etc.?

Eating out —
Some rules for diners

If you don't very often eat out in a restaurant, you may need some advice — as the latest issue of the *Good Food Guide* points out. Several rules for people eating out are given, some of which seem perhaps to favour restaurant staff more than they are likely to help diners! For example the *Guide* tells its readers to be sure to phone up and cancel any booking they make which they can't keep. The restaurant may otherwise be holding a table and ~~turning away~~ customers at its busiest time. Apparently this is a legal requirement, though how anyone could trace a Mr Smith or a Ms Jones who didn't turn up with a party of six is anyone's guess. The *Guide* also advises you to ring up if you're going to be delayed by more than a quarter of an hour; if you don't, your table may be given to someone else and it's only polite, according to the *Guide.*

Another rule they give is to let the restaurant know in advance if a member of your party has any special needs. So if you're eating with a small child, a very old person, a disabled person, a vegetarian or a Moslem let the restaurant know at least a day ahead so that you can all be sure of having better food and a happy time. A good restaurant owner will be only too happy to look after his guests' ~~individual requirements~~.

Before you go inside the restaurant, make sure you spend some time reading the menu outside quite carefully. Try to notice what the prices include and what they don't include. In *(cover- minimum)* particular look for any mention of cover charges, service charge and VAT. You might be in for a **nasty** shock when the bill comes if you haven't budgeted for these 'extras' and not all the menus you're shown at table mention these items. Once inside and seated comfortably at a table that suits you (and if you want a table by the window or in a quiet corner, do say so when you book) look at the menu carefully and insist that you're allowed enough time to decide at leisure what to order and to discuss with your companions what you're each going to have. There's nothing worse than being rushed into making a choice

good manner (etiquette)
common sense
accompaniments — extra

you'll regret later. By the way, don't be afraid to order two different dishes and to swop with a companion half-way through.

Another rule is to ask the staff questions: how is this dish cooked? what goes with what? what's that rather tasty looking dish the people at the next table are having? and so on. The *Guide* stresses that the people at the next table deserve consideration, too. If you want to smoke, you should ask them if they mind. This is more than just a polite formality since many people do object to breathing in other people's cigarette or, worse, cigar smoke while they're trying to appreciate good food.

While you're eating, someone will probably ask you 'Everything all right?' and probably expect the answer 'Fine, lovely!' but experienced diners should treat this as a serious enquiry and be prepared to offer compliments, criticisms (or both) honestly. Don't take any notice of companions who urge you not to 'make a fuss'. The trouble is, however, that you're usually asked this question when you have a mouth full of food, which makes it difficult to do more than nod and go 'Mmm'.

Finally, at the end of the meal, when you've been given the bill and are ready to pay you should thank the staff. Giving the waiter a big tip is no substitute for a warm thank you and a smile — if you've been served professionally and cheerfully you should reward the waiter with both gratitude and money! And if the food was poor, don't blame the waiter (it probably wasn't his fault — he wasn't the one who cooked the food) and don't refuse to give him a tip, either. In this case ask to see the manager and tell him you didn't really enjoy the meal and make sure you explain why.

By following these rules and guidelines, says the *Good Food Guide*, you can help yourself and others to enjoy better food. And if you do have a really good meal locally, tell your friends about it and encourage them to go to the same place. If you have a disastrous one, tell them about that too. After all, a good restaurant deserves to do good business and a bad one shouldn't be in business at all, perhaps.

(The Good Food Guide is published annually by the Consumers' Association)

136

A   Study these examples and fill the gaps with your own ideas:

-ing as the subject of a sentence:
Preparing a meal every day is hard work.   Eating out can be expensive.
.... abroad is interesting.   .... after a meal is boring.

-ing after prepositions:
Is anyone interested in joining me for a drink after work?
I'm looking forward to .... to Spain on holiday.
I can't get used to .... tea without milk.
I had an upset stomach after ....

Verbs + *-ing*:
can't help   enjoy   finish   dislike   avoid   give up   go on
don't mind   practise   delay
I've finished preparing the salad.
I avoid .... in expensive hotels.
I couldn't help .... when he fell over.
I'm trying to give up smoking.
I dislike .... after a meal.
I always enjoy .... new dishes.

Verbs + *to* —:
learn   manage   mean   choose   decide   forget   can't afford
help   pretend   need   didn't mean   expect   hope   offer   refuse
want   agree   promise   I'd like   recommend   encourage   train   try
teach   allow
I'd like you to give me a hand with the washing-up.
They promised to invite me to lunch.
I can't afford .... at the Ritz.
We managed .... a table by the window.
He didn't mean to spill the soup.
We decided .... a drink in the pub.
He tried .... the lid.

Verbs + *-ing* OR + *to* — with no difference in meaning:
begin   start   continue   intend   hate   like   love   prefer   propose
She began to eat/eating her meal.
I don't like .... alone in restaurants.
After the meal we continued ....
I love to eat/eating Chinese food.
Which dessert do you intend ....?
I .... black coffee.

Verbs + *-ing* OR + *to* — with a difference in meaning:
stop -ing and *stop to* —
Please stop making that noise, it's driving me mad! (= don't continue ...)
Their mother told them to stop ....
We stopped to get some petrol and have some lunch. (= stop in order to ...)
I was half-way through my meal but I had to stop .... the phone.

remember to — and *remember -ing*

Did you remember to buy the lettuce for dinner? (= not forget ...)
I don't remember you asking me to buy a lettuce. (= have a clear memory of ...)
You should have remembered .... Jill an invitation to the party.
I remember .... the letter yesterday evening after work.

to — after adjectives:

pleased glad surprised disappointed relieved shocked etc.
interesting kind hard essential difficult easy etc.

I was pleased to receive your invitation.   It was kind of you to invite me.
I was glad .... my old school friends again after so many years.
We were surprised .... a bill for £45.
It's easier .... from here to the centre by bus than .... by car.

too ... *to* — AND ... *enough to* —

We arrived early enough to get a seat.   My coffee is too hot to drink.
The tray was too heavy for me ....   Boiled eggs are easy enough ....

B   Rewrite these sentences, using the words on the right.

1 I'll be happy when I can see my friends on Friday.   I'm looking forward ...
2 If you want a table for ten you must phone the
   restaurant.   It's essential ...
3 I don't normally eat at restaurants.   I'm not used ...
4 You could sit by the window or outside on the terrace.   Would you prefer ...
5 They went on smoking all through the meal.   They didn't stop ...
6 I forgot to bring my wallet with me, have you got
   yours?   I didn't remember ...
7 Boiling an egg is not difficult.   It's ...
8 I'm very thirsty, could you get me some water, please?   I'd like you ...
9 Expensive restaurants are out of my price range.   I can't afford ...
10 You could share my pizza, if you like.   I don't mind you ...

C   Make all the changes and additions necessary to produce sentences
that together make a complete story. You may have to do an exercise like
this in the Use of English paper. The first is done for you as an example:

Dear Martin,
1 Last Sunday we go out / the country / visit my grandparents.
   *Last Sunday we went out into the country to visit my
   grandparents.*
2 I always look forward / go / see them and enjoy spend / day with them.
3 My grandmother like / grow all / own vegetables.
4 She never prepare / meal without / use fresh vegetables and / refuse / use any
   ingredients / have artificial additives.
5 When we arrive / we decide / go for / short walk before / sit down / lunch.
6 I love / walk in / country, even though I dislike / walk when I be in the city.
7 When we get back, / table be laid in / garden for lunch and we all begin / eat and talk
   and we go on / eat and drink all afternoon!
8 I be not used / eat a lot, / but everything be so delicious / I just can not stop / eat!
9 I manage / eat / great deal more than I intend / eat.
10 When we all finish / eat, we sit round / table and go on / talk / till it get dark.
    We all had a marvellous day,
                Best wishes, George

10.4 A memorable meal

A 🔲 You'll hear six people describing a meal they remember.
Decide whether these statements are true (**T**) or false (**F**).

1 Last Boxing Day **Judy** had invited all her family to dinner.
2 Her sister's children behaved very badly.
3 **Anne** was in the West Indies visiting some friends.
4 She arrived early in the morning.
5 The meal consisted of wonderful tropical fruit.
6 **Blain** was on holiday in Crete and loved the food.
7 When he returned to Britain he went straight to McDonald's.
8 While in Greece, **Jill** and her friends ate in the same restaurant every
  day.
9 The owner of the restaurant gave them wine instead of ordering a taxi.
10 They only had to pay for the wine, not the food.
11 **Ishia**'s meal in Italy consisted of twelve courses.
12 About half the courses were some kind of pasta.
13 **Coralyn** had invited four people to lunch at her flat.
14 The vegetarian couple fortunately had a sense of humour.
15 Her boyfriend saved the day by cooking everyone an omelette.

B Work in small groups. Ask your partners to recall a particular meal
they once had. It may be the food, the place or the situation they
remember.

10.5 *On* ... and *out of* ...

Prepositional phrases

Fill the gaps in these sentences with suitable phrases from the list below.

1 It's important to arrive .... if you're meeting someone ....
2 The lift is .... so we'll have to use the stairs.
3 When we're .... we always like to eat .... if the weather's nice.
4 Surely you don't want to sit .... – why don't you join us?
5 There was nothing to pay because Harry, the owner, said their meal was ....
6 Don't get angry, I didn't break the plate ....
7 Last year's diary is no use because it is ....
8 We're not ...., so I'll ring you from a public phone.
9 Frozen food is certainly convenient but, ..., fresh food tastes much better.
10 He lost his job last year and he's been .... ever since.
11 The frying pan is on the top shelf, it's ....
12 I couldn't get any ~~mustard~~ – it was .... at my local shop.
13 A policeman shouldn't join you for a drink if he's ....
14 .... I must say that I prefer eating at home to eating out.

on business   on duty   on purpose   on the other hand
on the house   on the telephone   on the whole   on holiday/vacation
on time   on your own   out of date   out of doors   out of order
out of reach   out of stock   out of work

139

A   Before reading the passage, work in small groups. Ask your partners these questions:
- Do you like potatoes or not? Why?
- How many different ways can potatoes be cooked or served?

The humble spud 马铃薯 (口)

Potatoes have been a staple food of the Old World for so long that it's easy to forget that they originated in the New World. The first ones came to England from Chile in 1586 and the new vegetable soon became popular and in parts of Europe replaced bread as the staple diet of the poor. The original potatoes were misshapen and full of large deep eyes, unlike 丑陋 modern varieties which have been bred to be disease-free, smooth-skinned and free from deep eyes. Potatoes tend to be either floury or waxy in texture, the former being good for 粉状. boiling whilst the latter are best for frying or eating cold. You can't do better than to grow your own, which is easier than you may think — you can even grow them in large flower pots on a balcony. If you buy potatoes in a greengrocer's, however, make sure you look for them with plenty of damp soil on them because they're likely to be fresher than the ones that have been around long enough to have been washed, graded and bagged in polythene! Flavour and nutrition are better retained if the potatoes are cleaned and then boiled in their skins, rather than peeled before boiling. New potatoes taste great, steamed and unpeeled with butter and salt. The four easy recipes that follow are for six people (or four hungry ones!).

Grilled potatoes
Boil or steam 1 kilo medium sized potatoes in their skins, drain and peel them while still warm. Cut each potato lengthways and brush with melted butter. Then put under a hot grill until golden brown. Serve with salt and freshly ground black pepper.

Potato salad
1 kilo medium sized waxy potatoes
2 tablespoons chopped chives, onion or parsley
mayonnaise or yoghurt dressing
Boil the potatoes in their skins and then peel and slice while still warm. Add the chives, onion or parsley to the dressing and coat the potato slices evenly. Leave to cool in the refrigerator before serving.

Potatoes with sesame seeds
1 kilo potatoes
6 tablespoons vegetable oil
2 tablespoons sesame seeds
about ¼ teaspoon cayenne pepper or chilli
   powder
1 teaspoon salt
juice of half a lemon
Boil or steam the potatoes in their skins, drain and peel. Cut into 2cm cubes and allow to cool. Heat the oil in a frying pan and when hot, throw in the sesame seeds. When they start to pop, add the potatoes and fry for 5 minutes, stirring all the time. Then add the cayenne pepper, salt and lemon juice and continue frying till crisp and brown.

Potatoes in their jackets
6 large potatoes
250ml sour cream
3 tablespoons chopped chives
oil
Preheat oven to 200°C. Wash the potatoes and rub them all over with the oil. Bake for 1 to 1½ hours, or until tender. (They'll cook faster if you put a skewer through each potato beforehand.) When cooked through, cut each potato in half lengthways and sprinkle salt and pepper on top, then let everyone spoon on the sour cream and sprinkle the chives on top.

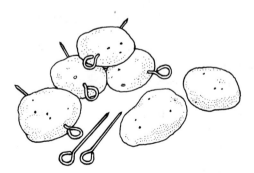

B   Choose the best alternative to complete each sentence.

1 The first potatoes .... modern ones.
   a) didn't taste as good as   c) were more healthy than
   b) weren't as smooth as   d) were smaller than
2 According to the passage, the best potatoes for eating cold are ...
   a) floury ones   c) large ones
   b) small ones   d) waxy ones
3 According to the passage, the best potatoes are ...
   a) bought locally   c) home-grown
   b) grown in flower pots   d) grown locally
4 It's best to buy ...
   a) clean potatoes   c) dirty potatoes
   b) potatoes in plastic bags   d) small potatoes
5 New potatoes are delicious ...
   a) cooked and eaten in their skins   c) cooked in their skins and then peeled
   b) eaten raw   d) peeled and then cooked

C   When should you ...
1 peel the potatoes to make 'Grilled potatoes'?
2 cut the potatoes to make 'Potato salad'?
3 remove 'Potatoes with sesame seeds' from the pan?
4 put the potatoes in the oven to make 'Potatoes in their jackets'?
5 take the 'Potatoes in their jackets' out of the oven?
6 put the sour cream on the 'Potatoes in their jackets'?

D   Work in small groups. Ask your partners these questions:
● What do people eat as basic foods in your country?
● How do cooks in your country make basic foods like rice more interesting?

10.7   In a restaurant   *Listening and Interview exercise*

A   Before you hear the recording, look at the questions below. Which of them
can you already answer, from your own knowledge of international food?
        Now listen to the recording and fill the gaps:

1 Before the meal, Philip has .... to drink and Anne has ....
2 A Greek salad is made of cucumber, ..., ... and cheese.
3 *Wiener Schnitzel* is a thin piece of .... coated in egg and ...., fried in oil.
4 A Spanish omelette is made of eggs, ... and ....
5 *Lasagne al forno* is thin .... of .... and .... sauce with a béchamel
   sauce, baked in the .... with .... on top.
6 *Moules marinière* are mussels cooked in .... with onions and a little ....
   You can have it as a .... or as a ....
7 *Rösti* is .... potatoes, ... and onions fried together. You can have it with
   two .... on top as a main course.
8 Anne orders .... as a starter and .... as a main course with a .... salad.
9 Philip orders .... as a starter and .... as a main course.
10 With the meal, Anne has .... to drink and Philip has ....

B Work in groups of three. Imagine that you are sitting together in a restaurant looking at this menu – the problem is that you don't understand some of the dishes. For more information, student A should look at Activity 7, student B at 35 and C at 48.

> *Could you tell me what … is?*
> *I'm not sure what … is.   I'd like to know what … is.*
> *Could I have … to start with and … to follow, please?*

LEO'S RESTAURANT

MENU
£11.99 for three courses, including VAT and service

STARTERS
Avocado with prawns
Home-made paté
Melon and orange salad

MAIN COURSES
Lancashire Hotpot with seasonal vegetables
Steak and kidney pie with new potatoes and vegetables
Cottage pie with seasonal vegetables
Chicken Madras with rice
Chicken Maryland with French fries
Nut and mushroom roast with brown rice
Omelette, plain or with your choice of filling

DESSERTS
Pancakes served with lemon juice and brown sugar
Sherry trifle with whipped cream
Blackberry fool
Bread and butter pudding
Chocolate mousse

All our dishes are prepared in our own kitchens, using the freshest ingredients.
ENJOY YOUR MEAL !

10.8 Compound words   *Word study*

A   Compound adjectives and compound nouns are formed from two parts. The best way to learn these words is to make a note of them when you read them or hear them. Usually, the meaning of a compound word can be worked out from the meanings of the words it is made from:

She is a kind-hearted person	(= she has a kind heart)
He is left-handed	(= he writes with his left hand)
A blue-eyed, red-haired boy	(= a boy with blue eyes and red hair)
This is my second-best suit	(= not my very best suit)
He uses a food processor	(= a kitchen machine that processes food)
I asked to see the wine list	(= the list of wines served in the restaurant)
She needs a tin opener	(= a gadget to open tins with)

Write down more examples of compound adjectives and nouns.

B   Look at these examples and fill the gaps, using the words listed below.

first	first cousin	first-class	....	....	....
high	high-speed	high-pressure	....	....	
home	home-made	....			
middle	middle-class	middle name	....		
second	second-class	second course	....		
self	self-control	self-defence	....	....	
well	well-done	well-informed	....	....	

-aged -best -class -discipline -grown -hand -known -level
-off -produced -respect -service -sized
floor name course cousin

★ Compound adjectives are usually (but not always) written with a hyphen, while compound nouns usually have no hyphen – but see section D below.

C   Combine the words in these two lists to make compound nouns. These are compound nouns that are normally written as TWO WORDS, with no hyphens. The first two are: *air travel* and *cake tin*.

air cake coffee exercise food instant intelligence railway
recipe restaurant salad savings sports story tea television
tennis tomato wholemeal yogurt

account bag beans book book bread carton coffee court
dressing ground owner processor set soup station telling
test tin travel

tea - caddy

D   Combine the words in these two lists to make compound nouns. These are compound nouns that are normally written as ONE WORD, with no hyphens. The first two are: *airport* and *boyfriend*.

air boy bread chair dish head house play post sea tax
tea tooth tooth tooth

ache ache brush crumbs food friend ground keeping man
man paste payer port pot washer

dental floss
tooth pick

★ Remember that a tea cup is a cup used for tea (perhaps empty), while a cup of tea is a cup full of tea. So a soup bowl and a bowl of soup are also different!

E   Fill the blanks in these sentences with a word that combines with the one given to make a suitable compound word.

1 We've got a new high-*speed* microwave oven.
2 I'm afraid I've chipped one of your coffee ....
3 Could you buy me a tube of tooth*paste* at the supermarket?   *dispenser*
4 He ate so much that he's got a stomach*ache* now.
5 My aunt's daughter is my first *cousin*
6 I'd like my steak well-*done*, please.   *rare – medium – well done*
7 Have you met Richard's new girl*friend*?
8 We always eat home-*grown* vegetables in the summer.
9 Some people prefer old-*fashioned* cooking to modern fast foods.
10 Could I have some salad *dressing* to put on my salad, please?

10.9 A nice cake

Listening

A   Before you hear the recording, look at the ingredients and list of instructions below. The instructions are in the wrong order: can you decide what might be the correct order? The first is done as an example:

RICH DUNDEE CAKE

220g flour

1½ teaspoons of mixed spice

(ground cinammon, nutmeg, cloves)

150g butter

150g sugar

3 eggs

300g mixed dried fruit

(raisins, currants, sultanas)

50g glace cherries

1 tablespoon of sherry

1 tablespoon of rum

50g ground almonds

50g split almonds

A	Remove cake from tin.
B	Test after 2 hours with knitting needle.
C	Beat eggs and add to creamed butter and sugar.
D	Arrange split almonds on top.
E	Add remaining ingredients.
F	Fold in flour and mixed spice.
1 G	Measure out all ingredients.
H	Allow to cool completely before cutting.
I	Cook in preheated oven (160°C) for 2½ hours.
J	If ready, remove from oven and allow to cool for 15 mins.
K	Grease a medium-size cake tin.
L	Pour mixture into cake tin.
M	Cream butter and sugar in large mixing bowl until light and fluffy.

B   Listen to the recording and rearrange the instructions in the correct order. Compare your answers with a partner and, if necessary, listen again to settle any disagreements.

C   The class is divided into an even number of pairs. Half the pairs should look at Activity 6, the other half at 29. You'll see some instructions on how to make two refreshing non-alcoholic drinks.

10.10   Revision exercise

Grammar

Rewrite each sentence using the words on the right:

1 Someone is preparing a meal for us now.   A meal ...
2 I've laid the table, so you can sit down now.   As the table ...
3 Brown bread is supposed to be better for you than white.   White bread ...
4 The worst meal I've ever had was at my brother's flat.   I've never ...
5 You've arrived too early, that's why the meal isn't ready. If ...
6 We'll get there early so that we'll be able to get a table. If ...
7 As there was no coffee left, we had to have tea.   If there...
8 I love chocolates but I'm on a diet – still, I'll just have one. Although...
9 There was a power cut while we were having dinner.   During ...
10 They'll arrive soon. I'll make some tea then.   When ...

144

When you're writing a composition, it's important to consider WHO is supposed to be your reader. In the exam, your real reader will be the examiner, but if the question says:

'Write a letter to a stranger ...' or 'Write what you would say to a child ...' or 'Write instructions for a friend ...'

– you'll need to suit your style of writing to the imaginary reader.

A   Look at these extracts. Who do you imagine is the reader or listener in each case?

1   Now, then. Let's suppose you want to make some old-fashioned lemonade. Well, it's quite easy really, but you might need a little bit of help with boiling the water. You need to make sure you've got four nice juicy lemons and some sugar, all right?

2   This is a favourite drink in our family and it's easy to prepare. All you need is four lemons and some sugar. All right? Well, first of all you have to peel the lemons, but very thinly so that you remove only the rind – that's the outside part of the peel, not the white part. OK, everyone? Good. Then you have to ...

3   You ought to try making your own lemonade, you know. It's ever so easy – anyone can do it! And it's much better for you than fizzy lemonade – and cheaper too. All you need is a few lemons and some sugar. Really, that's all, plus some water. Shall I tell you how to make it?

4   To make old-fashioned lemonade you need four lemons and 500 grams of sugar. The process is extremely straightforward and I'll explain it to you briefly ...

5   Unlike the commercial fizzy lemonade that is available in cans or bottles, home-made lemonade is pure, tasty and free from artificial additives. It contains only lemons and sugar and is simple to prepare. It is also considerably cheaper than commercial lemonade ...

6   ... Peel the lemons thinly, removing only the rind, and squeeze the juice into a large bowl. Add the sugar ...

B   Work in pairs. Imagine that a foreign friend has asked you for the recipe of a typical NATIONAL DISH that is a speciality of your country (or region), which he or she can prepare easily. Decide on a suitable national dish. What ingredients are needed and are they obtainable abroad, do you think? How is it made, step by step? Why have you chosen this particular dish? Use a dictionary, if necessary. Make notes.

C   Write a letter to an English-speaking friend who has asked you for the recipe of a national dish from your country or region. Explain why you have chosen this dish and how the dish can be prepared.

Show your completed composition to another student and ask for comments.

10.12   *Leave, let, pull* and *run*

A   Fill the gaps with suitable forms of LEAVE, LET, PULL or RUN:

1 Could you ....*let*.......... her know the news?
2 I'm not serious, I'm just ....*pulling*......... your leg.
3 Don't push the door, ...*pull*........ it to open it.
4 I asked him to ......*leave*...... me alone.
5 Let's ......*leave*...... the washing-up till tomorrow.
6 They .....*let*..... the flat for £200 a month.
7 When does the London train ....*leave*....... ?
8 She ....*ran*....... five kilometres before breakfast.
9 She was ....*left*....... £2,000 in her aunt's will.
10 I'm just going to ....*run*........ a bath.
11 The police ....*let*....... him go after questioning him.
12 My uncle ....*runs*........ a restaurant in the old city.

B   Fill the gaps with suitable forms of the phrasal verbs below.

leave + let
1 It's a very exclusive restaurant, they won't .... anyone .... wearing jeans.
2 I'm sorry that I ......*let*...... you ....*down*.... by arriving so late.
3 If you can't answer a question, don't .... it .... – guess the answer.
4 It's very dangerous to .... fireworks .... indoors.
   pull
5 You can't get on or off a bus when it .... at traffic lights.
6 If you've got toothache, you may have to have that tooth ....
7 It's a shame that all the old buildings have been ....
   run
8 He braked suddenly to avoid .... a dog but he lost control and .... a tree.
9 You won't believe this: the pub has .... beer.
10 We were walking past the farm when a large black dog started to .... us.
11 I .... an old school friend of mine the other day.
12 Mrs Brown has .... her best friend's husband.

leave out ~*omit*~   let down   let in   let off ~*explode*~
~*demolish*~ pull down   pull out   pull up ~*stop*~
run after   run away with   run into   run into   run out of   run over

leave out = omit

'Don't go to any trouble on my
account. I'll just have what
everybody else is having.'

146

11 Work and business

11.1 Earning a living

Vocabulary

A   Work in small groups. Ask your partners these questions:
- What do you do / plan to do for a living?
- What do the other members of your family do for a living?
- If you could choose any job in the world, what would it be? Why?

B   Choose the best alternative to fill each gap. As in the exam, there are four alternatives to choose between.

1 He has all the right .... for the job.
   certificates   degrees   diplomas   qualifications
2 She's looking for a better position with another ....
   association   firm   house   society
3 A doctor is a member of a respected ....
   occupation   profession   trade   work
4 It's wise to think about choosing a .... before leaving school.
   business   career   living   profession
5 If you want a job you have to .... for one.
   applicate   apply   ask   request
6 You'll probably have to .... an application form.
   fill down   fill in   fill on   fill through
7 And you'll need to give the names of two or three ....
   hostages   judges   referees   umpires
8 All the members of our .... are expected to work hard.
   personal   personnel   staff   gang
9 If you're a(n) .... you have to do what your boss tells you.
   director   employee   employer   manager
10 You can earn more money by working ....
   extraordinary hours   overhours   overtime   supplementary hours
11 It's difficult these days for a young person to find a well-paid .... job.
   eternal   permanent   reliable   stable
12 She was .... after three years with the company.
   advanced   elevated   promoted   raised
13 An apprentice is required to do several years' ....
   coaching   education   formation   training
14 In Britain, people are usually unwilling to tell other people how much they ....
   deserve   earn   gain   obtain
15 A retired person is paid a ....
   grant   pension   rent   scholarship
16 According to everyone in the ...., she is a very good boss.
   apartment   compartment   department   employment

147

17 Some of my work is quite interesting, but a lot of it is just ....
   habit   practice   routine   tradition
18 If you are paid monthly, rather than weekly, you receive ....
   revenue   a reward   a salary   wages
19 The purpose of running a business is to make a ....
   contribution   money   profit   service
20 The .... were delivered to the warehouse by lorry.
   data   goods   material   stuff

C   In these questions THREE of the alternatives are correct and TWO are wrong.

1 Ford is a multi-national corporation that .... motor vehicles.
   constructs   fabricates   makes   manufactures   produces
2 He was .... because he was an unreliable and lazy worker.
   dismissed   dispatched   fired   released   sacked
3 When the factory closed down, 500 people ....
   became unoccupied   became unemployed   lost employment   lost
   their jobs   were made redundant
4 A good worker is usually someone with the right kind of ....
   experience   experiences   experiment   personality   qualifications
5 Business letters are produced on a ....
   computer   printer   typist   typewriter   word processor

D   Work in small groups. Ask your partners these questions:
• People who work often say that students have an easy time. Do you agree?
• What is the most difficult job you can imagine?
• What is the most unpleasant job you can imagine? And the most pleasant?

11.2   How to create a good impression . . .   *Reading*

A   Imagine that a young friend is about to attend his or her first job
interview. Before you read the passage, decide which of these pieces of
advice are DOs and which are DON'Ts.

1 Find out as much information as you can about the job and the
   company.
2 Arrive early for the interview.
3 Make a list of reasons why you are suitable for the job.
4 Have something to eat before you go to the interview.
5 Go to the toilet before the interview.
6 Have a drink before the interview.
7 Take all your certificates and letters of recommendation with you.
8 Admit your ignorance if you don't know about the technical aspects of
   the job.
9 Show your best side only.
10 Shake hands with the interviewer.
11 Tell the interviewer about your shortcomings.
12 Ask about the pay you'll get if you're successful.

Then read the passage to see if your ideas are the same as the writer's.

148

YOUR FIRST INTERVIEW

With unemployment so high, and often scores of applicants chasing every job, you have to count yourself lucky to be called for an interview. If it's your first, you're bound to be nervous. (In fact if you're not nervous maybe your attitude is wrong!) But don't let the jitters side-track you from the main issue - which is getting this job. The only way you can do that is by creating a good impression on the person who is interviewing you. Here's how:

DO
Find out as much as you can about the job beforehand. Ask the job centre or employment agency for as much information as possible.

Jot down your qualifications and experience and think about how they relate to the job. Why should the employer employ you and not somebody else?

Choose your interview clothing with care; no one is going to employ you if you look as though you've wandered out of a disco. Whether you like it or not, appearance counts.

Make sure you know where the interview office is and how to get there. Be on time, or better, a few minutes early.

Bring a pen; you will probably be asked to fill in an application form. Answer all the questions as best you can. And write neatly. The interviewer will be looking at the application during the interview; he or she must be able to read it.

Have a light meal to eat, and go to the toilet. If you don't, you may well be thinking about your inside during the interview.

DON'T
Ever walk into the interview chewing gum, sucking on a sweet or smoking.

Forget to bring with you any school certificates, samples of your work or letters of recommendation from your teachers or anyone else you might have worked part-time for.

Have a drink beforehand to give you courage.

The interview
The interview is designed to find out more about you and to see if you are suitable for the job. The interviewer will do this by asking you questions. The way you answer will show what kind of person you are and if your education, skills and experience match what they're looking for.

DO
Make a real effort to answer every question the interviewer asks. Be clear and concise. Never answer 'Yes' or 'No' or shrug.

Admit it if you do not know something about the more technical aspects of the job. Stress that you are willing to learn.

Show some enthusiasm when the job is explained to you. Concentrate on what the interviewer is saying, and if he or she asks if you have any questions, have at least one ready to show that you're interested and have done your homework.

Sell yourself. This doesn't mean exaggerating (you'll just get caught out) or making your experience or interests seem unimportant (if you sell yourself short no one will employ you).

Ask questions at the close of the interview. For instance, about the pay, hours, holidays, or if there is a training programme.

DON'T
Forget to shake hands with the interviewer.

Smoke or sit down until you are invited to.

Give the interviewer a hard time by giggling, yawning, rambling on unnecessarily or appearing cocky or argumentative.

Ever stress poor aspects of yourself, like your problem of getting up in the morning. Always show your best side: especially your keenness to work and your sense of responsibility.

After the interview
Think about how you presented yourself: could you have done better? If so, and if you do not get the job, you can be better prepared when you are next called for an interview. Good luck!

B Find these words and phrases in the passage and work out their meanings from their **context** – don't use a dictionary. The first is done as an example:

1 scores of (line 1)
   a) a few   b) hardly any   c) a large number of ✓
2 chasing (line 2)
   a) escaping from   b) running after   c) applying for
3 count yourself (line 2)
   a) congratulate yourself for being   c) consider yourself to be
   b) feel proud that you are
4 the jitters (line 6)
   a) over-confidence   b) nervousness   c) lack of experience
5 side-track (line 6)
   a) distract   b) emphasise   c) interest
6 issue (line 7)
   a) argument   b) purpose   c) difficulty
7 Jot down (line 15)
   a) mention   b) type   c) note down
8 done your homework (line 62)
   a) practised being interviewed   b) worked hard at school
   c) found out as much information as possible about the company
9 get caught out (line 65)
   a) be found to be lying   c) be wasting your time
   b) be in danger
10 sell yourself short (line 67)
   a) are too nervous   b) are too modest   c) don't talk enough
11 giggling (line 74)
   a) arguing   b) coughing   c) laughing in a silly way
12 rambling on (line 75)
   a) talking for too long   b) going for a walk   c) hesitating
13 cocky (line 76)
   a) nervous   b) proud   c) over-confident

Now use a dictionary to look up the ones you couldn't guess from the context.

C Work in small groups. Ask your partners these questions:
- Which of the advice given in the passage would hold good for an FCE interview?
- How important/unimportant are job interviews in your country?
- Which of the advice given did you find most useful and least useful? Why?

'I'm basically a problem solver – as long as the problems are simple.'

11.3 Reported speech Grammar

A Reporting Statements

Look at these examples and fill the gaps. Imagine that your friend Helen was talking to you the other day and you want to tell someone else what she told you.

1 Helen said, "I'm looking for a new job."
 → Helen said that she was looking for a new job.
2 "I want a job that pays well."
 → She told me that she wanted a job that paid well.
3 "I haven't found a job that suits me yet."
 → She said that ....
4 "I'll telephone them and I'll ask them to send me an application form."
 → She told me ....
5 "I didn't get that job I applied for."
 → I found out ....
6 "I did very badly at the interview."
 → She admitted ....

These verbs are often used to report statements:
*add   admit   announce   answer   complain   explain   find out
inform someone   let someone know   reply   report   say   shout   state
suggest   tell someone   whisper*

- If the information is still relevant or true, the tense often isn't changed:
 My boss didn't let me know whether **I'm going to** get a pay rise next
  year.
 He told us that Jupiter **is** the largest planet.

B Reporting Orders, Promises, Offers, Requests and Advice

Look at these examples and fill the gaps. Imagine that your friend Michael was talking to you about applying for a job when you last met him.

1 I said to Michael, "Apply right away if you want to get the job."
 → I told Michael to apply right away if he wanted to get the job.
2 "You'd better write them a letter."
 → I advised him to write them a letter.
3 "Would you mind typing this letter out for me, please?"
 → He wanted me ....
4 "I'll do it on my word processor if you like."
 → I offered ....
5 "You must send it by first-class post."
 → I reminded him ....
6 "You will make a photocopy of it for me, won't you? All right?"
 → He persuaded ....

These verbs are often used to report orders, promises, offers, requests and advice:
*advise   encourage   invite   offer   order   persuade   promise
recommend   remind   threaten   want   warn*

Use whether ~~weither~~ when there are a lot of choice
He asked whether I liked tea or coffee

C   Reporting Questions

Look at these examples and fill the gaps. Imagine that you were talking to your friend Irene last month about an interview she was soon going to have.

1 I said to Irene, "What time do you have to be at the interview?"
   → I asked Irene what time she had to be at the interview.
2 "Have you had many interviews before?"
   → I wanted to know if she had had many interviews before.
3 "Is this your first interview?"
   → I asked her if it *was her first interview*
4 "What is the most important thing to remember at an interview?"
   → She asked me what the ~~was the~~ *most important thing to remember was*
5 "What are you going to wear for the interview?"
   → I wanted to know *what she was going to wear*
6 "How do you think you'll feel before the interview?"
   → I wondered *how she would feel before* *she ~~would feel~~*
7 When I saw Irene after the interview, I asked, "Did you get the job?"
   → I asked her if *she had got the job*
8 "Yes." "Why don't you look pleased, then?"
   → I tried to find out *why she didn't look pleased*
9 "Because it's not really the kind of work I want to do."
   → She said she was disappointed because *it was not really the kind of work she wanted to do,*

These verbs can be used to report questions:
ask   wonder   want to know   inquire   try to find out

■ Remember that when you're reporting times and places, these words usually (but not always) have to be changed:
   here→there   now→then   this→the   tomorrow→the next day
   yesterday→the day before   this week→that week
   last week→the week before
e.g. "Phone them tomorrow." → She told me to phone them the next day.

■ Remember that the actual words used can be omitted in reported speech:
   "I wonder if you'd mind helping me?"→She asked me to help her.
   "Why don't we have lunch together?"→He invited me to have lunch with him.

D   Rewrite these sentences, starting with the words on the right:

1 "I'm not enjoying my work," he said.   He said that ...
2 "I didn't remember to post this letter last night," he said.   He told me ...
3 "I want you to get here early tomorrow."   She said ...
4 "Have you already phoned our clients or will you do it later?"   She asked ...
5 "Don't forget to order the supplies I need," she said.   She reminded ...
6 "When will the delivery van arrive?" he asked.   He wanted to
                                                                                       know ...
7 "Don't you think it would be a good idea if we phoned them?"   She persuaded ...
8 "I think I'd better tell you that it was my fault."   He admitted ...
9 "If you don't all stop laughing, I'll scream."   She threatened ...
10 "I'll make that phone call first thing tomorrow."   He promised ...

152

11.4 Four candidates

A Work in small groups. Ask your partners what qualities and skills are required to be a good ...

manager   shop assistant   secretary   factory worker   waiter/waitress

B   [cassette] Listen to the conversation. Two colleagues are discussing the four candidates short-listed for a job in their department. Make notes as you listen.

be lacking in drive

	GOOD POINTS	BAD POINTS
Mr Anderson		
Miss Ballantyne		
Mr Collins		
Miss Davis		

C Work in pairs. Compare your notes and, if necessary, listen to the conversation again. Ask your partner these questions:
● Which of the candidates did get the job? Give your reasons.
● What was the job they were being interviewed for, do you think?

11.5 Fill the gaps

Fill each gap in this story with ONE word only:

One of 1 .... most enjoyable jobs I've 2 .... done was when I 3 .... a student. When you 4 .... what it was you may be a 5 .... shocked, but 6 .... I know it sounds unpleasant I can assure you that it was 7 .... fact delightful. Believe it or 8 ...., I was a grave-digger for a 9 .... summer. It was one of 10 .... hot, dry summers which made the 11 .... as hard as rock and it needed a great deal of 12 .... to dig the graves. Now, a grave-digger doesn't have 13 .... to do with dead bodies. All he has to do is dig two-metre deep holes and fill them in 14 .... when the coffin has been put in. As I 15 ...., it was a marvellous summer and I'm glad to say 16 .... I didn't have to work on my 17 .... I had a workmate who had been digging graves 18 .... 1950. In 19 .... of his depressing trade he was a cheerful character, always laughing and 20 .... jokes. He used to tell me 21 .... about his experiences and I 22 .... to him for hours on 连续 end. Mind you, we had to work quite 23 .... and usually there were two or three graves to dig every day. By the 24 .... I had to go 25 .... to college I was fitter, browner and in some 26 .... a wiser person.

★ In the exam there will be twenty gaps to fill. Make sure you read the whole story through BEFORE you start adding words. If you're unsure, leave a blank and come back to the exercise later.

INN ON THE PARK
requires
ROOM SERVICE ORDER TAKER

Previous experience would be an advantage, but the successful applicant will have a pleasant telephone manner and a good knowledge of food and beverage. Good salary, 40-hour week.
For further details please phone 01-499 2252.

ATTENTION!
Men, Women and Students

If you are new to London, temporarily discontinuing your education, recently discharged from the 服务 Services or for any reason seeking temporary or career work, consider this unique opportunity in our Publishing Sales Field Department.

You CAN EARN £250 PER WEEK

based on your productivity, commission plus incentives. The men and women we are looking for may be tired of typing, folding papers, warehouse jobs and working for a limited income.

Work with young people. Rapid advancement possible. If you are 18 or over and will be available to start work immediately, call Mr Allison, 606 1419 between 9 a.m. – 5 p.m.

TWO YEARS AGO
I WAS BROKE *no money*

Now I drive an Aston Martin, live in a 5-bedroom house, take my holidays abroad and earn a five-figure income. I need 2 ambitious people to share in my success, aged 22-40. Ring now, Terry Bilham, on 404 4522 or 404 0113.

THE SELFRIDGE HOTEL

01-408 2080
Personnel

The 4-star luxury Selfridge Hotel is currently seeking an experienced

DAY TELEPHONIST
(M/F)

Hours 7.30 am to 3 pm and 3 pm to 10 pm on a 5-day week rota. Knowledge of PABX3 switchboard is essential plus previous experience in a similar quality operation. Excellent salary, meals on duty plus benefits associated with a large hotel company.

A member of Thistle Hotel Group.
Interested applicants should telephone Personnel on the above number.

SECRETARY/ RECEPTIONIST WANTED

for language school. Essentials: fast typing, friendly calm personality, working knowledge of German or Greek. Will be in close contact with clients.
Tel. 489 8071 – ref. PDQ

STEWARDESSES

Adventure, travel, excitement aboard 41ft luxury charter and pleasure sailboat located in Miami cruising the Bahamas and Florida Keys, equipped for diving, live aboard, will train.

Salary plus travel expenses.

Send photo and resume to: T.W. Charters, Pier 3, Slip 9, Box L, Dinner Key Marina, Miami, Florida 33133, USA.

PART-TIME. If you are aged between 18-30, have a sparkling personality, intelligence, energy, and own a car, an interesting job awaits you on Sundays throughout the season. You can earn £100 plus for approx. 7 hours' work. No selling involved. Training given. – Tel. for interview B'mth 21362 Sunday 2 pm – 5.30 pm and 7 pm – 10 pm.

PART-TIME bar staff required. Please apply to – Personnel.

A   Look at the advertisements above and choose four jobs, one for each of the people who describe themselves below. Decide on the advantages and disadvantages of each of the jobs you have chosen.

ANNE: 'I'm 29 next birthday and I've been looking at the job ads in the evening paper lately. Alan and I are really short of cash these days and I'd like to get out of the house and earn a bit of money if I can. The trouble is that I can't leave the kids alone when Alan's at work – Alison's only 2½ after all – but at weekends when Alan's at home, I could do something. I could use the car at weekends, too.'

BOB: 'I'm 21 now and I've just left college. Unfortunately, I kept getting these headaches in my final year and I couldn't concentrate on my studies, so I failed the exams. The problem now is how to earn a bit of money and decide what to do with my life. I still feel awfully mixed-up. 混乱的迷惑 I don't think I ought to make any hasty decisions about a career at this stage. I'd like a job I can do fairly mechanically while I look around for something more rewarding and try to sort myself out.'

CHERRY: 'I'm 23 now and I've done all sorts of secretarial work, you know, apart from the obvious shorthand and typing, I've used word processors and worked the switchboard and done reception work. My last-but-one job was good because there was such a variety of work to do. But then I left them for a much better paid job in another firm and then two months later they went bankrupt! So now here I am looking for something which is going to be interesting and where I can use all of the skills I've learned.'

DORIS: 'Unlike the others, I've still got a job but I'm getting more and more bored with it. I'm 24 now and I mainly do clerical work, filing, sorting out documents, answering the phone, you know, stuff like that. I can't type and I did quite badly at school – I'm not stupid, mind you, it's just that I got bored with what we did there. I want to find a job that'll give me a chance to do something more exciting. I've got no ties or responsibilities, so I could go anywhere.'

B Write four paragraphs (about 50 words each) about each job you have selected, beginning as follows:

'The best job for Anne ...'
'Bob would ...'
'Cherry might ...'
'Doris should ...'

11.7 Word stress + Joining up words   *Pronunciation*

A It's important to stress the right part of a word. Mark the stréssed sýllables in these words and read the examples aloud. The first three are done as examples:

	Verbs and -ing forms	*Nouns and adjectives*
conduct*	I was condúcted round the museum.	I disapprove of their bad cónduct.
contract*	Metal contrácts when it gets cooler.	They signed the cóntract.
export	We expórted the goods to the USA.	Tourism is an invisible éxport.
import	These bananas are imported.	Imports have risen this month.
insult	He insulted me.	That was a terrible insult.
object*	I object to being insulted.	Unidentified Flying Object
perfect	They perfected a new method.	Your work is not quite perfect.
permit	Smoking is not permitted.	You need a permit to fish in the river.
progress	His work is progressing well.	Progress to First Certificate
protest	They protested about the situation.	They held a protest meeting.
record	Listen to the recording.	Have you heard their new record?
suspect	He is suspected of the crime.	He is the main suspect.

* In these cases, the meanings are different.

In verbs + "ing" forms, the stress is on 2
In nouns + adjectives the stress is 1st

≫→

155

B   When a word has more than two syllables, it's sometimes difficult to remember where the main stress is placed – especially when there is a similar word in your own language.

Look at these words and **márk** the main stressed **sýllable** in each one like this:
empl**óy** empl**óy**er empl**óy**ment employ**ée** appl**ý** applic**á**tion

employ   employer   employee   employment   apply   application
advertising   advertisement   attraction   certificate   comfortable
communication   deputy   desert   dessert   desirable   details
development   experience   girlfriend   himself   information   intelligence
machine   permanent   photograph   photography   qualification   receptionist
reservation   secretarial   secretary   telephone   telephonist   temporary
themselves   toothache   vegetable   yourself

C   Generally speaking, grammatical words (modal verbs, articles, prepositions, etc.) are not stressed in a sentence. Content words (nouns, adjectives, verbs and adverbs) are stressed. Listen to these examples and márk the stréssed sýllables:

1 Stress is just as important in a conversation as when you're reading something aloud.
2 Knowledge of at least one foreign language is required in this job.
3 The unemployment figures are higher again this month, it says in the paper.
4 I heard on the news that exports are up again this year.
5 Male secretaries were replaced by women in the First World War.
6 Find out as much as possible about the job beforehand.
7 Show some enthusiasm when the job is explained to you.
8 No one is going to employ you if you look as if you've wandered out of a disco.
9 The way you answer will show what kind of person you are and if your education, skills and experience match what they're looking for.
10 It takes most people a long time to perfect their pronunciation in English.

D   If you're quoting a sentence from a letter or book, it's important to read in such a way that people can understand you easily.

It   is   very   hard   to   understand   someone   if   they   pause   between   each   of   the   words   in   a   sentence.
Normally, the words in a sentence are 'joined up', like this:
The words in a sentence are joined up when the last sound in a word is a consonant and the first sound in the next word is a vowel.

1 Mark the places in the sentences in C above where the words are joined up, when spoken.
2   Listen to the recording again and compare your marks with the voices on the tape.
3 Work in pairs. Take it in turns to read each of the sentences aloud.

E   Look again at the passage about interviews in 11.2 and find:
● the most useful piece of advice given
● the least useful piece of advice given
● the most obvious piece of advice, that everyone already knows
Mark where the words in the sentences you have chosen are joined up and then read them aloud.

11.8 First jobs

Listening

A [cassette] You'll hear four people describing the first jobs they had.
Decide which of the alternatives best completes each sentence.

1 **Jill** first worked in a design studio as ...
   a) a clerk   b) a designer   c) a secretary   d) a typist
2 She left the job ...
   a) when her boss returned from holiday   c) after she had returned from holiday
   b) while her boss was on holiday   d) after she had taken a day off
3 Some weeks later, when her boss wrote her a letter, ...
   a) she didn't return to the studio   c) the horrible woman had been sacked
   b) she returned to the studio   d) the horrible woman was on holiday
4 **David** enjoyed himself in the library by ...
   a) giving people the wrong books
   b) guessing what books people were going to borrow
   c) hiding books
   d) putting books on the wrong shelves
5 **Richard** found that the other postmen in Berlin used to ...
   a) arrive early for work   c) take his mail
   b) help him   d) think he was strange
6 His journey to work took about ...
   a) 30 minutes   b) one hour   c) 90 minutes   d) five hours
7 Compared with an English postman's work, the work of a German postman seemed
   to be more ...
   a) enjoyable   b) exciting   c) responsible   d) tiring
8 If **Jocelyn** didn't sell any encyclopedias, she ...
   a) didn't earn any money   c) earned just enough to live on
   b) didn't earn enough to live on   d) earned very little
9 She found that the key to success in the job was ...
   a) having a sense of humour   c) talking about encyclopedias
   b) not being shy   d) talking to people
10 She earned enough to ...
   a) buy a car   c) pay for her education
   b) pay for a holiday   d) support her family

B If anyone in your class has worked (even only holiday work) get them
to describe their first job. Ask them questions like these:
● What did you have to do?
● What was enjoyable/dull about the work?
● How hard did you have to work?

★ In the exam, some of the listening comprehension questions may be
very difficult. Remember that you don't have to get ALL the answers right
in order to pass, just most of them. As you'll hear each recording twice,
you'll always get a second chance to try to answer the difficult questions.

11.9 The secretary

Reading

WORKFACE

Jane McLoughlin

IN OLDEN DAYS, when a glimpse of stocking was looked upon as something far too shocking to distract the serious work of an office, secretaries were men.

Then came the first World War and the male secretaries were replaced by women. A man's secretary became his personal servant, charged with remembering his wife's birthday and buying her presents; taking his suits to the dry-cleaners; telling lies on the telephone to keep people he did not wish to speak to at bay; and, of course, typing and filing and taking shorthand.

Now all this may be chang-ing again. The microchip and high technology is sweeping the British office, taking with it much of the routine clerical work that secretaries did.

"Once office technology takes over generally, the status of the job will rise again because it will involve only the high-powered work — and then men will want to do it again."

That was said by one of the executives (male) of one of the biggest secretarial agencies in this country. What he has predicted is already under way in the US. One girl described to me a recent temporary job placing men in secretarial jobs in San Francisco, she noted that all the men she dealt with appeared to be gay so possibly that is just a new twist to the old story.

Over here, though, there are men coming onto the job market as secretaries. Classically, girls have learned shorthand and typing and gone into a company to seek their fortune from the bottom — and that's what happened to John Bowman. Although he joined a national grocery chain as secretary to its first woman senior manager, he has since been promoted to an administration job.

"I filled in the application form and said I could do audio / typing, and in fact I was the only applicant. The girls were reluctant to work for this young, glamorous new woman with all this power in the firm.

"I did typing at school, and then a commercial course. I just thought it would be useful finding a job. I never got any funny treatment from the girls, though I admit I've never met another male secretary. But then I joined the Post Office as a clerk and fiddled with the typewriter, and wrote letters, and thought that after all secretaries were getting a good £1,000 a year more than clerks like me. There was a shortage at that time, you see.

"It was simpler working for a woman than for a man. I found she made decisions, she told everybody what she thought, and there was none of that male bitchiness, or that stuff 'ring this number for me dear,' which men go in for.

"Don't forget, we were a team — that's how I feel about it — not boss and servant but two people doing different things for the same purpose."

Once high technology has made the job of secretary less routine, will there be a male takeover? Men should beware of thinking that they can walk right into the better jobs. There are a lot of women secretaries who will do the job as well as they — not just because they can buy negligees for the boss's wife, but because they are as efficient and well-trained to cope with word processors and computers, and men.

A Decide which alternative best completes each sentence, according to the text.

1 Before 1914 female secretaries were rare because they ...
   a) were less efficient than men
   b) wore stockings
   c) were not as serious as men
   d) would have disturbed the other office workers
2 A female secretary has been expected, besides other duties, to ...
   a) be her boss's memory
   b) do everything her boss asked her to
   c) clean her boss's clothes
   d) telephone her boss's wife

158

3 Secretaries, until recently, had to do a lot of work now done by ...
   ✓a) machines   b) servants   c) other staff   d) wives
4 A secretary in the future will ...
   a) be better paid   ✓c) have higher status
   b) have less work to do   d) have more work to do
5 John Bowman is now a ...
   a) junior manager   c) male secretary
   b) member of the administrative staff   d) senior manager
6 He was given his first job as a secretary because ...
   a) he had the best qualifications   c) he wanted to work for a woman
   b) he was lucky   d) no one else applied
7 He did a commercial course because he ...
   a) couldn't think of anything else to do
   b) thought it would help him to find a job
   c) had done typing at school
   d) wanted to become a secretary
8 When he was a post office clerk, secretaries were better paid because ...
   a) not many were looking for jobs   c) they had greater responsibility
   b) they were better trained   d) they worked longer hours
9 He found that working for a female boss was less ...
   a) boring   b) easy   c) complicated   ✓d) frustrating
10 The writer believes that before long ...
   a) men and women will be secretaries
   b) men will take over women's jobs as secretaries
   c) men will be better with machines
   d) women will operate most office machines

B   Work in small groups. Ask your partners these questions:
● Is your job (or the job you plan to do when you finish studying) often
  done by someone of the opposite sex? Can it be done just as well by
  men and by women?
● In your country, which of these jobs are normally done only by men or
  women:
      secretary, clerk, shop assistant, bus driver, train driver, airline pilot,
      taxi driver, ship's captain, building worker, doctor, schoolteacher,
      receptionist, politician?
● Would you rather work for a female boss or a male boss? Give your
  reasons.

11.10　A typical working day

A　🔲　Listen to the recording and try to guess the speakers' jobs.

B　🔲　Listen to the recording again and decide which of these
statements about Albert Wilson's work are true (**T**) or false (**F**):

1 He always has to get up at 4 a.m.
2 The work he does makes him feel
　tired.
3 He spends all his working life below
　ground.
4 The work is unhealthy because it
　strains the nerves.
5 He really enjoys his work.

6 He is able to talk to his workmates
　after every journey.
7 He thinks he is well paid.
8 He prefers working on the evening
　shift.
9 He gets one day off per week.
10 The members of his family don't
　have to pay for transport in London.

C　🔲　Decide which of these statements about Gordon Spencer's
work are true (**T**) or false (**F**):

1 He works at home.
2 No one can disturb him when he's
　working.
3 He begins each day by typing notes.
4 He never leaves work unfinished until
　the next day.
5 He only stops working to have lunch.

6 He goes to work by bicycle.
7 As soon as he arrives home, he has a
　meal.
8 It takes seven weeks to write a book.
9 He writes one book a year.
10 He travels round the world mainly
　for pleasure.

11.11　Writing a formal letter

A　It's important, when writing a composition, to include only ideas and
information that are relevant – if you're writing a composition about 'my
ideal job', there's no point in writing about all the jobs you would *hate* to
do!

Work in pairs. Imagine that you or a friend wants to apply for this job:
• What kind of information would be RELEVANT in your letter?
• What kind of information would be IRRELEVANT?

PART-TIME IMPORT/EXPORT CLERK

We are looking for an intelligent, self-confident young person who is
fluent in at least one foreign language. The work involves answering
correspondence, using a typewriter or word processor, and dealing on
the phone with clients abroad. The working week will be 20 hours per
week Monday-Friday, mornings or afternoons only.
A good salary will be paid to a suitable applicant.

Apply in writing to Ms Brown, ACME Enterprises, 13 Armada Way,
Brookfield BF2 7LJ.

B   Look at these two letters. What important information is missing from each of them? Which of them do you prefer and why?

```
                                    c/o Mrs Grey
                                    15 Green Road
                                    Brookfield
                                    (Tel. 345678)

                                    1 April 199#
Dear Sir,
    After reading your advertisement in the Evening
Chronicle, I wonder if I might be suitable for the part-
time post advertised. I am a Greek national, and I am
studying in England for a year. My typing is quite good
and I enjoy dealing with people.
    Please let me know if you think I may be suitable for
the post. I can come for an interview at any time
convenient for you.
    Yours sincerely,
```

```
                                    c/o Mrs Green
                                    51 Grey Road
    Ms Brown                        Brookfield BF8 9DN
    ACME Enterprises
    13 Armada Way
    Brookfield BF2 7LJ

    Dear Ms Brown,
        I am interested in applying for the post of Part-time
    Import/Export Clerk.
        I am 20 years of age and in my third year studying business
    administration at Brookfield Polytechnic. As my lectures
    take place only in the mornings and evenings I would be
    available to work in the afternoons from about 1.30 or 2 p.m.
        I speak and write fluent Italian and some German, as
    well as English. I have had some experience of office
    work in my own country. I am available for interview any
    afternoon and would be pleased to discuss my suitability
    for the post on the telephone.
        I look forward to hearing from you.
        Yours sincerely,
```

★ In the exam you'll have to write two compositions in 90 minutes – that's 45 minutes per composition INCLUDING time for planning, making notes and checking your work through afterwards.

C   Time how long it takes you to write this composition:

Write a letter of 120–180 words applying for the job advertised on the next page. (Make sure your letter is laid out in the appropriate style with your address at the top, today's date in the right place, etc. These words shouldn't be counted as part of the composition.)

Remember to make notes before you start.
Check your work through afterwards and correct any mistakes you notice in SPELLING and GRAMMAR.

TEMPORARY HOTEL RECEPTIONIST
Pleasant medium-size hotel in the heart of Cambridge
seeks young person with pleasant personality to assist
in reception office.
Previous experience an advantage but not essential.
Knowledge of at least one foreign language required.
Good pay for someone who can work sensibly and
cheerfully in our team. Apply in writing to
College Hotel, King's Parade, Cambridge.

★ If you took longer than 45 minutes, you'll need to improve your speed.
If you only took 25–30 minutes, you may not be spending enough time planning
beforehand or checking afterwards.

★ In the exam, if you write too many words the examiner will only look closely at
the first 180 words of your composition. Although you may get some credit for
relevant material at the end of the composition, it's not worth the risk.

11.12 *Set, stand* and *turn*   *Verbs and idioms*

A Fill the gaps with suitable forms of SET, STAND or TURN.

1 The house .... on a hill.
2 The weather .... cloudy.
3 Our agreement still ....
4 She .... a good chance in the exam.
5 What time does the sun .... ?
6 He .... his back on her.
7 Can you .... on your head?
8 The novel is .... in New York.
9 I can't .... the way he laughs.
10 Please .... the table for dinner.
11 She .... the page.
12 I .... my alarm clock for 6 a.m.
13 Go straight on and then .... left.
14 The milk .... sour.

B Fill the gaps with suitable forms of the phrasal verbs below:

set
1 As they had a long way to go, they .... early in the morning.
2 An organisation was .... to help unemployed people and their families.
3 The union rule book .... the rules all members must follow.
stand
4 While the boss is away, her assistant is .... her.
5 I will not .... such terrible behaviour.
6 I'm not afraid to .... the boss if I know I'm right.
7 What's the name of the man who .... President in the USA in 1988 and lost?
8 A good friend will .... you in good times and bad.
9 Everyone .... while the national anthem was played.
turn
10 There's no need to make an appointment, you can .... at any time.
11 If you .... the next page, you'll see exercise 12.1.
12 He was happy in his work and .... the offer of promotion.

set off/set out   set out   set up
stand by   stand for   stand for   stand in for   stand up   stand up to
turn down   turn over   turn up

162

11.13 Different kinds of jobs
Interview exercises

★ In the Interview in the exam, the activities you'll have to do (Talking about pictures, Discussion/Communication activity, etc.) will all be based on a single topic. If you're lucky, this topic will be one that you've discussed in *Progress to First Certificate* – but not necessarily.

A Work in pairs or small groups. Ask your partners these questions about the photos:
● What kind of work does each of these people do?
● What sort of people are they?
● What does each one do on a 'typical working day'?
● Which of their jobs would you most like to do AND least like to do? Why?
● What kind of work do you do? OR would you like to do one day?
Can you think of any other questions you could ask them?

★ Remember that the purpose of the questions in this exercise is to encourage you to speak and express your ideas – NOT to test your knowledge of specialist vocabulary to describe all the objects in the picture.

B Work in groups of three. Ask your partners these questions:
● Which of these occupations are well paid and badly paid?
● Which should be paid most?
● What would be the attractions of the jobs?
● What would be the drawbacks of the jobs?

AUTHOR   CARPENTER   GOVERNMENT MINISTER
NURSE   POSTMAN/WOMAN   SALES REPRESENTATIVE
SECRETARY   SHOP ASSISTANT   TAXI DRIVER

For more information, student A can look Activity 26, student B at 30 and C at 45.

12 In the news

12.1 The press, politics and crime   *Vocabulary*

A   Work in small groups. Ask your partners these questions:
● Where do *you* find out about the news: local newspaper, TV or radio?
● Do you find the news depressing, interesting, annoying or amusing?

B   Choose the best alternative to complete each sentence.

1 I read an interesting .... in the paper the other day.
    article   information   news   reporting

2 I've only had time to read the .... in this morning's paper.
    columns   headings   headlines   sections

3 A newspaper's opinions are given in its ....
    cartoons   editorial   reports   titles

4 The person who reads the news on TV is called a(n) ....
    announcer   commentator   journalist   newsreader

5 The terrorists who hijacked the plane last night are still holding ten ....
    casualties   hostages   pedestrians   victims

6 I read in the newspaper that there has just been a .... in Transylvania.
    revelation   revolting   revolution   revolver

7 Over a thousand people are believed to have died in the ....
    bomb   earthquake   earthwork   explode

8 Only a small number of countries possess nuclear ...., thank goodness.
    ammunition   equipment   guns   weapons

9 Does that newspaper .... the government or oppose it?
    advantage   assist   encourage   support

10 In a .... everyone over a certain age is allowed to vote.
    democracy   dictatorship   nation   state

11 In some countries it is compulsory to vote in a(n) ....
    choice   constituency   election   selection

12 In the USA the most important person in the .... is the President.
    bureaucracy   civil service   government   state

13 In Britain the leader of the majority party in Parliament is the ....
    Chancellor   President   Prime Minister   Sovereign

14 The police have .... the man who is suspected of committing the murder.
    arrested   captivated   imprisoned   punished

15 Over £2 million was .... in the robbery.
    ceased   liberated   robbed   stolen

16 The arrested criminal admitted nothing and said that he wanted to see his ....
    accountant   advocate   lawyer   supervisor

17 The burglar was sentenced to 20 years in ....
    dock   goal   jail   trial

18 He was found .... of the crime and fined £500.
    convicted ✓guilty innocent responsible
19 In a British law court a case is heard by a judge and a .... of twelve people.
    cabinet committee ✓jury panel
20 He's a .... and so he always votes for the Labour Party.
    conservative liberal ✓socialist ~~socialite~~ 社会名流

C Work in small groups. Ask your partners these questions:
- What have been the main national and international news stories during the past week? How many can you remember?
- What is the most awful thing that has happened in the last week?
- What is the most amusing thing that has happened in the last week?

12.2 The robber gendarme   *Reading*

A Work in pairs. Before you read this article, look at the headline. What do you think the story is going to be about?

Bingo brings down the robber gendarme [dʒɑːnˈdɑːm] 宪兵

Derek Brown in Brussels

DAVID Saucez's bank robbing was as bad as his bingo. Desperate to pay off his gambling debts, he held up his local bank, and made off with around £2,000 before turning up for work – as a member of the Belgian gendarmerie.

It was the easiest arrest his colleagues could have possibly expected. For Saucez not only used his service pistol in the hold-up, but also made his get-away in his own easily recognised family car. 逃脱

The car's number was taken by the manager of the Sud Belge bank in the Brussels suburb of Schaerbeek. He witnessed the hold-up, but was unnoticed by Saucez.

The unhappy gendarme told colleagues who arrested him that he had run up a debt of 60,000 Belgian francs (around £800), playing bingo. He was also paying off a home loan, and his wife – who works in another bank – did not know of his gambling.

Saucez, described as a "model gendarme" with six years' service, said he considered robbing the same bank the week before. His nerve failed at the last moment, and he ended up asking for advice on a loan.

On Monday this week he returned to the same bank, and the same temptation. This time it was too much.

He told arresting officers: "I had no intention of committing a hold-up. I left the barracks to go to the bank and request a delay in repaying my loans. It was on the way there that I decided to 撤款/抢款 take action."

He was well equipped for the job, if not the getaway. Producing his service pistol, he demanded and got the money and then made off in his distinctive red Vauxhall.

He was already late for duty, but paused on the way to pay off 20,000 francs of his debt. By that time the net was inevitably closing in.

The gendarmerie, having answered the manager's alarm call too late to catch the robber red-handed, at least had the information to catch him red-vehicled.

They traced the car number to Saucez, alerted his unit in Brussels, which said he had been on duty but was now absent. A few minutes later he turned up complete with the hold-up weapon, the getaway car, and the remainder of the loot in his pocket.

B Here are the main events in the story. Rearrange them into the correct sequence and number them 1–9. The first is done as an example:

Alarm raised by manager   Arrested   Decided to rob bank
Found himself in debt   Paid part of his debts Played bingo 1
Reported for duty   Robbed bank   Was afraid to rob bank

C Decide which of the alternatives best completes each sentence:

1 David Saucez's wife works ...
   a) as a policewoman   c) in the bank he robbed
   b) as a security guard   d) in another bank
2 David Saucez's wife ...
   a) disapproved of his gambling
   b) tried to help him to give up gambling
   c) was unaware that he was so heavily in debt
   d) was worried about his debts
3 David Saucez used ...
   a) a borrowed car   c) a red car
   b) a car with false number plates   d) a stolen car
4 The previous week, David Saucez had planned to rob the bank, but ...
   a) asked them to lend him some money
   b) asked them what he should do about borrowing money
   c) paid some money into his account there
   d) didn't dare to go inside
5 The police knew about the robbery because ...
   a) David Saucez admitted his guilt
   b) David Saucez had parked his car outside the bank
   c) David Saucez was unlucky
   d) the bank manager made an alarm call
6 David Saucez arrived late for duty because he ...
   a) stopped to pay back some of the money he owed
   b) was afraid to report for duty
   c) was going to rob the bank
   d) was trying to escape

D Work in small groups. Ask your partners these questions:
- If you had been David Saucez, what would you have done differently?
- If you had been his wife, what would you have done?
- If you were in debt, how could you avoid getting involved in crime?

'You won't get away with this!'

A Adverbs
Look at these examples, showing where the adverbs are normally placed in the sentence:

Before	*Mid*	*After*
Recently he was arrested.	He was recently arrested.	He was arrested recently.
Unexpectedly, he was arrested.	He was unexpectedly arrested.	He was arrested unexpectedly.
—	He was never arrested.	—
Certainly he was arrested.	He was certainly arrested.	—
Yesterday he was arrested.	—	He was arrested yesterday.
—	—	He was arrested by the police.

B   Notice the following points:
- We DON'T normally say or write:
    By the police he was arrested. ✗   Never he was arrested. ✗
but we CAN say or write:
    He certainly was arrested.   He never was arrested.   He recently was arrested.

- Notice where these adverbs are placed when there is a modal verb in the sentence:
    He will certainly be arrested.   He will never be arrested.
    NOT: He will be certainly arrested. ✗   He will be never arrested. ✗

- Normally, an adverb is not placed between a verb and a direct object:
    I like very much tennis. ✗   or   He drove very fast the car. ✗

C   Decide where each of the adverbs below can be placed in these sentences:

They	**didn't**	**arrive on time**	.
She	**was**	**able to finish her meal**	.
We	**knew**	**that the work**	**would**	**be very difficult**	.

almost   always   hardly ever   just   nearly   never   rarely   seldom

as usual   certainly   definitely   frequently   maybe   normally
obviously   often   one day   on Friday   perhaps   possibly   probably
really   still   usually   yesterday

D   Place the adverbs in suitable positions in these sentences:

1 She worked to finish the essay.	hard
2 You read about my country in the newspapers.	hardly ever
3 It was a hard task that took a long time to finish.	unexpectedly
4 He walked into the room and clapped his hands.	slowly
5 They did the work on their own.	very well

》》→

6 There is not much news in the paper.   normally   on Saturday
7 We will hear the election results on TV.   definitely   on Sunday
8 We listen to the evening news on the radio.   always   during dinner

E   IT and THERE used at the beginning of a sentence

Look at these examples and fill the gaps. Notice the word order:

2,000 people were in the crowd.	→	There were 2,000 people in the crowd.
Everyone applauded at the end.	→	There was ....
John told me the news.	→	It was John who told me the news.
I didn't break the window.	→	It wasn't me who ....
The other person is to blame.	→	It's the other person who is to blame.
The tall man started the fight.	→	It was ....
Hearing only bad news is depressing.	→	It's depressing to hear only bad news.
Good news is also interesting to read.	→	It's also ....
They believe he will win the election.	→	It is believed that he will win the election.
People say that crime is increasing.	→	It is said ....

F   Rewrite these sentences, using the words on the right.

1 Rewriting sentences is not as easy as it looks.   It isn't ...
2 The election was won by the right-wing party.   It was ...
3 Thank you for helping me.   It was kind ...
4 You needn't read the paper unless you want to.   There's no ...
5 The policies of the two parties are very similar.   There isn't ...
6 Unexpectedly, the left-wing candidate was elected.   It was ...
7 Unfortunately, no one survived the air disaster.   There were ...
8 George Bush was elected President in 1988.   It was ...
9 100 people have been killed, according to reports.   It is believed ...
10 The weather is probably not going to change.   There will ...

'Yes, but is there any news of the iceberg?'

12.4 What happened?

Composition

As the Composition paper is the one that causes most candidates most difficulties, there are two composition sections in this unit.

A Work in pairs.
1 Look at these photographs and decide what's happening in each one. What happened before and what is likely to happen next?
2 Work out a story which includes at least THREE of these events within the same story. The people involved could include yourselves and/or friends of yours.

B In 45 minutes, without using a dictionary, write the story in 120–180 words.
- Make notes before you start.
- Check your work and correct any mistakes in spelling and grammar.
  (Remember to check verb forms and endings, prepositions and articles.)

★ In the exam, the examiner will be looking at:
how well you have communicated, how accurate your writing is, and the
variety of structures and vocabulary you have used.

But remember that short sentences and simple vocabulary may be more
effective than wrongly-used complicated sentences or misused 'advanced'
vocabulary – it may be better to keep your sentences short.

12.5   Better safe than sorry! *Listening*

A [cassette icon] You'll hear part of a talk about crime prevention. Choose the correct
alternatives and fill the gaps, according to the information given in the talk.

1 According to the speaker, ... of crimes are against property, not against people.
   80%   85%   90%   95%
2 A recent survey showed that .... of homes do not have window locks.
   6%   16%   60%   66%
3 .... of all burglars get in through windows.
   one third   one half   two thirds   three quarters
4 To increase the security of your home, you should make sure that ...
   a) you have .... on all windows.
   b) there is a lock on the .... that can only be opened and closed with a ....
   c) you have a .... on the front door.
   d) your property is ....
5 In Britain over .... cars are broken into or stolen each year.
   ½ million   1 million   1½ million   5 million
6 According to the speaker, if you regularly park your car in a city street, there is a
   .... chance it will be stolen or broken into.
   4%   20%   25%   40%
7 When you leave your car you should always ...
   a) lock all the .... and the ....
   b) take your .... with you or lock them in the ....
   c) close the .... completely.
   d) make sure you park in a .... street at night.
8 When you leave your bicycle don't use a combination lock because ...
   a) you may ....
   b) and it only takes a thief .... minutes to open one.

B   Work in small groups. Ask your partners these questions:
- What advice do you think the speaker gave the audience on personal safety?
- Suppose you wanted to reassure an old lady who is afraid of being
  attacked when she goes out. What advice would you give her?
- What are the commonest crimes that are committed in your city:
  theft, robbery, murder, mugging, shop-lifting, etc.?
- Which crimes are on the increase?

12.6 Opposites

Word study

A First, some revision. Write down the opposites of these words. The first two are done as examples:

accurate ↔ *inaccurate*   painful ↔ *painless*

accurate painful agree approve comfortable harmless honest
kind legal lucky polite regular relevant safe willing

B Now write down the opposites of these words. The first two are done as examples:

difficult ↔ *easy*   bright ↔ *dull*

difficult bright arrogant beautiful cheap cruel defeat fail
follow freeze hate ill lose noisy rude stale tight wide awake

C The opposites of some of these words are formed by adding a suffix or prefix, while others are different words. In some cases there may be more than one possibility. Look at the examples first:

ashamed ↔ *proud*   like ↔ *dislike, hate*

ashamed like cooked dangerous different fiction hollow
mature necessary oppose personal pleasant polite rough true
visible winner wrong

★ When you're writing a composition and you can't think of the right word to express your idea, try thinking of the OPPOSITE – it may help you to remember the right word. If not, leave a gap in your composition and come back to it later.

'Look, I'd sit down if I were you.
Have you got a drink? Now, it's
nothing to worry about, really it
isn't ...'

meteorologist

A Read the newspaper article and answer the questions on the next page.

Texas prepares for the worst

Michael White in Washington

ON network television yesterday a south Texas property developer stood on the still tranquil sea front at Corpus Christi and brushed **1** aside the alarm of city dwellers in the temperate north about the onslaught of Hurricane Gilbert.

"I'd rather be standing here . . . than sitting on a freeway in Los Angeles that could **2** be destroyed by an earthquake," he said.

Few parts of the US are free from brutal reminders of nature's power. Hailstones the size of a man's fist, tornadoes, **3** floods, droughts, fires, all reflect a weather system often at the mercy of tropical or Arctic extremes.

Unlike impoverished citizens of Jamaica or Yucatan, cleaning up yesterday after Gilbert's devastation, Americans enjoy all the benefits of satellite pictures and a communications network which **4** gives them ample time to flee the path of a storm and the means – cars and cash – to do so.

Nowadays most do and those who stay behind are warned that they are on their **5** own.

The death toll in Jamaica is now put at somewhere between nine and 25 – chiefly **6** by drowning – with widespread damage caused to airports and hotels.

Flimsier structures, inhabited by the poor, inevitably suffered most, with some estimates putting the homeless at 500,000 of the island's 2.5 million people, with 20 per cent of homes destroyed and 80 per **7** cent left roofless. Waves as high as 23 feet were reported. As relief supplies began arriving damage was estimated at $300 million. Sugar and banana farming also suffered badly.

Venezuela and the Dominican Republic were the first to suffer. The British dependency of the Cayman Islands **8** was also hit by the storm – which touched 175 mph on Tuesday. No lives were lost.

Mexico's Yucatan peninsula also sustained less damage than was expected, though at **9** least 25 people are feared dead and many more are missing.

As elsewhere on Gilbert's 1,800-mile westward path across the Caribbean – **10** including southern Cuba – tourists were removed to safety.

Yesterday Gilbert was crossing the Gulf of Mexico towards the Corpus Christi area – 300 miles south of Galveston – and, on present projections, was expected to **11** make a landfall by midmorning today on either the US or Mexican side of the Rio Grande basin whose major coastal town is Brownsville.

Described as "the mightiest storm to hit the Western hemisphere in this century," Gilbert's eye was described by air force weather analysts as unusually narrow, just eight **12** miles rather than 20–25 miles – and thus more like a tornado, a smaller but more devastating type of storm which arises on land.

The effect of a narrow low pressure eye, sucking warm wind from the ocean to altitudes of 50,000 feet, is to **13** intensify surrounding winds and with it the high waves which cause most death and damage.

The National Hurricane Centre on the frontline in **14** Miami is taking a very grave view.

The only other Category 5 hurricane to hit the US took 408 lives in Florida in 1935. In 1979 Hurricane David killed 3,000 in the Caribbean but **15** swept ashore harmlessly in South Carolina. Allen in 1980 killed 200 people in Haiti but only 28 in the US.

Yesterday people could be found planning to stay and sit out the experience because Allen had not been as bad as expected. "Everyone got **16** ready – and then, nothing," said another citizen of Corpus Christi. But by then most people had already left town.

Hurricane Gilbert's Path

Location Thursday:
22.0 N., 91.5 W.
Moving 15 mph, west northwest
120 mph maximum winds

Corpus Christi · Gulf of Mexico · Thursday · Yucatan Peninsula · Wednesday · Tuesday · Monday · Sunday · Saturday · Friday · CUBA · Atlantic Ocean · DOMINICAN REP. · PUERTO RICO

172

1 According to the person interviewed on TV in South Texas, ...
   a) Los Angeles is a less dangerous place than Texas
   ✓b) Texas is a less dangerous place than Los Angeles
   c) the hurricane will destroy the city
   d) hurricanes are not dangerous
2 In the USA, extreme weather conditions are experienced in ...
   a) all parts of the country   c) few parts of the country
   ✓b) almost all parts of the country   d) the northern states
3 American citizens are in a better position than Jamaicans because they have ...
   a) better roads and stronger houses
   b) better weather
   c) faster cars
   ✓d) transport and money to escape from a storm
4 Those Americans who don't escape from the storm are ...
   a) insured against the danger   c) unaware of the danger
   b) made aware of the danger   d) protected from the danger
5 According to the report, Hurricane Gilbert will reach the coast at around ...
   a) 8 a.m. today   c) 12 noon today
   b) 10 a.m. today   d) 2 p.m. today
6 A tornado usually ...
   a) ✓causes less damage than a hurricane   c) travels faster than a hurricane
   b) causes more damage than a hurricane   d) travels more slowly than a hurricane
7 When a hurricane strikes, most damage is caused by ...
   a) ✓high winds   b) falling trees and buildings   c) rain   d) the sea
8 In the past, hurricanes have killed ...
   a) fewer people on Caribbean islands than in the USA
   b) more people on Caribbean islands than in the USA
   c) the same number of people on Caribbean islands as in the USA
   d) very few people on Caribbean islands and in the USA
9 In 1980, Hurricane Allen turned out to be ...
   a) as serious as expected in the USA
   b) less serious than expected in the USA
   c) more serious than expected in the USA
   d) unexpectedly serious in the USA
10 The total number of lives lost in Hurricane Gilbert (up to the date of
    this report) is about ...
    a) 9   b) 25   c) 50   d) 200

B Find the words or phrases in the article that have the following
meanings. The numbers show which paragraph you should look at. The
first is done for you as an example:

quiet (1) tranquil   number of people killed (6)
refused to take seriously (1)   reach the coast (11)
attack (1)   make more extreme (13)
poor (4)   serious (14)

★ Remember that when you're reading a passage without a dictionary,
there are sure to be some words you don't understand. Always try to work
out their meaning from the context.

12.8 Exam practice

Make all the changes and additions necessary to produce sentences which make a complete story. The first is done for you as an example:

1 USA / many criminals become as famous / politicians.
  In the USA, many criminals have become as famous as politicians.
2 You hear / story / Edwin Chambers Dodson?
3 He be antique dealer / Hollywood / customers include / many famous film stars.
4 He lead / secret life / bank robber.
5 He rob more banks / any other man / American history.
6 He hold up more banks / Jesse James / Bonnie and Clyde.
7 He take part / 64 robberies / California and make $300,000.
8 He / be known / 'Yankee Bandit' because he wear / blue New York Yankees baseball cap / most / his robberies.
9 He / send / prison / 15 years after he plead guilty / eight robberies.
10 He still be / prison now.

★ In this kind of exercise there may be passives and other difficult verb forms to cope with. Make sure you check your completed sentences through, just as carefully as you check your composition.

12.9 Here is the news ...   *Listening*

     You'll hear a news broadcast. Decide whether the following statements are true (T) or false (F), according to the broadcast.

1 The drug arrests in Bolivia were made in the north of the country.
2 The arrests were part of a joint operation between Bolivia, the USA and the UN.
3 Three planes crashed during the operation.
4 Nearly 2½ tons of cocaine were found by the authorities.
5 In Europe more storms are expected soon.
6 In 24 hours there should be no more delays with air traffic.
7 In 24 hours there should be no more problems on the roads.
8 Next weekend is a holiday and traffic will be held up.
9 Damage in France is estimated to be over 15,000 million francs.
10 No foreign cars can travel through Switzerland during the weekend.
11 The hijackers of the airliner left the plane late last night.
12 The plane will be flown back to Athens by Captain Georgiou.
13 129 people were held hostage during the hijacking.
14 The hijackers have already left Algiers.
15 Prices of shares in Tokyo have gone up.

A   When you're writing a composition that asks you to give your opinion about a topic, you'll probably need to explain what you mean.
Write two more sentences, adding an explanation or reason to each opinion.

1   I hardly ever read a newspaper ...
   because I find that I get a much better picture of what is going on in the world by watching the news on television. Television news is also much more up-to-date than a newspaper and only the most important items of news are reported.
2   It would/would not be a better world if there were no nuclear weapons ...
3   Nuclear power stations are a good/bad thing because ...
4   The government should change/not change the law on drugs ...
5   If a criminal has committed a very serious crime ...
6   The only solution to terrorism ...

B   Here are four typical exam questions. Work in pairs and make notes of the points you could make if you wrote these compositions:

1   How does the problem of pollution affect your country and what can be done to improve the situation?

2   Should young people take a break of one or two years between leaving school and continuing with further education?

3   Very few women are members of parliament or government ministers. Why is this so and should it be changed?

4   What do you think of the view, expressed in some countries, that marriage is going out of fashion?

C   Write 120–180 words on ONE of these topics beginning as follows:

1   'One of the most serious problems facing the world today is ...'

2   'One of the most serious problems facing my country today is ...'

3   'I read in the paper/heard on the news that ...' (Choose a topic or event that is in the news at the moment and give your opinions about it.)

As in 12.4, time yourself as you write this composition. With this kind of composition, it's absolutely essential to make notes before you start writing. And don't forget to check your completed work through when you've finished.

★   The examiner will be assessing the quality of your English, not your ideas. But if you ignore the question and introduce irrelevant material (or include a passage you seem to have learnt by heart), you will lose marks.

12.11 Exam practice

★ The purpose of the Interview in the exam is to give the examiner a chance to hear you speaking English. If you don't say very much (because you're feeling shy or nervous) the examiner won't be able to hear how good your English normally sounds. That's why it's essential to do some practice interviews 'under exam conditions'.

Work in pairs for these activities and imagine you're taking part in the exam. One of you could play the role of examiner, perhaps. 🔲

A

Answer these questions about the photographs:
- What's happening in the pictures?
- What do you think has just happened?
- What do you think will happen next?
- How do you think each of the people is feeling?
- Which of the people would you support in such a situation?
- What could you say to each of them if you were there?
- How often do such things happen in your country?

B   Look at these newspaper headlines. Which of the articles would you be interested in reading and why? What do you think each article is about?

Royal baby shock
Film star's guilty secret
800 metre record broken
Peace talks break down
Jumbo crashes in Mediterranean
Prime minister dies in air disaster
Hurricane hits Mexico
Holiday sunshine traps drivers in nationwide traffic jams

C   Look at these cases where the law is being broken.

1 Put them in ORDER of seriousness and explain the REASONS why you consider some to be less serious than others.

2 What PUNISHMENT do you think should be given to someone who breaks the law in each case? (If you think 'it all depends', what does it depend on?)

- A motorist drives faster than the permitted maximum speed
- A passenger travels by train without a ticket
- A motorist parks on a double yellow line
- A motorist isn't wearing a seat belt
- A gang of youths attack an old lady and take her purse
- Someone keeps your wallet which fell from your pocket
- A group of terrorists kill one of their hostages
- An office worker takes some stationery home from the office
- A motorist drives after drinking a couple of glasses of wine
- A burglar breaks into your flat and steals your valuables
- A company doesn't declare all its income for tax
- A shopper takes some goods from a large department store without paying
- A husband kills his wife's lover
- A motorist drives after drinking a whole bottle of wine
- A student sells drugs to fellow students

12.12   *Have* and *give*   *Verbs and idioms*

A   Which of the endings below go with these beginnings? Some of them go with more than one of the beginnings, sometimes with a different meaning:

Alex had …	**Charlie gave us** …
Barry was having …	**Carol gave** …

a quarrel with Tim   an order   a sigh   a good time   permission
a good performance   a meal   a drink   his/her opinion   a headache
his/her hair cut   a chance   a look   an interview   a good idea
the information   never been abroad   an accident   a rest   a swim
the details   a newspaper   no imagination   better be careful

B   Fill the gaps with suitable forms of the phrasal verbs below:

give
1 When I'd read the books I .... them .... to her.
2 Smoking again? I thought you .... smoking.
3 A man was standing on the corner .... leaflets to everyone.
4 This information is secret, don't .... it .... to anyone.
5 The criminal .... himself .... to the police.
6 Check your work through before .... it .... at the end of the exam.
7 After a bloody battle, the defeated army .... and peace talks began.
   have
8 He .... his best suit .... for the interview.
9 When you've finished with the cassette, I'd like to .... it .... again.
10 It's been very nice .... you .... Do come and see us again!

give away   give back   give in   give in   give out   give up   give up
have round   have on   have back

13 People

13.1 It takes all sorts . . .   *Vocabulary*

A Work in small groups. Ask your partners these questions:
- What kind of person do you think you are?
- What sign of the zodiac were you born under? Do you think this affects your character?
- What kind of people do you get on with best?
- What kind of people do you find it hard to get on with?

B Choose the word or phrase that best completes each sentence.

1 She's a very .... person – always smiling and in a good mood.
  cheerful delighted glad pleased
2 He's a very .... person – I wish he was a bit more easy-going.
  bad-tempered furious mad wild
3 Don't tell her off – she's very .... and she may start to cry.
  responsive sensible sensitive sympathetic
4 People enjoy his company because he's extremely ....
  adorable likeable lovable sympathetic
5 If you've got a problem, go and talk to her – I'm sure she'll be ....
  patient sympathetic tolerant warm-hearted
6 He has excellent taste in clothes and always dresses ....
  cleanly healthily smartly tastily
7 When his wife started seeing more of the tennis coach, he became very ....
  arrogant envious jealous selfish
8 The twins keep pretending to be each other – they're such .... children!
  evil miserable naughty wicked
9 Thank you for my beautiful present. It was very .... of you to buy it for me.
  charitable generous loyal reliable
10 If you give him a message make sure he writes it down because he's very ....
  absent forgetful mindless preoccupied
11 You have to be quite .... to stand up in front of an audience.
  self-confident self-conscious selfish self-satisfied
12 She's a very .... little girl – her parents give her everything she asks for.
  consented discriminating generous spoilt
13 He's a dreadful person – I can't .... him.
  stand suffer support swallow
14 Everyone agrees that he's a very .... man.
  beautiful gorgeous handsome pretty
15 When she first went to work in another city, she felt very ....
  abandoned alone lonely single

178

16 Most people feel .... before an examination.
absent-minded anxious eager nervy

17 How long has Sarah been .... with Peter?
going back going in going out going up

18 They fell in love at first ....
glimpse look sight viewing

19 How long have they been .... ? 妇闭一次婚 (to (betrothal)
betrothed engaged financed intended

20 When are they going to .... ?
get married marry them marry each other marry themselves

21 Peter has asked Michael to be his .... at the wedding. 思信枘 bridesmaid
best man bridesmaid eyewitness godfather

22 Sarah has invited all her .... to the wedding.
compatriots in-laws parents relations 亲属

23 Her parents have been married for 25 years and today is their .... ?
anniversary birthday jubilee marriage

24 The people in the flat upstairs are always having noisy ....
debates discussions noises rows

25 When her mother remarried, she got on very well with her new ....
ancestor forefather foster-father step-father

26 A diagram that shows the members of a family and their relationship is called a
family ....
branch line river tree

★ In the exam there may be two answers that both appear to you to make
sense in the context provided – if in doubt, choose the one that fits BEST.

C Work in pairs. Draw your own family trees, showing your
grandparents, uncles and aunts, brothers and sisters, nieces and nephews.
Then join another pair and tell them about your partner's family, while
your partner tells them about yours.

D Work in small groups. Describe the following people, but not in this
order. DON'T name them because your partners should try to guess the
name of each person you describe, or their relationship to you.

● One of your favourite relatives
● A well-known public figure
● One of your closest friends
● Someone your partners don't know
● One of your favourite film stars, singers or musicians

E Work in small groups. What qualities do you admire most in other
people?
Put these qualities into order of importance:

Ambition	Creativity	Good looks
Honesty	Independence	Intelligence
Loyalty	Sense of humour	Strength
Tenderness	Understanding	Warmth

● What other important qualities are missing from this list?

13.2   What is Dateline? *Reading*

A   Read this text and answer the multiple-choice questions on the next page.

What is **Dateline**

Dateline is the computer dating service that takes the chance element out of man-woman relations. In a single flash of electronic brilliance it provides a supply of partners who are absolutely right for you — partners whose looks and conversation appeal to you from the first and with whom you feel quickly at ease, friends who are likely to grow closer with every meeting.

How's it done? Simple. By taking careful note of what you are like and following your guidance on the kind of man or woman you get along best with, we select, from the tens of thousands of profiles in our store exactly those who are destined to be your kindred spirits.

There's nothing magic about it. It's a matter of applying science to nature. By the laws of probability there are certainly people in the world who are physically and mentally right for you, just as there are stars in the universe similar to ours. All one has to do is to find them. Dateline has the unique power — thanks to modern computer science — of finding the few-in-thousands who can communicate with you at a deep level of understanding.

■ The Age We Live In

Dateline — the most significant advance in modern relations between the sexes. It is part of the new life-style. It combines all that is new and socially advanced with the traditional ideas of restraint and integrity that belong to any organisation dealing in personal relationships.

Take the Dateline questionnaire. It has been carefully compiled with the aid of experts in psychology and social sciences, using the most up-to-date research of British and American universities, to provide the most accurate and least prying method of assessing personalities.

Take the Dateline computer system. It's a variation on the systems used for launching missiles and rationalising the operations of banks. You can't get more accurate or more impartial than that. It's our own computer too, programmed and operated only by our own experts.

Altogether Dateline is the most exciting social

advance for single people since the granting of the vote. Join it and your days will really come alive.

■ The Shifting Society

Social life is changing more rapidly than ever before. The older generation spent their lives more or less in one place.

School, work and family life grew out of the same environment people were born in. You knew everyone in your district and it wasn't too difficult to pick the friends who suited you, and who shared your interests. Even so, when society was more static the opportunities for widening your circle were still restricted, and life wasn't so varied as it is today.

Now we're in the space age. The old 'school-work-early marriage' syndrome is disappearing. A whole new generation of mobile young people is at large in the world. They're people with initiative, independent of their home background, able to change jobs and locations, to take up studies and pastimes, and to pursue their careers all over Britain and overseas if they want to. Many do just that, taking their freedom in both hands and making the most of the world's opportunities. Dateline is for them, and in this case, 'them' means you.

■ What Sort of People join Dateline?

Everyone joins Dateline: showbiz personalities, artists, Lords, musicians, soldiers, cooks, stockbrokers, property-men, models, nurses, athletes, business executives of all kinds, teachers, secretaries, students, librarians, dancers. The only qualification you need is to be unmarried.

Most of our members are busy, successful, intelligent people with enquiring minds and varied interests. They've usually got plenty of their own friends, who, perhaps, they know too well to get romantic about. Others, through pressure of work, or through a shy disposition, or because they find themselves in a strange new career environment, are short of interesting company, and want to make a fresh social start. Through Dateline they can do it. Dateline puts you in touch with new faces, a different crowd, and completely refreshes your social life.

180

More important for many people is the scientifically-based probability of meeting the man or woman you've always dreamed about, and simply falling in love. Yes, it does happen: so frequently you shouldn't be surprised when it hits you personally. Every week Dateline receives scores of letters from happy couples matched by our computer. Already more than ten thousand known marriages can be attributed to Dateline, and perhaps thousands more that we haven't been told about.

■ How Do You Join Dateline?

Complete our questionnaire. Designed by experts in computer sciences and psychology, it takes about 15 minutes to fill in, longer if you're in an extra-thoughtful mood, but it's fun. The 200 questions are very thorough and for a good reason. The more you tell us about yourself and the kind of people you most like, the more accurate our computer can be and the closer to your ideal will be your dates.

■ What Kind of Questions?

First, basic straightforward questions on your age, physical build, appearance and social background. Then a few on education, social habits and occupation. Next a chance to list all your special interests. And finally, the personality test in three parts. There's also a space for any additional information about yourself that you care to give.

Side by side with the profile of yourself formed by the answers to this set of questions, you fill in a profile of your chosen man or girl, marking the qualities you prefer from the list given. All this careful planning goes a long way to ensure that the people you meet through Dateline will be exactly your kind.

Send for your questionnaire, and from there on, Dateline takes over.

1 Finding your ideal partner is like finding
   A a needle in a haystack. 干草堆   C the answer to your prayers.
   B a star like ours in the universe.   D 50 pence when you've lost 10 pence.
2 Dateline's computer will find you a partner who
   A looks like you.   C will laugh at your jokes.
   B will like you.   D looks attractive.
3 Dateline's computer is
   A only used by Dateline's own staff.   C also used by banks.
   B also used for launching missiles.   D only used for arranging dates.
4 Life nowadays is different because
   A older people don't move around much.
   B young people have the vote.
   C young people travel abroad a lot.
   D marriages happen later in life.
5 Compared with the past, it is now
   A less difficult to find friends.   C much more difficult to find friends.
   B much easier to find friends.   D no more difficult to find friends.
6 The world is full of
   A accidents for young people.   C jobs for young people.
   B chances for young people.   D risks for young people.
7 Most of Dateline's members
   A have too many friends.   C dislike their acquaintances.
   B are lonely.   D have lots of friends.
8 Dateline couples
   A generally fall in love.   C sometimes fall in love.
   B regularly fall in love.   D often fall in love.
9 Dateline is responsible for thousands of marriages
   A a day. B a week. C a month. D a year.
10 In the questionnaire there are 200
   A accurate questions.   C exhaustive questions.
   B complete questions.   D nosy questions.

B Work in small groups. Look at this coupon and then ask your partners the questions below.

```
┌─────────────────────────────────────────────────────────────────────┐
│  FREE                    ● 'All you need is love' (a Sphere paperback) — stories of real │
│                            people matching and meeting through Dateline.                  │
│  START HERE ▼1           ● A full colour guide to how Dateline can work for you.          │
│  I am over 17            ● Details of just one of the many Dateline members who could    │
│  Single ⌐Widowed ⌐Divorced ⌐   be your 'Perfect Partner'.                                 │
│  (gender) Your Sex ⌐ put M or F          I enclose 3 first class stamps.                  │
│  Your Height ⌐ft ⌐ ins.                                                                    │
│  Your age ⌐ yrs          2 Tick ✓ which     3 Tick ✓ those activities you enjoy, put a   │
│  Age you would like to meet ⌐ min    characteristics best    X against those you dislike, and leave │
│  BLOCK CAPITALS ⌐ max    describe you.      blank those where you have no preference. X   │
│  First Name _____                                                                         │
│  Surname _____          ARE YOU:          DO YOU ENJOY:                                  │
│  Address _____          Warmhearted       Wine bars/Eating out  Jazz/Folk music         │
│  _____                  Serious           Pubs                  Classical music          │
│  _____                  Considerate       Sports/Keep Fit       Theatre/Arts             │
│  _____                  Shy               Politics/History      Watching TV              │
│  _____                  Romantic          Reading               Smoking                  │
│  _____                  Fashion conscious Travelling            Drinking                 │
│                          Practical         Science/Technology    Being with children      │
│                          Conventional      Cinema                Homemaking               │
│                          Reliable          Pets/Animals          Gardening                │
│  Occupation _____       Adventurous       Pop/Rock music        Countryside              │
│  Religion _____         Dateline  Dept ( SEN )  23 Abingdon Rd.                          │
│                                            London W8 6AH. Tel: 01 938 1011.               │
└─────────────────────────────────────────────────────────────────────┘
       THE WORLD'S LARGEST AND MOST SUCCESSFUL AGENCY
```

- Would you be honest about filling it in? Or would you make yourself out to be more attractive, interesting or intelligent?
- Can one find a perfect partner for life through an agency like Dateline?
- Is it possible to find a perfect partner for life by an arranged marriage (where your spouse is chosen by your parents)?

13.3 Difficult questions   *Grammar*

A Rewrite the sentences in such a way that they still mean the same:

1 You should be very careful.	You'd better ...
2 I'm not very happy.	I wish ...
3 Please use a dictionary.	I'd like ...*to*
4 You told me to do that.	It was ...
5 It's advisable to arrive a few minutes early.	I suggest ...
6 Why haven't you done the work yet?	It's time ...

Did you find those tricky? Well, questions like those do come up in the Use of English paper. If you try to remember the grammar points in this section, you should be able to cope with questions like those. But don't forget that losing a couple of marks on questions like those may not be a great disaster – it's the questions you CAN answer that will help you to succeed in the exam.

B Look at these examples and fill the gaps with your own ideas:

bare infinitive

better AND best

You'd (had) better do some revision.   = You should / I strongly advise you to ...
It's better to revise carefully than trust to luck.   = better of two alternatives

182

It'd (would) be better to do question 2 before 1.   = better of two alternatives
It's best to make notes before you start writing.   = best of several alternatives
You .... several pens to the exam, not just one.
It .... the answer than to leave a blank space if you don't know.
It .... early on the day of the exam.

I'd rather / prefer / like

I'd (would) rather wear a sweater than a jacket. *(bare infinitive)*
I'd rather you didn't smoke in here. *(Simple past)*
We'd prefer you not to smoke, if you don't mind.
They wouldn't like you to use a dictionary.
Would you rather I .... today or tomorrow? *?*
Would you like me .... for you?

wish, if only AND hope

He wishes he were/was more intelligent.
He wishes (that) he had worked harder, but it's too late now.
I wish they wouldn't smoke – it makes me cough.
I wish to make a complaint.   Who do you wish to speak to?
She wishes she .... on holiday.
I wish .... more time before the exam, but there isn't.
If only there wasn't/weren't so little time left!
If only we .... in advance what questions would be asked!
I hope to get the job.   I hope (that) I get the job.
I hope we all ....

It's time

It's time to go home.   It's time we went home.
It's time .... some revision.   It's time .... a break.

suggest

I suggest (that) you (should) use a dictionary.
He suggested using a dictionary.
They suggested .... not worry about the exam.
What do you suggest .... after it's all over?

C   Rewrite these sentences, beginning with the words on the right.
1 Please don't interrupt me when I'm speaking.   I'd rather ...
2 It would be a good idea to phone and ask for information.   We suggest you ...
3 Don't be so frank – be tactful.   It's much better ...
4 Please let me know your decision today, not tomorrow.   I'd prefer ...
5 Staying at home would be better than going out tonight.   I'd rather ...
6 Please fill in this questionnaire.   I'd like ...
7 We ought to find out how much it's going to cost.   It's time we ...
8 They should book early if they want tickets for the concert.   They'd better ...
9 I've got so much to do today.   I wish ...
10 What a shame you didn't tell me earlier!   If only ...

★ If there are a few difficult questions you can't answer in the exam,
DON'T PANIC – just leave a blank, put a pencil mark in the margin to
remind you where they are and come back to them later. Rub out the
pencil mark.

13.4 Synonyms

Word study

A Look at these examples. What is the difference between them?

1 She's a very *nice* person. It was *nice* of her to help me and she was *nice* to you too, wasn't she?
2 She's a very *likeable* person. For example, it was *kind* of her to help me and she was *friendly* to you too, wasn't she?

★ Some words that are perfectly all right in conversation are best avoided if you want to make your writing more interesting.

B Work in pairs.

1 Write down at least TWO synonyms that can be used in place of:
 nice good bad thing like dislike

2 Write down at least TWO synonyms you can use instead of these adjectives (to avoid having to repeat the same word in a paragraph):
 large small important intelligent interesting strange
 unpleasant beautiful

3 Write five sentences for your partner (or for another pair) to rewrite more interestingly or more clearly.
4 Join another pair and compare your ideas.

C Sometimes you may not be able to think of exactly the right word you need:
 'The carpenter wanted to tighten the screws, so he used a you know, a whatchamacallit.'
 But it's sometimes possible to use another word which still shows what you mean:
 'He used a special tool to tighten up the screws.'

In these examples, what is the word that can be used to describe all the items in the list? The first is done for you as an example:

screwdriver hammer spanner **tools**

sister cousin uncle	suit socks sweater
bread cake meat	dollar pound franc
grass cactus bush	rugby tennis squash
rabbit lion mouse	photography stamp-collecting reading
lamb beef chicken	medicine law accountancy
bus train lorry	parrot goldfish cat
house flat room hotel	wheat rye oats
parrot sparrow pigeon	rose carnation daisy
copper steel iron	ant bee wasp
breakfast supper lunch	book newspaper brochure
autumn spring winter	

184

13.5 'Due to a computer error...' *Problem solving*

The problem:

Six people joined a computer dating service but there was a computer error. Instead of giving them their perfect partners, it matched them with partners who had the same initials! Not realising this, all the people turned up for their first dates with high hopes.

A Work in pairs. Discuss these questions and make notes:
- How badly mismatched were the couples, do you think?
- What did they have in common and how well do you think they got on?

Name ANDREW APPLEBY Age 29
Occupation: CIVIL SERVANT
How would you describe yourself?
  CREATIVE, OUTDOOR TYPE
What do you enjoy? POLITICS,
  CLASSICAL MUSIC, TRAVELLING,
  GOOD FOOD
What do you dislike?
  POP MUSIC, JAZZ, PUBS, DISCOS

Name ANNE AMIS Age 25
Occupation: SECONDARY SCHOOL
  TEACHER
How would you describe yourself?
  PRACTICAL, OUTDOOR TYPE, SHY
What do you enjoy?
  SPORT, FOLK MUSIC, READING,
  TRAVEL
What do you dislike?
  POLITICS, JAZZ, FASHION,
  MEANNESS

Name BILL BANKS Age 34
Occupation: ACCOUNTANT
How would you describe yourself?
  EXTROVERT, PRACTICAL
What do you enjoy?
  GOOD FOOD, TRAVEL, PUBS, SPORT
What do you dislike?
  POETRY, CLASSICAL MUSIC,
  READING, ART

Name BRENDA BOOTH Age 24
Occupation: MEDICAL STUDENT
How would you describe yourself?
  CREATIVE, ADVENTUROUS,
  EXTROVERT
What do you enjoy?
  POP MUSIC, FASHION,
  CONVERSATION
What do you dislike?
  SPORT, POETRY, JAZZ

Name COLIN COOMBS Age 24
Occupation: ART COLLEGE LECTURER
How would you describe yourself?
  SHY, CREATIVE, PRACTICAL
What do you enjoy?
  MUSIC (ALL TYPES), READING,
  SPORT
What do you dislike?
  TELEVISION, PUBS, POETRY

Name CAROLE CLARKE Age 19
Occupation: LAW STUDENT
How would you describe yourself?
  GENEROUS, SHY, OUTDOOR TYPE
What do you enjoy?
  READING, ART, POP MUSIC,
  POLITICS
What do you dislike?
  SPORT, CLASSICAL MUSIC,
  SCIENCE

B Write four paragraphs of about 50 words each, based on your discussion in A, beginning:

'On their first date, Andrew and Anne ...'
'Although Bill and Brenda ...'
'Colin and Carole probably ...'
'Of the people described, the one I'd most like to meet myself is ......
because ...'

13.6 Using your brain

You'll hear part of a talk about the human brain. Answer the questions below.

callosum corpus

1 The left-hand side of the brain normally controls the .... side of the body.
2 What functions do the two hemispheres of the brain control?

LEFT (rational side)理性面、推理   RIGHT (irrational side) 无理的
language   rhythm

....
linearity ['liniæriti] 线性,直线性 ....
analysis
                                            ....
....   space: three dimensions
                                            seeing .... of things as a whole
....
sequencing

3 In left-handed people, these priorities are often ....
4 The .... is the link between the two hemispheres.
   It is the key to ....
5 The first question the speaker suggests you ask in the experiment is: 'What's
   ....?'
6 The second question is: 'What piece of furniture is ....?'
7 While someone is trying to answer the first question they will .... to prevent
   themselves being distracted by ....
8 Unfortunately, the experiment will not be successful if they ....
9 As we get older our memories ....
10 You forget things more easily if your brain doesn't have enough .... or ....
11 Your brain can deteriorate if you don't get enough .... or if your .... is
    unhealthy.
12 The three Golden Rules of brain power are:
   1 Use your senses and don't only think .... Imagine a problem ....
   2 Use .... of your brain.
   3 Don't say .... because your brain is .... as anyone else's.

★ In the exam, if you haven't got time to write a complete answer down
during the first listening, just write the first few words and come back to it
later. Otherwise you may not hear the answer to the next question.

A   Read this text and answer the multiple-choice questions on the next page.

CHAPTER ONE

My first impression was that the stranger's eyes were of an unusually light blue. They met mine for several blank seconds, vacant, unmistakably scared. Startled and innocently naughty, they half reminded me of an incident I couldn't quite place; something which had happened a long time ago, to do with the upper fourth form classroom. They were the eyes of a schoolboy surprised in the act of breaking one of the rules. Not that I had caught him, apparently, at anything except his own thoughts: perhaps he imagined I could read them. At any rate, he seemed not to have heard or seen me cross the compartment from my corner to his own, for he started violently at the sound of my voice; so violently, indeed, that his nervous recoil hit me like repercussion. Instinctively I took a pace backwards.

It was exactly as though we had collided with each other bodily in the street. We were both confused, both ready to be apologetic. Smiling, anxious to reassure him, I repeated my question:

'I wonder, sir, if you could let me have a match?'

Even now, he didn't answer at once. He appeared to be engaged in some sort of rapid mental calculation, while his fingers, nervously active, sketched a number of flurried gestures round his waistcoat. For all they conveyed, he might equally have been going to undress, to draw a revolver, or merely to make sure that I hadn't stolen his money. Then the moment of agitation passed from his gaze like a little cloud, leaving a clear blue sky. At last he had understood what it was that I wanted:

'Yes, yes. Er – certainly. Of course.'

As he spoke he touched his left temple delicately with his finger-tips, coughed and suddenly smiled. His smile had great charm. It disclosed the ugliest teeth I had ever seen. They were like broken rocks.

'Certainly,' he repeated. 'With pleasure.'

Delicately, with finger and thumb, he fished in the waistcoat-pocket of his expensive-looking soft grey suit, extracted a gold spirit-lighter. His hands were white, small and beautifully manicured.

I offered him my cigarettes.

'Er – thank you. Thank you.'

'After you, sir.'

'No, no. Please.'

The tiny flame of the lighter flickered between us, as perishable as the atmosphere which our exaggerated politeness had created. The merest breath would have extinguished the one, the least incautious gesture or word would have

>>>→

destroyed the other. The cigarettes were both lighted now. We sat back in our respective places. The stranger was still doubtful of me. He was wondering whether he hadn't gone too far, delivered himself to a bore or a crook. His timid soul was eager to retire. I, on my side, had nothing to read. I foresaw a journey of utter silence, lasting seven or eight hours. I was determined to talk.

'Do you know what time we arrive at the frontier?'

Looking back on the conversation, this question does not seem to me to have been particularly unusual. It is true that I had no interest in the answer; I wanted merely to ask something which might start us chatting, and which wasn't, at the same *t*͘ either inquisitive or impertinent. Its effect on the remarkable. I had certainly succeeded in arous-

1 The stranger at first looked
   A frightened. B harmless. C shocked. D surprised.
2 When the writer first spoke, the stranger
   A gasped. B got up. C jumped. D screamed.
3 The writer had
   A sat down beside the stranger.   C walked across to the stranger.
   B sat down opposite the stranger.   D walked up behind the stranger.
4 The writer asked the stranger for a light
   A once. B twice. C three times. D four times.
5 Before the stranger replied, he
   A adjusted his waistcoat.   C thought for a while.
   B looked for his lighter.   D wondered if the writer was a thief.
6 The stranger gave the writer a
   A delicate smile. B nervous smile. C pleasant smile. D wicked smile.
7 The writer gave the stranger
   A a cigarette. B a light. C a reassuring smile. D his hand.
8 The stranger seemed to be afraid that the writer might be a
   A dull companion. B murderer. C foreigner. D policeman.
9 The writer wanted to start a conversation because he
   A found the stranger fascinating.   C had nothing else to do.
   B found the stranger interesting.   D respected the stranger.
10 The meeting described in the passage took place
   A in a café. B on a bus or coach. C on a plane. D on a train.

B   Work in small groups. In your own words, describe the stranger. Then ask your partners these questions:
- Why would you have chosen or not chosen to start a conversation with the stranger?
- Have you ever had a conversation with a total stranger on a long journey or in a public place? How did the conversation start and what did you talk about?
- How usual is it for people to start speaking to strangers on trains or buses in your country?

★ If you don't know the answer in a multiple-choice test, you should guess – remember that you have a one-in-four chance of guessing right!

A, C, C B, C C, A, A, C, D

13.8 Exam practice

Passage with gaps

Fill each gap with ONE WORD only.

The first thing you notice *1* .... him is his smile. He's slim, quite tall and very athletic. He talks fast and is very funny. He's *2* .... actor, but he usually plays the same kind *3* .... roles. *4* .... fact, it's difficult to separate the character *5* .... the man *6* .... the characters he plays *7* .... his films. You know that he's going to win every argument and get *8* .... of any difficult situation *9* .... getting hurt. He's *10* .... of today's most popular American film stars.

You can't help *11* .... impressed by her good looks and her voice. Her style is modern and *12* .... clothes are always very unusual: she sets the fashion *13* .... than following it. She's not only *14* .... popular with young people, but she's so talented *15* .... even older people appreciate her. The break-up of her *16* .... came as no surprise to anyone – she *17* .... so much publicity that it's impossible for someone *18* .... her to have a private *19* .... When ordinary people have similar problems, it's only their friends and *20* .... who get to hear about it.

13.9 Five students

Listening

A 🔊 You'll hear a conversation between two English teachers. Barbara is telling Chris about some of her students who will be joining his class. As you listen, note down her comments on each student.

	Appearance	Good points	But be careful!
PAUL	*Tall,*	*Helpful,*	*Makes mistakes,*
SUSAN			
MARIA			
HELEN			
PETER			

B Work in small groups. How do you think your teacher would describe each of YOU to a colleague?

C 📺 Work in pairs. One of you should look at Activity 38, the other at 49. You'll each have a picture of people to describe to your partner.

13.10 Describing people *Composition*

A It's generally easier to write short sentences rather than long ones. Often short sentences are easier to read and understand too.
Which of these three paragraphs do you prefer?

1 He is a tall dark-haired man with attractive brown eyes, whose clothes are always smart and who always behaves charmingly even when people are not pleasant to him.
2 He is a tall dark-haired man with attractive brown eyes. His clothes are always smart. He always behaves charmingly even when people are not pleasant to him.
3 He is a tall dark-haired man. He has attractive brown eyes. He always wears smart clothes. He always behaves charmingly. People are not always nice to him.

B Write four short paragraphs, using these ideas:

1 He is ... overweight mid thirties selfish dishonest
  loses his temper people disagree with him
2 She is ... thin late fifties absent-minded
  delightful sense of humour helps other people with problems
3 He is ... 18 athletic loves sport favourite game football
  spare time: going out with friends + going to cinema
4 She is ... 16 studious enjoys reading 4 brothers + 2 sisters
  hopes to go to university wants to study engineering

★ In questions like 1 to 3 in C below, the examiner is interested in how well you can express yourself, not in how truthful you are. Imaginary ideas may be more interesting or easier to describe. Try to use words you know, and don't experiment with words you're unsure of.
  For example, you could describe a wonderful imaginary aunt in 3 or write about an exciting imaginary meeting in 1 – you needn't even tell the truth about yourself in 2! (NB: In 4 below, you do have to tell the truth.)

C Write 120 to 180 words on TWO of these topics:

1 Describe your first meeting with someone who became a close friend OR who later became an enemy.
2 Write a letter to a new pen friend. Imagine this is your first letter and give your friend a good idea of your appearance, interests and personality.
3 Describe two people you admire or like OR two people you dislike very much. Explain why you feel this way about these people.
4 If you have read one of the prescribed books, explain which of the characters you liked best OR which of the characters you found least attractive.

Write the two compositions together in $1\frac{1}{2}$ hours or separately in 45 minutes each. Don't use a dictionary.
● Make notes before you start.
● Decide how you will begin and end each composition.
● Check your work through afterwards.

13.11 That's a problem!

Interview exercises

A Work in small groups. Look at these pictures. What's going on? What
has happened? How can the people solve their problems?

B ◼️ Work in groups of three. Student A should look at Activity 31,
student B at 36 and C at 50. You'll each have a problem, which your
partners must help you to solve.

Here are some useful expressions:

> *Why don't you … ?*
> *You could …*
> *If I were you I'd …*
> *The best thing to do would be …*

> *That wouldn't work because …*
> *That's not really possible because …*
> *I'd like to do that but I can't, because …*

13.12   Grammar revision

A   Rewrite each sentence, starting with the words given below.

1 You must be more polite to people.
    It's ....

2 She wrote me a letter to tell me she never wanted to see me again.
    The letter ....

3 He's so dull that people fall asleep while he's talking.
    He's such ....

4 Although she's the daughter of a rich man, he doesn't want to marry her.
    In spite ....

5 You'll lose touch with him unless you write to him.
    If ....

6 'I'm leaving and I'm never coming back!' she said to me.
    She told ....

7 She's much more amusing than her brother.
    Her brother ....

8 They first met ten years ago.
    They have ....

9 During her husband's absence she was very lonely.
    While ....

10 He's a liar and a cheat but everyone still seems to like him.
     Everyone ....

B   Complete the unfinished sentences in this dialogue.

Chris: Hi, Robin.
Robin: Hello, Chris, what's up? Are 1 .... ?
Chris: Not really, no. I feel a bit depressed.
Robin: Oh dear. Why 2 .... ?
Chris: It's my family again. My Uncle George is staying with us again.
Robin: I see, but what 3 .... ?
Chris: Oh, *he's* all right. It's just that my father doesn't get on with him.
             If they're in the same room one of them starts an argument.
Robin: Can't 4 .... ?
Chris: They wouldn't take any notice of me. And to make matters worse,
             Uncle George is sleeping on the spare bed in my room.
Robin: Why 5 .... ?
Chris: He snores and I can't get to sleep.
Robin: How 6 .... ?
Chris: He arrived on Sunday.
Robin: And how 7 .... ?
Chris: Another three weeks at least. Until he gets another ship.
Robin: What 8 .... ?
Chris: He's a merchant seaman. He always stays here when he's on leave.
Robin: Well, you'd better 9 .... ?
Chris: Yes, I'll have to, I suppose! I'm going to be spending a lot of time
             away from home, until he goes back to sea.
Robin: You could 10 .... ?
Chris: Really? That'd be wonderful. Thanks a lot.

14 The past

The exercises in this unit are organised in the same order as in the exam:

14.1 to 14.3 will help you to revise for Paper 1 Reading Comprehension.
14.4 will help you to revise for Paper 2 Composition.
14.5 to 14.9 will help you to revise for Paper 3 Use of English.
14.10 to 14.12 will help you to revise for Paper 4 Listening Comprehension.
14.13 will help you to revise for Paper 5 Interview.

14.1   Vocabulary and grammar   *Reading comprehension*

The first part of Paper 1 consists of 25 questions on vocabulary and on grammar. In the exam, allow yourself at least 25 minutes for this exercise – each question is worth one mark out of a total of 55 for the whole of Paper 1.

1   If you can't remember, let me try to .... your memory.
     A arouse   B awaken   C refresh   D stimulate
2   Most of what she learnt at school she's now ....
     A forgotten   B lost   C mislaid   D omitted
3   Aristotle was alive in the fourth century ....
     A AC   B BC   C CD   D DC
4   Her husband claims he is a(n) .... of Queen Victoria.
     A ancestor   B descendant   C follower   D heir
5   Queen Victoria's been dead for about 90 years, ...?
     A has she   B hasn't she   C is she   D isn't she
6   The castle was built in the 12th century and the church beside it is equally ....
     A ancient   B antique   C elderly   D old-fashioned
7   Despite their age, her grandparents are still very ....
     A alive   B childish   C lively   D living
8   My sister's son, Jimmy, is my favourite ....
     A cousin   B nephew   C niece   D uncle
9   The train was delayed so we had to wait for ....
     A ages   B a moment   C a second   D long times
10 I didn't expect you to arrive so soon. How long did the journey ....?
     A continue   B endure   C go   D take
11 We talked about her trip and she said that she .... there before.
     A had never been   B had never come   C never came   D never went
12 It was very kind of you to do the washing-up, but you .... it.
     A didn't have to do   B hadn't to do   C mightn't have done
     D mustn't have done

193

13 Because of the bad weather we had to .... our picnic.
   A put aside   B put off   C put out   D put up
14 We thought we'd missed the bus but, of course, it arrived ....
   A at the end   B conclusively   C in conclusion   D in the end
15 If you're not sure what the date is today, look at your ....
   A almanac   B calendar   C dairy   D day-book
16 Don't worry, you'll get an answer to your letter ....
   A at last   B one of those days   C sooner or later   D when all's said and done
17 He hasn't come yet, but I'm expecting him to arrive ....
   A at any time   B at no time   C at one time   D at this time
18 It was my first proper holiday for years, so I was really .... it.
   A anticipating   B expecting   C looking forward   D looking forward to
19 It was supposed to rain yesterday, according to the weather ....
   A forecast   B oracle   C prediction   D warning
20 She told me she knew exactly what would happen, but I wasn't ....
   A certainly   B convinced   C secure   D surely
21 I wish I .... more attention in my history lessons at school.
   A had paid   B have been paying   C paid   D was paying
22 We agreed to .... in the main square at 7.30.
   A meet   B meeting   C meet together   D meet us
23 Remember that exams never start late, they always start ....
   A ahead of time   B at the last moment   C in time   D on time
24 I haven't .... an exam for two years.
   A made   B taken   C took   D set
25 Exams are never enjoyable, ...?
   A are there   B are they   C aren't there   D aren't they

★ In the exam, if you can't answer a question, leave a blank, make a
pencil mark in the margin and come back to it later. If you still can't
answer it, make a guess – you've got a 25% chance of being right!

14.2   1900   *Reading comprehension*

★ Each of the comprehension questions on the passages in Paper 1 is
worth two marks – in all there will be fifteen questions making a total of
30 out of 55. In the exam, there may be three or four passages and there
will be fewer questions than you have had to answer in this book.

★ It may be best to read the questions through before you read the
passage, so that you know what you have to find out. Alternatively, you
may prefer to read the text quickly through (to get an idea of what it's
about) before you read the questions and then look for the answers in the
text.
   If you spend too long trying to find a particular answer you may run out
of time – it may be best to make a pencil mark beside a tricky question and
come back to it at the end.

Read the passage and answer the questions below.

... the nineteenth century brought about the greatest expansion of wealth the world had ever known. Its sources lay in the industrialisation of Europe and the techniques for assuring the continuance of this growth were by no means exhausted or compromised in 1900. There had not only been a vast and accelerating flow of commodities available only in (relatively) tiny quantities a century before, but whole new ranges of goods had come into existence. Oil and electricity had joined coal, wood, wind and water as sources of energy. A chemical industry existed which could not have been envisaged in 1800. Growing power and wealth had been used to tap seemingly inexhaustible natural resources, both agricultural and mineral. Railways, electric trams, steamships, motor cars and bicycles gave millions of men a new control over their environment; they accelerated travel from place to place and eased transport for the first time since animals had been harnessed to carts thousands of years before. In terms of consumption, or of the services to which they had access, or in the enjoyment of better health, even the mass of the population in developed countries were much better off in 1900 than their predecessors a hundred years before.

In spite of this cheerful picture, doubts could break in. Even if what might happen in the future were ignored, contemplation of the cost of the new wealth and doubts about the social justice of its distribution were troubling. Most people were still terribly poor, whether or not they lived in rich countries where the illogicality of this was particularly more striking than in earlier times. Another change in the way men thought about their condition arose over their power to get a livelihood at all. It was not new that men should be without work. What was new was that situations should suddenly arise in which the operation of blind forces of boom and slump produced millions of men without work concentrated in great towns. This was 'unemployment', the new phenomenon for which a new word had been needed. Nor were the cities themselves yet rid of all the evils which had so struck the first observers of industrial society. By 1900 the majority of western Europeans were town-dwellers and they lived in more than 140 cities of over 100,000 inhabitants in 1914. In some of them, millions of people were cramped, ill-housed, under-provided with schools and fresh air, let alone amusement other than that of the street, and this often in sight of the wealth their society helped to produce. 'Slums' was another word invented by the nineteenth century.

(from *The Hutchinson History of the World* by J. M. Roberts)

1 Oil and electricity became available as sources of energy
   A after 1900.
   B before 1900.
   C in about 1800.
   D in about 1900.

2 In the 19th century travel became
   A cheaper and easier.
   B cheaper and faster.
   C cheaper, easier and faster.
   D faster and easier.

3 In 1900 life was better for
   A everyone in the world.
   B most people in Europe.
   C only the rich.
   D non-Europeans.

4 Before 1900 very large numbers of men were
   A always without work.
   B never without work.
   C often without work.
   D rarely without work.

5 The word 'slums' was invented to describe
   A bad housing.
   B poverty.
   C unemployment.
   D wealth.

JORVIK –
LOST VIKING CAPITAL

A thousand years ago York was one of the largest, richest and most famous cities in the whole of Britain. A monk at that time described it as packed with a huge population, rich merchandise, and traders 'from all parts, especially Danes'. People in the 10th century called it Jorvik, and knew it as the capital of the North of England, and one of Europe's greatest trading ports. It owed its prosperity to the hard work and commercial enterprise of Viking settlers from Scandinavia who had captured it in AD 866 and almost totally rebuilt it.

Most of the city's buildings were made of wood, and have long since been demolished, or have burnt down or rotted away. In some parts of modern York, however, near the rivers Ouse and Foss which run through the centre of the city, archaeologists have found that remains of Jorvik do still survive. They are buried deep below the streets and buildings of the 20th century city. Here the damp soils have preserved the timber buildings. Whole streets of houses, shops, workshops and warehouses are to be found, often still standing shoulder high. All the debris and rubbish left by the people of Jorvik in and around their homes is still there, awaiting discovery.

Between 1976 and 1981 archaeologists from the York Archaeological Trust excavated a part of this lost and all-but-forgotten city. The dig took place in Coppergate, before the city's new Coppergate Centre was built. Four rows of buildings were found, running back from Coppergate itself, almost exactly in the same positions as their modern successors. The remains were so well preserved – even down to boots and shoes, pins and needles, plants and insects – that every aspect of life at the time could be reconstructed.

JORVIK VIKING CENTRE

THE MOST EXCITING JOURNEY IN A THOUSAND YEARS
Coppergate, York YO1 1NT. Tel: (0904) 643211.

York Archaeological Trust decided to try to tell the story of Jorvik as it was a thousand years ago. To do so it built the Jorvik Viking Centre in the huge hole created by the dig. Two of the rows of buildings were reconstructed as we think they were. A further two were preserved just as the archaeological team discovered them, the ancient timbers set out as they were found in the late 1970s, deep below the new shopping centre, where they have lain for centuries.

In the Jorvik Viking Centre people from the 20th century journey back in time to the 10th century. The journey is done in time cars, which silently glide back through the years, past some of the thirty or so generations of York's people who have walked the pavements of Coppergate, until time stops, on a late October day in 948. For a while modern time travellers explore Coppergate and a little alley, Lundgate, which runs off it. The neighbourhood is full of the sights and sounds and smells of 10th century Jorvik. Townspeople are there, buying and selling, working and playing.

Choose the answer that best completes each sentence about the passage.

1 1,000 years ago York was
   A more important than present-day York.
   B the most important city in Britain.
   C the most prosperous city in Britain.
   D the principal city of Northern England.

2 Jorvik was first established
   A before the Vikings came to England.
   B 1,000 years ago.
   C in the 8th century by the Vikings.
   D in the 9th century by the Vikings.

3 The buildings that the Vikings built at Jorvik
   A are all still beneath the streets of modern York.
   B have all been destroyed.
   C have not all disappeared.
   D have all vanished.

4 Some of the streets of Viking Jorvik discovered by archaeologists
   A still had walls 1½ metres high.
   B were buried in rubbish.
   C were completely as they were in Viking times.
   D were paved with stone.

5 Coppergate is now
   A a museum   B a park   C a shopping centre   D a street

6 Archaeologists were able to discover exactly
   A how life was lived 1,000 years ago.
   B how the Vikings captured Jorvik.
   C how the Vikings constructed their buildings.
   D what kind of clothes the Vikings wore.

7 Jorvik Viking Centre was constructed .... the place where the dig
   had taken place.
   A at   B near   C some way from   D a long way from

8 Jorvik Viking Centre contains .... buildings.
   A two   B four   C two rows of   D four rows of

9 Visitors to Jorvik Viking Centre
   A have to queue up for a long time.
   B must be quiet in the museum.
   C should allow plenty of time for their visit.
   D travel back in time.

10 Visitors to Jorvik Viking Centre can
    A buy souvenirs of Viking Jorvik.
    B ask the staff questions about Viking Jorvik.
    C touch the exhibits if they like.
    D walk through the steets of Viking Jorvik.

14.4 Under exam conditions   *Composition – 1 ½ hours*

★ In the exam it's important to follow the instructions exactly. If the instructions say 'Write a letter to a friend ...', for example, your work must look like a personal letter and NOT like a business letter! This may sound obvious, but it's easy to overlook important instructions when you're in a hurry. So, before you start writing:

1 Make sure you fully understand the instructions for each question. If you don't quite understand a particular question, it's best not to answer it.
2 Decide which of the questions are the easiest for you to answer.
3 Check which grammatical structures may be needed for the subject: conditionals, modal verbs, past/present perfect, etc.
4 Make notes on both questions. If at this stage you find you haven't got enough ideas on one of them, there may be time to choose a different one.

A Choose TWO of the following composition questions. Allow yourself 90 minutes, including time to make notes beforehand and check your work through afterwards. Each composition should be between 120 and 180 words in length. You may not use a dictionary.

1 Write a short story that includes this phrase:
'... everything seemed to be going well until ...'

2 What was life like in your country 20 years ago? Describe the changes that have taken place and explain how the quality of life has improved and got worse.

3 Imagine that some friends have invited you to go on holiday with them some-time during the next six months. Write a letter explaining why you must turn down the invitation and describing what you will be doing instead.

4 Write a description of a place you once visited and the people you met there.

5 You have been chosen by the other members of your class to present a gift to your teacher and make a speech. Explain why you have chosen this particular gift and thank your teacher for all he or she has done for you. Write down what you would say in your speech.

6 If you have read one of the prescribed books, explain why you enjoyed OR didn't enjoy reading it.
OR Your teacher will suggest a question on the particular book you have read.

B Your teacher will give you a final mark for the two compositions and also point out what particular points you should be careful about in the exam.

● What are *your* typical 'careless mistakes' of spelling and grammar, which you should notice when checking your work?
● What types of questions do you feel more confident about (e.g. writing a narrative) and which do you dislike (e.g. writing an essay)?

★ In the exam it's a good idea to leave wide margins and to leave two or three lines between each paragraph. Start your second composition on a new page. Then, if you want to add anything or cross a sentence out and rewrite it, you'll have plenty of space.

14.5 Fill the gaps

Fill each of the numbered blanks in the following passage. Use only one word in each space.

Many years ago when the summers seemed longer and life was .... (1) complicated, we had rented a cottage by a river in the heart of the country where we were going to .... (2) three weeks' holiday. There were four of us: me (age 9), Mum and Dad and Mum's .... (3), Auntie June. Oh, and I mustn't forget to .... (4) Spot, our little dog. I was allowed to go off by .... (5) all day, ... (6) that I promised to be careful and took Spot with me for .... (7).

   One day I was out fishing with Spot when we heard a lot of shouting in the .... (8) followed by a scream and a splash. I was a bit .... (9) so I called Spot and we both hid .... (10) a bush where we could see but not be .... (11). After a few moments a straw hat came floating down the river, followed by an oar, a picnic basket and .... (12) oar. Then came the rowing boat itself, but it was floating .... (13) down! A few seconds later my Dad and Auntie June came running .... (14) the river bank, both wet .... (15). Spot started .... (16) so I came out of hiding and said hello. My Dad got really angry with me for not .... (17) to catch the boat as it went past. Luckily, however, the boat and both the oars had been caught by an overhanging tree a little further downstream, but not the hat or the picnic basket. So I had to let them .... (18) my sandwiches. Dad and Auntie June both made me .... (19) not to tell Mum what had happened in .... (20) she was worried.

★ Before you fill any blanks in this kind of exercise, read the whole story through to find out what it's about. Then start filling the gaps. If you're not sure of an answer, pencil it in lightly or leave a blank and come back to it later.

'Mum and dad, can I borrow the wheel tonight?'

14.6 Grammar revision

A   When you check your compositions through for mistakes, you need to notice spelling errors and grammatical mistakes. Some of these may just be careless mistakes or slips of the pen – others may be harder to recognise.

Work in pairs. Find the mistakes in these sentences and correct them – in some cases there are two or more mistakes.

1 Careless mistakes and slips of the pen:

A The castle contain many treasure and painting.
B I wonder wich of the misteaks is most serius.
C My brother and sister has brown eyes but my eyes be blue.
D Could you tell me what time does it opens?
E Who did paid for the ticket?

2 Mistakes that are harder to notice:

A After visiting the museum he had not very much time left.
B His hair is very long, it's time for him to have cut it.
C I am waiting for you since four hours.
D They never visited Rome before their first visit in 1987.
E She never wrote a letter by hand since she has bought a word processor.
F I am learning English during five years.
G A suspicious is questioning by the police.
H Before they had gone out they had been watched the news on TV.

B   Finish each of the sentences in this exercise in such a way that it means exactly the same as the sentence printed before it.

1 I'll be busy working while you're on holiday.
   During ....
2 I haven't seen my old school friend for ages.
   It's ages ....
3 It was my first visit to North America.
   I ....
4 The ancient Egyptians built the Pyramids.
   The Pyramids ....
5 It'll be necessary for her to give up her job soon.
   Soon she ....
6 CLOSED DUE TO ILLNESS said the notice on the office door.
   We found out ....
7 In spite of the heat it was an easy climb to the top of the hill.
   We managed ....
8 I'll get ready before your arrival.
   By the time ....
9 It wasn't a good idea for you to put so much salt in the soup.
   You ....
10 I'm afraid it's far too salty for me to eat now.
   It's so ....

200

★ If there is a word-building exercise in the exam (there may not be), you may have to add both a prefix AND a suffix to the root word. AND you may well have to change the form of a verb to fit the sentence.

A   Work in pairs. Here are some examples of tricky questions for you to try. Form another word from the words in capitals to complete each sentence.

1 She got very angry but later she apologised for her	PATIENT
2 He is very generous and everyone admires his	SELF
3 I didn't want my money back, I wanted a	PLACE
4 His boss told him off because he had behaved	RESPONSIBLE
5 I read an article about .... among school-leavers.	EMPLOY
6 Her parents .... her to apply for the job.	COURAGE
7 They had a quarrel after .... about who was responsible.	AGREE
8 This knife is very blunt. It needs	SHARP

B   Now try this revision exercise.
The words in capitals at the end of each sentence can be used to form a word that fits suitably in the blank space. Fill each blank in this way.

1 In some places the weather changes so quickly that it's very	PREDICT
2 We had a marvellous holiday and our trip to the mountains was	FORGET
3 Two of these tablets should be taken	DAY
4 He remembers every detail of it because he has a .... memory.	PHOTOGRAPH
5 I expect she'll get the job, at least there's a fairly high	PROBABLE
6 I'm not sure at all, I really can't say with	CERTAIN
7 There's no .... of the government calling an early election.	LIKELY
8 The day she got married was a .... occasion.	MEMORY
9 Nobody wears clothes like that any more – they're terribly	FASHION
10 They all passed their exams without the slightest	DIFFICULT

★ Before you take the exam, make sure you get some practice in doing exercises like these in an Examination Practice book:

It be quite difficult / do / exercise like this / exam.
It is quite difficult to do an exercise like this in the exam.

and

A: Are ....?
B: Yes, I'm feeling quite confident now.

★ One of the exercises in the Use of English paper may be new to you, but the work you have done so far on Vocabulary, Word study, Prepositions and Verbs and idioms will help you to cope with these. Here are three exercises to give you some practice. The golden rules with an unfamiliar type of exercise are:

1 Read the instructions carefully – twice!
2 Look at the examples very carefully.

A   Complete these sentences with an expression formed from **make** or **do**. A preposition or particle may or may not be necessary.

EXAMPLE: I'm afraid I have ....**made**.... a mistake.

1 I didn't believe their story, I was sure they had ....
2 There was no wine to drink so we had to .... water.
3 You haven't .... your shoelaces – you might trip over.
4 The robbers .... over £1 million.
5 Have you .... all your work yet?
6 We told the driver we were .... the coast and asked for a lift.

B   Complete the following sentences with ONE appropriate word connected with the subject of **books**.

EXAMPLE: This book has 210 .**pages.**.

1 The .... of this book is *Progress to First Certificate*.
2 He made notes beside the text in the left-hand ....
3 You can use the .... at the end of a book to find where the information is given.
4 Most dictionaries have two .... on a page.
5 The complete novels of Charles Dickens take up twenty ....
6 Use this card as a .... so that you can find your place again easily.

C   Complete these sentences with one word related in meaning to the number given.

EXAMPLE: It was the ....**third**.... time I had seen that film.   3

1 We're going away on holiday for a   14
2 I've been to that place .... of times.   12
3 The admission prices have .... since I was last there.   2
4 20% is the same as one   5
5 If you cut the apple into pieces, we can each have a   4
6 In the year 2000 a new .... begins.   100

★ In the exam you are sure to find that there are some questions that you can't answer. Don't get depressed about this. If all the questions were easy, everyone would get 100%!

A   Read this information and consider these questions:
- Which of the cities would suit them best?
- What could they do together – or separately – during a day in the city?

Mr and Mrs Meier and their two children Helen (14) and Richard (16) are staying in London and want to spend Sunday in either York or Cambridge. The Meiers have chosen these cities because they are all interested in history, but they don't all share the same tastes: Helen is artistic and likes looking at paintings, Mrs Meier doesn't like walking, Mr Meier doesn't like museums and Richard likes railways.

In a day, allowing time for travel and meals, there would only be time to see two or three of the sights – not all of them.

York Historic city with many ancient buildings

- Roman city walls — walk around the city
- York Minster: one of the largest churches in Europe, stained glass windows
- Jorvik Viking Centre: experience the sights, sounds and smells of daily life in Viking times
- The Shambles: old street lined with fascinating shops
- Castle Museum: contains a reconstructed street with shops of various periods
- National Railway Museum: historic engines, carriages and history of railways in Britain

Journey time from London 2 hours — weekend return £45, day return £32

CAMBRIDGE
Historic university city with old colleges

- ◼ King's College Chapel: tall windows and superb ceiling
- ◼ Colleges – many are open for the public to walk through: peaceful courtyards
- ◼ Fitzwilliam Museum: paintings and antiquities
- ◼ Kettle's Yard: delightful artist's house full of paintings and beautiful furniture
- ◼ River Cam: walk beside river or hire a boat

Journey time from London 1 hour – weekend return £24, day return £16

B   Write about 100 words, explaining which city they should go to and what they would do there together (or separately) once they got there.

》》⟶

203

★ Directed writing is probably one of the hardest parts of the exam. Make sure you read the instructions very carefully (twice). Select the information you think is relevant. There is no perfect answer in this kind of exercise – as long as you can explain and justify your decisions your answer will be satisfactory.

   Remember that this exercise only counts for 20–25% of the marks in the Use of English paper – about the same as the Fill the gaps exercise, which is usually question 1 – so don't spend too long on it.

   Maybe do it first of all – you can answer the questions in any order you like.

14.10   I remember . . . *Listening comprehension*

You'll hear two people talking about a childhood experience. Answer the questions or choose the alternative that best completes each sentence.

1 Liz's brother is
   A about the same age as her.
   B much older than her.
   C slightly older than her.
   D younger than her.

A	
B	
C	
D	

2 They used to go together to the
   A funfair.
   B park.
   C playground.
   D shops.

A	
B	
C	
D	

3 While she was on one of the swings she realised that
   A it was getting cold.
   B it was starting to rain.
   C she was alone.
   D she was lost.

A	
B	
C	
D	

4 Which of these pictures best shows what happened?

A	
B	
C	
D	

5 The dog tried to
   A bite her.
   B get her teddy.
   C chase her.
   D pull her off the swing.

A	
B	
C	
D	

6 In the end the dog
  A was caught.
  B was hit with a stick.
  C was killed.
  D ran away.

A	
B	
C	
D	

7 After that experience she always
  A avoided the playground if it was empty.
  B told her brother not to leave her.
  C went with her mother to the playground.
  D went to a different, safer playground.

A	
B	
C	
D	

8 Now she realises that her brother had really
  A forgotten about her.
  B gone home to fetch help.
  C left her to be eaten.
  D lost his way home.

A	
B	
C	
D	

9 This experience
  A has almost been forgotten.
  B has had a big influence on her life ever since.
  C has had no effect on her life.
  D still affects her attitude.

A	
B	
C	
D	

10 Which of these pictures best shows what happened?

A	
B	
C	
D	

★ In the exam, you will normally hear each recording twice. Make sure you read the questions through carefully while you're waiting for the recording to be played to you.

★ If you are slightly unsure about any questions, put a light pencil mark beside the answer you think might be best, then listen carefully for the answer to that question on the second listening.

If you have no idea about an answer, don't leave a blank – guess!

'That's the deal then. We give you our gold and you give us something called Spanish omelette.'

14.11 The slave trade

Listen to the radio interview with Professor Nicholson. Put a tick
(✓) beside the true statements and a cross (✗) beside the false statements.

1 Professor Nicholson has made a TV film about slavery. ☐
2 According to him, there are still slaves in the world today. ☐
3 The first African slaves were seen in Europe in 1534. ☐
4 Before 1700 the slave trade was dominated by Portugal. ☐
5 Slaves were needed to work on the plantations in the New World. ☐
6 The French and English dominated the slave trade in the 18th century. ☐
7 Six million people were sent from Africa between 1700 and 1800. ☐
8 The plantations in America produced fruit and rubber. ☐
9 Sugar, cotton and tobacco were sent to Europe. ☐
10 Many slaves did not survive the awful journey across the Atlantic. ☐
11 Conditions in the plantations were better than on the ships. ☐
12 The anti-slavery movement started in Europe. ☐
13 English ships stopped carrying slaves in 1809. ☐
14 Slaves in British colonies were set free in 1865. ☐
15 Slaves in the United States were set free in 1833. ☐
16 Some slave owners voluntarily gave their slaves freedom. ☐
17 Liberia was set up as a home for freed slaves who returned to Africa. ☐
18 This interview is about the slaves who were sent from Africa to America. ☐

14.12 Gipsy signs

You'll hear a talk about gipsies and the signs they used to leave for
each other outside people's houses. Listen to the recording and DRAW the
signs beside their meanings. The first is done for you as an example:

1 Beware of the dog △

2 Fierce dog

3 Friendly people

4 Friendly, generous people

5 Very friendly, generous people

6 Work to be had here

7 Gipsies not liked

8 Nothing to be had

9 Work available with good pay

10 These people will buy from you

11 This place has been robbed

⊙ ┼ ⊖ △ ≡ ⊙

/// ○ △ ∓ ⊖

14.13 A long time ago . . . *Interview exercises*

A ⚡ Work in pairs. One of you should look at Activity 14, the other at 21. You will each see different photographs, showing a scene from the past. Find out about your partner's photograph by asking questions.

B Work in pairs. Look at the brochure and answer these questions:
- Would you like to visit this place? Why/Why not?
- What would you enjoy most about it?
- What historical buildings or monuments have you visited? What did you find interesting about them?
- What buildings or monuments should a visitor to your city or area go and see? Why?

"The loveliest castle in the world."

LORD CONWAY

Leeds castle, Kent. Named after Led, Chief Minister of Ethelbert IV, King of Kent, in AD 857.

It is situated about 4 miles to the East of Maidstone on the A20 London-Folkestone Road, in some of England's loveliest countryside.

Built on two islands in the middle of a lake, the Castle was originally a stronghold until it was converted into a Royal Palace by Henry VIII.

Beautifully furnished and lovingly restored, its truly historic atmosphere gently reminds one that it was a Royal Residence for over 300 years.

The surrounding parklands offer many magnificent views and walks as well as a charming woodland garden.

Lunch, tea and light refreshments are available and picnics are welcome in the grounds surrounding the car park area.

Leeds Castle, Maidstone, Kent.

C Work in pairs or small groups. Ask your partner(s) these questions:
- Why do people study history?
- In what ways is studying history relevant to our present-day lives?
- What important historical events have happened in the history of your country? (In Britain everyone learns what happened in 1066 and 1588, for example. What equivalent 'memorable dates' are there in your country's history?)
- What would have happened if those events had turned out differently?
- If someone who had emigrated from your country or city twenty years ago returned now, what changes would they notice?

≫→

★ In the exam, the examiner will give you marks for the following aspects of your spoken English:

- **fluency** – Do you speak without too much hesitation?
- **grammatical accuracy** – Do you speak without making too many mistakes?
- **pronunciation** – Can people understand you easily?
- **communication** – Do you communicate your ideas effectively in a conversation?
- **vocabulary** – Do you know enough words to be able to express your ideas?

★ Remember that in the interview you should try to be as relaxed as possible – and as talkative as you normally are in class. The best way to do this is to PRACTISE by taking part in 'mock' interviews.

14.14 Good luck!

In Papers 1 to 4 of the exam,
- keep cool and don't get depressed if there are some questions you can't answer
- use your time sensibly
- read all the instructions and examples very carefully
- check all your written work and correct any careless mistakes you've made
- show the examiners how much you know!

Best of luck and good wishes from

Leo Jones

208

Communication activities

1 Dictate these names, addresses and phone numbers to your partner. Spell out the difficult names, if you're not sure how to pronounce them. Ask your teacher for help, if necessary.

Ms Fiona Davison, 13 Gloucester Rd, Cheltenham GL9 6GT (0242 819232)
Mr Thomas Twining, 70 St Andrews St, York YO1 8AR (0904 678999)
Mrs G. K. Fuller, 115 W. Harbour Drive, Portsmouth PO3 2PJ (0705 414332)
Miss Helen Konstantinides, 170 El. Venizelou Street, 114 27 Athens, Greece
M. Jean-Pierre Martin, 135 quai de Southampton, 76600 Le Havre, France

2 Here are some ideas you might like to mention to your partners:

> More people will use bicycles in the future:
> no fuel required   no pollution   no traffic jams
> healthy exercise for all   cheap and available for young and old
> heavier traffic will discourage people from using their cars
> everyone can go wherever they want

3 The original version of the story uses the past tense, making it seem true, rather than fiction. Its lack of detail makes it very dull.

What makes the following version of the story better than the one on page 29?
Underline the extra information that helps to improve the story.

'CASABLANCA'
The story is set in Morocco during the war. Rick (Humphrey Bogart) is an American who owns a night club in Casablanca. His ex-girlfriend, Ilsa (Ingrid Bergman), arrives at Rick's with her new husband, Victor Laszlo (Paul Heinreid). Laszlo is in danger there and has to escape to Lisbon, but although they can get plane tickets, they are unable to get visas. Ilsa persuades Rick to help her 'for old time's sake' and he manages to get two visas on the black market but has to sell his club to pay for them. At the end of the film Rick and the chief of police, Renault (Claude Rains) watch the plane take off, carrying Ilsa and Laszlo to freedom.

4 What are the differences between these notes and the notes you made?

GIFT IDEAS FOR CHRIS

Alarm Wallet ✓ - Chris going to USA, doesn't want to lose the money earned at the vacation camp. Would be pleased to receive it. Quite expensive though.
Beach Chair ✗ - Probably not suitable, Chris seems active person, not the sort who would want to lie on the beach reading.
Shopper Calculator ✓? - Chris enjoys supermarkets - maybe a possible gift, fairly cheap, not very exciting though.
Voice Over ✗ - Not suitable, Chris not interested in music.

GIFT IDEAS FOR JO

Alarm Wallet ✗ - Probably not suitable, though if shopping for family might need to make sure money not lost.
Beach Chair ✓ - Suitable for Jo: likes reading + going to the beach. Half the price of Voice Over but more expensive than Shopper Calculator.
Shopper Calculator ✓? - Possibly suitable to make shopping easier, but not what a friend should give Jo. Maybe suggest this to a member of Jo's family??
Voice Over ✓ - Could be suitable - Jo likes music and singing: could enjoy composing own songs perhaps? Quite expensive though.

5 Dictate these words to your partner:

hopeless   abbreviation   butter   lucky   juice   charming   ready   surprise   social   telephone   half

Silent letters: thorough   debt   soften   knot   chalk   scared   vehicle

6 Look at this recipe with your partner and make sure you understand it. Is this something you'd like to make and/or drink?

LASSI – a refreshing Eastern yogurt drink

¼ litre yogurt
¼ litre milk (or water)
juice of 1 lemon
ice cubes
sugar to taste

1 Crush the ice cubes or put them in a food processor.
2 Put all the ingredients, except the sugar, into the food processor or liquidiser and blend well.
3 Add the sugar little by little until the liquid is sweet enough. It should NOT be too sweet!
4 Serve immediately in tall glasses with drinking straws.

Join another pair and explain this recipe to them IN YOUR OWN WORDS.
They will be telling you how to make a different refreshing drink.

7 Here are explanations of some of the items on the menu on page 142, so that you can help your partners to understand them. DO NOT just read these descriptions out loud – try to remember them, so that you can answer your partners' questions.

When you're all clear about everything, decide what to order for each course.

Steak and kidney pie   A traditional English pie containing beef and kidneys in a rich sauce – delicious!

Chicken Maryland   Fried chicken, coated with breadcrumbs and garnished with fried bananas – rather strange!

Sherry trifle   Cooked fruit and cake, soaked in sherry and topped with vanilla sauce and cream – very fattening!

8 Here are some ideas you might like to mention to your partners:

> More people will use electric vehicles in the future:
> no petrol needed   no pollution
> small, lightweight batteries will be developed
> quiet and fast enough for city driving
> petrol and diesel vehicles will be banned from city centres

9 The original version of the story contains so little detail that it's impossible to get interested. As it's a personal story, there should be personal details to explain why the night was unforgettable. The exact times and distances are distracting and irrelevant.

What makes this version of the story better than the one on page 29? Underline the main changes that have been made.

I'll never forget the night our car broke down. We were on our way home after a marvellous evening out with some friends. It was well after midnight and we were still miles from home. We tried to get the engine started again, but in vain. There was no traffic on the road at all, so we couldn't get a lift and had to walk all the way home. To make matters worse it started to rain and by the time we arrived we were wet through. But worse was yet to come! It was then that we discovered that we'd left our front door key in the car.

We had no choice but to break a window and climb in. Unfortunately, just as we were doing this, a police car stopped in the road. At first, of course, the policeman didn't believe our story and wanted to take us to the police station, but in the end we convinced him that we were telling the truth. By the time we got to bed it was past three o'clock and we were cold, wet, miserable and absolutely exhausted.

10 Dictate these names, addresses and phone numbers to your partner. Spell out the difficult names, if you're not sure how to pronounce them. Ask your teacher for help, if necessary.

Mr Anthony Fitzgerald, 150 King William Sq., Edinburgh EH2 7JQ
  (031 552 1265)
Mrs Anne Greene, 16 Acacia Ave, Wimbledon, London SW19 4KE
  (01 331 4499)
Mr Mark Butcher, c/o Mrs Finch, 13 North St, Ramsgate CT13 7YZ
  (0843 662701)
Sig. Giorgio Rossi, Via Garibaldi 118, 40125 Bologna, Italy
Mr James Rockford, 4352 Ocean Boulevard, Malibu, CA 40781, USA

11 This is the rest of the passage, with pauses and stressed syllables marked.

Equípment requíred: |
a 30 cm rúler, | stícky tápe, | páper, | scíssors and a pén. |

Procédure: |
Óne. | Cút oút a píece of páper the sáme síze as thís páge. |
Twó. | Yóu will seé alóng the síde of the páge | a scále with divísions márked on it. | Eách divísion shóws a tíme ínterval. | Thése represént fráctions of a sécond. |
Thrée. | Cópy the scále cárefully onto the síde of the píece of páper you have cút oút | and thén tíghtly wráp it roúnd the rúler | só that the scále is vísible. | The bóttom énd of the scále | shóuld be at the bóttom énd of the rúler. | Fíx it secúrely with stícky tápe. |
Fóur. | Whíle you hóld the rúler at the poínt márked | 'HÓLD HÉRE', | gét the pérson to pláce hís or hér thúmb and fórefinger | on eíther síde of the zéro líne on the scále. | Téll them to cátch the rúler as soón as it begíns to fáll. | Íf they gríp the rúler *befóre* it begíns to fáll, | thís resúlt is nót cóunted. |
Fíve. | Withoút létting the pérson knów whén you are aboút to dróp it, | reléase the rúler. | The tíme that it toók the pérson to reáct | is shówn in séconds on the scále at the poínt they cáught it. |
Síx. | Repéat the expériment séveral tímes with eách pérson | and récord the resúlts in a chárt. |

12 Unfortunately, delays are quite common on long journeys:
• Alain's ferry might be two hours late, because of rough seas.
• And Bobby's flight could land three hours late, due to fog at the airport.
• And Conny may miss the 06.17 train via Birmingham, if her alarm clock doesn't go off.

Decide what advice you will give to each of them to allow for these situations.

13

Imagine that you've seen this advertisement in the street. Describe it to your partner.

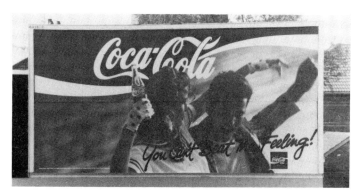

14

Ask your partner these questions about his or her photo, which was taken in 1940.

- What does your photograph show?
- What is happening?
- What has happened?
- What is going to happen?
- What would it be like to be one of the children in the picture?
- What are the differences between life now and life at the time the photograph was taken?
- Would you like to have been alive then? Why not?

1933

15

THE GUARDIAN   Thursday June 23

Yesterday's summary
Wednesday's weather
(Lunch-time reports)

	C	F			C	F			C	F			C	F
Algiers	C	26	79	B Aires	S	19	66	Glasgow	S	18	64	Montreal	R	23	73	Seoul	S	28	82
Amsterdam	C	18	64	Cairo	S	31	88	Helsinki	S	25	77	Moscow	C	25	77	Singapore	F	31	88
Athens	F	17	63	Cape Town	S	27	81	Hong Kong	C	30	86	Munich	S	14	57	Stockholm	F	22	72
Bahrain	S	35	95	Casablanca	S	23	73	Innsbruck	C	16	61	Naples	S	29	84	Strasbourg	S	19	66
Bermuda	S	30	86	Chicago	C	32	90	Inverness	S	18	64	New Delhi	F	31	88	Sydney	F	15	59
Barcelona	Th	22	72	Cologne	F	16	61	Istanbul	F	23	73	New York	F	36	97	Tangier	F	24	75
Berlin	C	13	55	Copenhagen	F	19	66	Karachi	S	35	95	Nice	S	24	75	Tenerife	F	23	73
Biarritz	C	23	73	Corfu	S	28	82	Las Palmas	S	24	75	Oslo	Sl	4	40	Tokyo	F	26	79
Birmingham	S	21	70	Dublin	S	21	70	Lisbon	F	21	70	Paris	F	21	70	Tunis	S	32	90
Bombay	Dr	27	81	Edinburgh	S	19	66	London	S	22	72	Peking	C	24	75	Valencia	S	27	81
Bordeaux	S	25	77	Florence	S	29	84	Los Angeles	F	17	63	Perth	C	21	70	Vancouver	C	18	64
Boston	R	29	84	Frankfurt	S	18	64	Luxembourg	S	15	59	Prague	R	10	50	Venice	F	25	77
Bristol	S	24	75	Geneva	Fg	14	57	Madrid	F	21	70	Reykjavik	R	8	46	Vienna	F	17	63
Brussels	H	15	59	Gibraltar	S	25	77	Majorca	F	30	86	Rhodes	S	26	79	Warsaw	C	15	59
Budapest	C	19	66					Malaga	F	29	84	Riyadh	S	41	106	Washington	F	37	99
								Malta	S	28	82	Rome	S	25	77	Wellington	R	12	54
								Manchester	S	18	64	Salzburg	C	12	54	Zurich	F	18	64
								Melbourne	C	15	59								
								Mexico City	C	16	61								
								Miami	F	31	88								

C, cloudy; Dr, drizzle; F, fair; Fg, fog; H, hail; R, rain; Sl, sleet; Sn, snow; S, sunny; Th, thunder.

16 Imagine that you are going to give advice to someone who is going to buy A NEW CAMERA or A PERSONAL STEREO (Walkman). They have never owned one before. What would you tell them? Make some notes.

When you're ready, join another pair.
1 Ask for their advice on buying a new bicycle or a new watch.
2 Then offer them your advice on buying a camera or a personal stereo.

17 Here are three scenes from a film. Your partners have more scenes from the same film. How did the story start, continue and finish? Where do these scenes fit in?

1 Explain your version of the story, beginning: 'This is what happened ...'
2 When each of you has given your version, look at each other's scenes and decide on a version of the story that includes all the pictures.

18 Tell your partner this story – as if it really happened to some friends of a friend of yours. DON'T read it aloud word-for-word.

These friends of mine went to the woods to gather mushrooms. They were afraid they might be poisonous, so they fed one to their cat. The cat still seemed OK a few hours later, so they cooked the mushrooms and ate them. When they'd just finished, they looked out of the window and saw the cat lying dead on the pavement. In panic, they rushed to hospital to have their stomachs pumped. On their return they found a note through their door from a neighbour who had accidentally run the cat over in the road.

19 Imagine that you and your partners need a break. Why don't you go away somewhere together? This advertisement in the paper has caught your eye – it seems a wonderful idea.

Tell your partners why they would enjoy a few days at the Springs Hotel.

20 Imagine that you've seen this advertisement in the street. Describe it to your partner.

21 Ask your partner these questions about his or her photo, which was taken in 1933.

- What does your photograph show?
- Why has he got the sign on his bike, do you think?
- What has happened?
- What is he going to do?
- What would it be like to be the man in the picture?
- What are the differences between life now and life at the time the photograph was taken?
- Would you like to have been alive then? Why not?
- How serious a problem is unemployment in your country today?

1940

22 Dictate these words to your partner: .

approximately beauty matter quickly edge cheerful wreck lazy information cough halve

Silent letters: height doubt whistle knowledge calm heart exhibition

23 Imagine that you are going to give advice to someone who is going to buy A NEW BICYCLE or A NEW WATCH. They have never owned one before. What would you tell them? Make some notes. When you're ready, join another pair.
1 Offer them your advice on buying a bicycle or watch.
2 Then ask for their advice on buying a new camera or a personal stereo.

24 Here are three scenes from a film. Your partners have more scenes from the same film. How did the story start, continue and finish? Where do these scenes fit in?

1 Explain your version of the story beginning: 'This is what happened: ...'
2 When each of you has given your version, look at each other's scenes and decide on a version of the story that includes all the pictures.

25 These are the correct spellings of the words on the tape:

slipping sleeping   trouble robber   total putting
address doubled   request Christian   angle ignorant
engine average   adventure butcher   careful million
often sudden   immense coming   worry railway   please assistant
pleasure insurance   laughing rough   convince live   theory themselves
twelve while   university yawning

26 Here are just a few ideas on the attractions and drawbacks of some of the jobs listed on page 163. Your partners have different ideas.

AUTHOR: ✓ ✓ ✓ Working at home, no boss
CARPENTER: ✓ ✓ ✓ Your own boss, working with your hands
GOVERNMENT MINISTER: ✗ ✗ ✗ 18 hours a day, no holidays
NURSE: ✗ ✗ ✗ Long hours; work can be upsetting
POSTMAN/WOMAN: ✗ ✗ ✗ Not so good in bad weather, dogs may be a problem
SALES REPRESENTATIVE: £££ Excellent, if successful
SECRETARY: £££ Quite good
SHOP ASSISTANT: £££ Not very good
TAXI DRIVER: ✓ ✓ ✓ You're your own boss

When you've looked at these notes, go back to page 163 and continue your discussion – DON'T read the notes aloud.

27 Compare these model paragraphs with your own work.

The ideal gift for Chris would be the Alarm Wallet. As he is likely to earn a lot of money while he is working in the USA, the wallet will keep the money safe. During his journey around the country he needs to be sure that his money isn't stolen and that he doesn't lose it accidentally. I'm sure that Chris would be pleased to receive this as a gift and that it would be very useful. It has plenty of room inside for tickets and loose change – and all the dollars he'll earn in the USA!

As Jo likes music and singing, the ideal gift would be the Voice Over. However, this is very expensive and I could only afford it if several of us shared the cost. So it seems that the Beach Chair would be the best present for her. Jo enjoys reading and going to the beach, so she would certainly find it very useful. There's room in it for keeping drinks and sandwiches cool and, I suppose, for a couple of books. Once she gets to the beach she can unfold it and sit comfortably in the sun.

28 Here are some ideas you might like to mention to your partners:

More people will use public transport in the future :
one bus can take 100 people   a train can take 1,000 people
one car can take only 4 (maximum)
private cars will be banned from city centres
heavier traffic will discourage people from using their cars

29 Look at this recipe with your partner and make sure you understand it. Is this something you'd like to make and/or drink?

OLD-FASHIONED LEMONADE – a refreshing drink, rich in vitamin C

4 juicy lemons
500g sugar (brown or white)
1 litre water

1 Peel the lemons thinly, removing only the rind, and squeeze the juice into a large bowl. Add the sugar.
2 Boil the lemon rind in the water for a few minutes.
3 Remove the rind and pour the water over the juice and sugar. Mix well to dissolve the sugar.
4 Pour the liquid into clean bottles and put them in the refrigerator.
5 Shake well before serving. Dilute with cold water to taste.

Join another pair and explain this recipe to them IN YOUR OWN WORDS. They will be telling you how to make a different refreshing drink.

30

Here are just a few ideas on the attractions and drawbacks of some of the jobs listed on page 163. Your partners have different ideas.

AUTHOR: ✗ ✗ ✗ Income is not regular, no workmates
CARPENTER: ✗ ✗ ✗ Physically tiring
GOVERNMENT MINISTER: £££ Excellent, but only when in office
NURSE: £££ Not good enough
POSTMAN/WOMAN: £££ Not good
SALES REPRESENTATIVE: ✓ ✓ ✓ Meeting people; being out of the office
SECRETARY: ✓ ✓ ✓ Can be interesting, comfortable conditions
SHOP ASSISTANT: ✓ ✓ ✓ Meeting people, working in a team
TAXI DRIVER: ✗ ✗ ✗ Unhealthy; some passengers can be difficult

When you've looked at these notes, go back to page 163 and continue your discussion – DON'T read the notes aloud.

31

This is your problem. Tell your partners about it:

– locked yourself out of your car
– keys inside, including house keys – all your money inside – 2 o'clock in the morning.

Begin like this: 'Oh no, what am I going to do? ...'

Try to think of drawbacks and objections to each suggestion that is made!

32

Tell your partner how to draw this diagram on page 27.

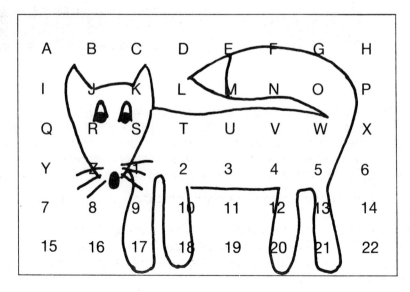

33

Imagine that you and your partners need a break. Why don't you go away somewhere together? This advertisement in the paper has caught your eye – it looks a great idea.

Tell your partners why they would enjoy a few days in an English Country Cottage.

34

35

Here are explanations of some of the items on the menu on page 142, so that you can help your partners to understand them. DO NOT just read these descriptions out loud – try to remember them, so that you can answer your partners' questions.

When you're all clear about everything, decide what to order for each course.

Cottage pie   Minced beef in gravy topped with mashed potato – could be nasty!

Nut and mushroom roast   Nuts, mushrooms and rice made into a kind of loaf and cooked in the oven – tasty and suitable for vegetarians!

Blackberry fool   Cooked blackberries and sugar whipped up with fresh cream and served cold.

36

This is your problem. Tell your partners about it:

– middle of holiday in foreign country – run out of cash – no traveller's cheques – no credit cards – no friends in this country

Begin like this: 'Oh dear, what can I do? ...'

Try to think of drawbacks and objections to each suggestion that is made!

37

CORRECTED VERSION of 1.10 C. As there are no firm rules for punctuation in English, there are a number of possible variations to this version.

Every Tuesday, Friday and Saturday in our part of the city, there's an open-air market in the main square which everyone goes to. Farmers come in from the countryside to sell their fresh vegetables and fruit. Other stalls sell all kinds of things: cheese, jeans, fish and even second-hand furniture. It's almost impossible to carry on a conversation above the noise and shouting as customers push their way to the front, trying to attract the stall-holder's [or stall-holders'] attention and demanding the ripest, freshest fruit or the lowest prices.

38

Take it in turns with your partner to describe each person in your photos – their appearance AND the kind of people they seem to be. Make notes on what your partner tells you.

Start with the person on the left of the group in your photo.

39 With your partner, study the details below and prepare to explain to another pair how SOAP works. What questions do you think you may be asked? Don't join another pair until you have familiarised yourselves with the process.

When you're ready to start, close your book and explain the process FROM MEMORY. Draw a diagram as you explain, if necessary.

SOAP AND WASHING POWDER

1 Soap is made up of millions of tiny parts called molecules. Each contains two parts.

2 One part is the head which attracts water, the other, the tail, is repelled by it.

3 In soapy water the tails attach themselves to dirt to get away from the water.

4 The tails pull the dirt away from the cloth. This makes the cloth clean and the water dirty.

5 What soap does to water. The tails of the soap molecules try to get out of the water. They break up the drops of water.

6 Soapy water spreads out. Water without soap stays in drops.

40 Tell your partner how to draw this diagram on page 27.

41

Villa Don Carlos
Marbella, Spain

August 30

Dear John,
    It's really lovely here in Spain. The sun's blazing hot
and the weather has been perfect. The food's really good too
— yesterday we had a marvellous 'paella'. The people too are
ever so friendly — we made friends with an old man the other
day who helped us to do our shopping (in Spanish) and afterwards we talked to him for ages and he was really interesting.
    There are plenty of interesting places to visit nearby.
On Sunday we went to a town in the mountains called Ronda,
which is full of ancient buildings and was fascinating to
explore. We went there by bus which took hours! It was an
exciting journey but it's a pity we haven't got a car here,
then we could explore the countryside properly. It's such a
long drive from England that the best thing would be to hire
a car here for a few days.
    It really is a shame you couldn't come with us — perhaps
next year you'll be able to. As I said, it's a wonderful
place and we're having a great time.
    Love,
        Jenny and Bill x

17 Cherry Tree Avenue
Greenwich
London SE11 4IZ

The Manager
Hotel Romantica   April 1 199#
Sea Road
Felixstowe

Dear Sir,
    Your hotel has been recommended to me by Mr Charles
Brown, who is a regular guest of yours and who has told me
quite a lot about the hotel.
    I wish to reserve two twin-bedded rooms and one single
room for myself and my family (3 adults and 2 children) for 7
nights from July 7th. We should like to have quiet rooms with
a bath or shower and which have sea views, preferably with
balconies. Would you please inform me of the cost of the rooms
with half board and enclose a brochure describing your hotel?
    One member of my party is my father-in-law, Mr Black,
who will be occupying the single room. He has a small dog
which he would like to sleep in his room. Please confirm that
this will be convenient. He is also a vegetarian, so please
also confirm that you can provide suitable meals for him.
    I look forward to hearing from you.
    Yours sincerely,
        Alan Green

42

Tell your partner this story — as if it really happened to some
friends of a friend of yours. DON'T read it aloud word-for-word.

These friends of mine wanted a new carpet, so they went to
the shop and chose one and the carpet-fitter came round to fit
it while they were out at work. When he had finished he found there was a
bump right in the middle. He realised this must be a pack of cigarettes that
he'd put down absent-mindedly, so he jumped up and down on the bump till
it was flat. The family got home and admired the carpet. Then they asked the
man if he had seen their pet canary which was missing. It was then that he
noticed his cigarettes on the hall table!

222

43 Imagine that you and your partners need a break. Why don't you go away somewhere together? This advertisement in the paper has caught your eye – it looks a really nice idea.

Tell your partners why they would enjoy a few days in a villa in Italy.

44

45 Here are just a few ideas on the attractions and drawbacks of some of the jobs listed on page 163. Your partners have different ideas.

AUTHOR: £££   Good, but only if you're successful
CARPENTER: £££   Not very good
GOVERNMENT MINISTER: ✓ ✓ ✓ Power, serving his/her country
NURSE: ✓ ✓ ✓ Looking after people, belonging to a team
POSTMAN/WOMAN: ✓ ✓ ✓ Popular with the public, fresh air
SALES REPRESENTATIVE: ✗ ✗ ✗ Insecure job, a lot of travelling
SECRETARY: ✗ ✗ ✗ A bad boss can be difficult to work with
SHOP ASSISTANT: ✗ ✗ ✗ Long hours, some customers can be difficult
TAXI DRIVER: £££   Good, but only when business is good

When you've looked at these notes, go back to page 163 and continue your discussion – DON'T read the notes aloud.

46

Here are three scenes from a film. Your partners have more scenes from the same film. How did the story start, continue and finish? Where do these scenes fit in?

1 Explain your version of the story, beginning: 'This is what happened: ...'
2 When each of you has given your version, look at each other's scenes and decide on a version of the story that includes all the pictures.

47

With your partner, study the details below and prepare to explain to another pair how A CASSETTE works. What questions do you think you may be asked?

Don't join another pair until you have familiarised yourselves with the process. When you're ready to start, close your book and explain the process FROM MEMORY. Draw a diagram as you explain, if necessary.

1 Two spools. Tape passes behind this window. When the recorder is going, tape winds from one spool to the other.

2 The plastic tape is covered with thousands of tiny magnets, too small to see.

3 Tape head pushes against the tape. When you play the tape the magnets make electric signals in the tape head as they move past.

4 The electronic circuit sends electric signals to and from the tape head.

5 Electric signals come along these wires. The loudspeaker changes the signals into the sounds of voices and music you hear.

6 Your voice makes part of the microphone shake. The microphone turns sounds into electric signals.

48 Here are explanations of some of the items on the menu on page 142, so that you can help your partners to understand them. DO NOT just read these descriptions out loud – try to remember them, so that you can answer your partners' questions.
When you're all clear about everything, decide what to order for each course.

Lancashire Hotpot   Lamb and vegetables cooked in the oven with a layer of potatoes on top – very tasty!
Chicken Madras   Chicken pieces in an Indian curry sauce – very hot!
Bread and butter pudding   Layers of bread and butter with raisins and cream, baked in the oven till crisp and chewy – delicious!

49 Take it in turns with your partner to describe each person in your photos – their appearance AND the kind of people they seem to be. Make notes on what your partner tells you.
Start with the person on the left of the group in your photo.

50 This is your problem. Tell your partners about it:

– on an excursion – coach has left without you – in the middle of nowhere – no public transport – money and raincoat on the coach – just started to pour with rain

Begin like this: 'Oh my goodness, what shall I do? …'

Try to think of drawbacks and objections to each suggestion that is made!

Index

Grammar

Word study and pronunciation

Composition

Prepositions

Verbs and idioms